D1355949

PROBLEMS IN STOICISM

Problems
in Stoicism

Edited by
A. A. LONG
Lecturer in Greek and Latin at
University College London

UNIVERSITY OF LONDON
THE ATHLONE PRESS
1971

Published by
THE ATHLONE PRESS
UNIVERSITY OF LONDON
at 2 Gower Street London WC1
Distributed by Tiptree Book Services Ltd
Tiptree, Essex

Australia and New Zealand
Melbourne University Press

U.S.A.
Oxford University Press Inc
New York

© *A. A. Long*, 1971

ISBN 0 485 11118 7

Printed in Great Britain by
ROBERT MACLEHOSE AND CO LTD
GLASGOW

PREFACE

This book brings together a set of papers by different hands on problems in Stoicism. Most of the material is published here for the first time, and it deals with problems of Stoic epistemology, logic, metaphysics and ethics. In more than one sense this book is a statement of work in progress. Several of its topics take up questions already treated in recent literature, and further publications on Stoicism by most of its authors are current or forthcoming. More particularly, half the chapters of the book were presented at a series of seminars in the Institute of Classical Studies, University of London, and we are deeply grateful to its Director, Professor E. W. Handley, for offering us such a congenial forum for discussion and for suggesting publication in this form.

The problems in Stoicism are vast, and they vary greatly in type over a long period of time. This book makes no claim to treat more than some of them, much less to give a comprehensive account of Stoicism. But its collection of papers does cover topics of considerable philosophical and historical importance, and through the treatment of these much of the coherence and significance of Stoicism as a whole can be seen. Because we are concerned here with a school of Greek philosophy, and its Roman inheritance, part, sometimes a large part, of the discussion turns on matters of philology. But with the help of translation and transliteration it is hoped that the book will be found intelligible and interesting to those who have no knowledge of Greek and Latin. A short bibliography gives full details of most of the works on Stoicism cited in the notes and often referred to there by abbreviated titles.

As convenor of the seminar and editor I have incurred many debts. Without the enthusiastic support of the other authors of the book, and the continuous interest of many who contributed actively to the seminar but are not named here, neither project

would have got off the ground. I hope that this book is a just
reflection of their cooperation. If it has serious defects they
should be attributed to me. I cannot try to thank individually
all those who have taken part, but they will understand why I
single out for mention Professor A. C. Lloyd and Professor
F. H. Sandbach. For their kindness and encouragement at
different stages of this work I am especially grateful. Acknow-
ledgements are also due to the Cambridge University Press for
permission to print the chapter by Professor J. M. Rist, and to
the Clarendon Press for a similar courtesy concerning Chapters
II and VII: these two are reprinted with minor changes from
the *Classical Quarterly* xxiv (1930) 45–51 and v new series (1955)
181–94.

London   A.A.L.
July 1969

NOTE ON TRANSLITERATION

Most Greek words which occur as isolated terms or short phrases in
the main text have been transliterated. In general, the corresponding
letters of the Roman alphabet are used to transliterate Greek
characters, but where the Greek υ occurs, except in diphthongs, it is
rendered by *y*. This accords with the English spelling of Greek
derivatives, e.g. syntax from σύνταξις. On the first occurrence in
each chapter of a transliterated word an η or ω is indicated by ē or
ō. Diacritic signs are only added to subsequent occurrences of the
same word if their sense or inflection might otherwise be
misinterpreted.

CONTENTS

Introduction

Modern scholarship has extended knowledge of ancient philosophy in many directions, but one major school of thought,
Stoicism, has received little of its attention. This neglect of the
most influential system of later antiquity is particularly notable
in English-speaking countries. Reasons for it, if scarcely com-
pelling, are not hard to seek. Stoicism suffers severely from a
lack of evidence in its crucial, formative period. No complete
work by Zeno, Cleanthes or Chrysippus has survived, and a
knowledge of their thought must be gleaned, where it can,
from summaries or occasional quotations by writers, many of
them hostile, who lived anything from two to eight centuries
later. So, for the most part, we lack detailed Stoic arguments,
and philosophy lives by argument. From the Roman period
there is copious writing by Stoics. But the 'monumental
moralizing dullness', in Gerard Watson's phrase, of much of it
is uncongenial to modern taste and false to the dialectical rigour
with which Chrysippus' name was associated. The early Stoics
should not be judged by Seneca and Marcus Aurelius. Though
vitally concerned with designing a system which defined man's
place in the world, their achievements in logic and physics
went far beyond what was required to support a purely
practical ethic. In spite of the many gaps in our knowledge
enough of the whole system can be reconstructed to prove the
Stoics' philosophical importance and provide a context in
which to place their more practical teaching.

The main justification for this book is the lack in English of
works which discuss specific problems in Stoicism. Where so
much remains doubtful and obscure there is a need for detailed
studies as well as general appraisals. During the last few years
the tide for Stoicism has happily begun to turn. Thanks to

S. Sambursky (*The Physics of the Stoics*, London 1959), Benson
Mates (*Stoic Logic*, Berkeley 1953), and William and Martha
Kneale (*The Development of Logic*, Oxford 1964) Stoic physics
and logic have been given an authoritative treatment previously lacking. For Stoic ethics there is no comparable recent
work to set alongside that of Bréhier and Pohlenz. But specialist
studies of time by Victor Goldschmidt (*Le système stoïcien et
l'idée de temps*, Paris 1953) and epistemology by Gerard Watson
(*The Stoic Theory of Knowledge*, Belfast 1966) also throw much
new light on Stoic ethics. The aim of the present book is to
treat some specific problems in Stoic epistemology, metaphysics,
psychology and ethics and provoke further discussion of them.
If physics as such receives no special treatment, that is not
because the authors underrate its significance but because this
book reflects their current research interests. We make no claims
to have given a comprehensive treatment of Stoicism. But
through the detailed discussion a coherent view of Stoicism does
emerge, which may be more accurate because it is presented by
different authors in different ways.

In fact the book arises directly from a series of seminars at the
Institute of Classical Studies of London University during
1967–8. It seemed to some of us that some corporate work on
Stoicism might be valuable. Half the chapters in this book were
presented formally or informally to the seminar, and all the
authors have declared interests in the subject. The ten meetings
which took place provided a most useful forum for the exchange
of views, and the book owes several debts to scholars whose
names do not appear in the list of authors. Most of the material
is published here for the first time, but J. M. Rist's chapter on
the Stoic Categories will also be found in his book *Stoic Philosophy*
from Cambridge University Press; and two papers by I. G. Kidd
and F. H. Sandbach which deserve wider dissemination are
reprinted with minor changes from the *Classical Quarterly*
('*Ἔννοια* and *Πρόληψις* in the Stoic Theory of Knowledge':
vol. xxiv (1930) 45–51, and 'The relation of Stoic intermediates
to the *summum Bonum* . . .': vol. v new series (1955) 181–94). The
fact that only two chapters have previously appeared as articles
is in no way intended as an adverse judgement on other recently
published work. It would be perfectly possible to compile a

volume which consisted entirely of papers already available in
journals or extracts from books. But that was not our intention.
The chapters of this book which are not new were chosen both
for their merit and also because of their bearing on other parts
of the book. There has been no attempt to impose any uni-
formity of outlook on the authors, and the attentive reader will
notice certain points on which they differ. I have drawn attention in editorial notes to some passages where a comparison of
views is relevant and interesting.

Stoicism naturally raises far more problems than those which
are discussed in this book. It may therefore help those who are
encouraged to read on if I say something briefly about the place
in Stoicism of the topics treated.

The changing nature of reality, on which the Stoics laid such
stress, is reflected in the history of the Stoic school. By convention we refer to doctrines as 'Stoic' and in this reflect, as we
must, the practice of ancient doxography. But Stoicism is a
broad term, broad enough to admit divergence and development in a variety of fields. Numenius tells us that internal disagreement and argument were features of Stoicism from the
beginning (ap. Eusebium *Praep. ev.* xiv, p. 728a), and much
modern research, particularly by Pohlenz, has concerned itself
with plotting the contributions of individual Stoics. As a
heuristic principle it is clearly desirable to note those texts in
which views are attributed by name to individual Stoics, but
these are fewer than we should like and a 'Zeno says' is no
necessary guarantee that the doctrine which follows derives
specifically from the founder of the school. Some of the difficulties which arise when an unwarranted emphasis is placed on
alleged differences between Zeno and Chrysippus are exposed
by Sandbach in his chapter on the *katalēptikē phantasia*.
Undoubtedly Chrysippus refined and developed much in the
teaching of Zeno and Cleanthes, and he was traditionally
regarded as the standard of Stoic orthodoxy. There is every
reason to think that the majority of doxographical reports of
'the Stoics' derive ultimately from Chrysippus. In this book
then the term Stoic, unless otherwise indicated, should be taken
to mean his views which will often have been those of the Old

Stoa. But on some topics, especially logic, it is quite impossible to date or attribute much of our evidence, and it must remain only a probable hypothesis that Chrysippus is the source of our knowledge. When later Stoicism is under discussion it is more important, and often easier, to distinguish individuals, for instance Panaetius or Posidonius. In this book they are considered mainly in the chapters by I. G. Kidd.

The first part of the book deals with topics which later Stoics would classify largely under *logikē*, a term considerably broader than 'logic'. F. H. Sandbach examines two central problems in Stoic epistemology. His first chapter on the *kataleptike phantasia* analyses some of the evidence on this most controversial term and sets it in the general context of Stoic psychology. He shows what the Stoics meant when they made *kataleptike phantasia* the test of a true presentation, and argues against Pohlenz that there is no good reason for seeing any difference between Zeno and Chrysippus on this question. The second chapter is Sandbach's now classic article on *ennoia and prolēpsis*. It is reprinted here with minor changes and a postscript by the author. Sandbach argues that the terms *ennoia* and *prolepsis* are not identical in sense and that among orthodox Stoics neither term refers to innate ideas or *a priori* concepts. In the course of this discussion Sandbach does much to illuminate the nature of Stoic empiricism and its similarities, in certain respects, to Epicureanism.

The Stoics were materialists, and their theory of knowledge rested on the assumption that men possess an accurate means of perceiving the objects which constitute the external world. But while they confined existence to bodies, they also recognised, at least for the purpose of philosophical exposition, a class of things designated 'incorporeal'. These include *lekton*, a term very difficult to translate, which appears to correspond approximately to the sense or meaning of an utterance. The place of such incorporeals in Stoicism is obscure and fraught with difficulties, not least the inadequacy of our evidence. But the importance which the Stoics ascribed to *logos* makes it imperative to come to grips with their theories of language and rational processes; for which reason the next three chapters are mainly attempts to elucidate problems connected with *lekta*.

In the third chapter J. M. Rist raises some basic questions

concerning the status of incorporeals, and then proceeds to examine the (so called) Stoic categories, which are taken to be examples of *lekta*. He argues that the four categories constitute a set of philosophical questions which enable the enquirer to place and identify particular things in the framework of Stoic ontology. On this interpretation the Stoic categories have a reference to physical objects or the states of physical objects and constitute ways of describing and classifying reality.

A. C. Lloyd, in the following chapter, while agreeing that the categories have this descriptive function, argues that as *lekta* they are connected with the parts of speech and should be classified in Stoicism under dialectic and grammar not physics. Beginning with an account of the subjects which dialectic embraced for the Stoics he shows that they had an 'unstable division' between language as sound and language as what is said. Lloyd points to certain crucial difficulties in the Stoic theory of meaning which arise from their view of the *natural* relation between sound and what it signifies. He also applies his study of Stoic grammar to the system in general and its metaphysical basis.

Though much good work is now available on the formal aspects of Stoic logic little has been written concerning its internal relation to other aspects of Stoicism. The Stoics divided philosophy into three parts, physics, ethics and logic, but the division was a convenience for exposition rather than an affirmation of independent subjects. The organic unity of Stoicism was emphasised in similes to illustrate the interdependence of its subject-matter, e.g. an egg which has logic as its shell, ethics as its white and physics as its yolk (Diogenes Laertius, VII 40). In the fifth chapter I have offered an essay on what might best be described as applied logic. The principal subjects discussed are the *lekton*, which is compared with Aristotle's theory of meaning, and the Stoic view of truth. No account of these topics can avoid some logical treatment of a formal kind, but I have been chiefly concerned to find their context in Stoicism as a whole. So the chapter has an intentional ethical slant in its conclusion, and thus looks forward to the later part of the book.

A basic problem for the Stoics, and one which has caused

perennial difficulty in philosophy, is the derivation of moral concepts. Nature (*physis*) has both a factual reference to the world and a moral reference as the criterion of value. Man is required to live in accordance with nature, but can he fail to do so? If he can, nature seems to become an ambiguous if not vacuous term; if he cannot, the validity of praise and blame is at once called in question. Furthermore the Stoics, who denied innate ideas or *a priori* concepts, had to derive their morality from experience and this led them inevitably to analyse the psychology and evolution of man, the experiencing subject. They also found it necessary to define man's place in the total scheme of things, his relation to members of his own and other species, and to develop some kind of social principles. For Stoicism, however esoteric parts of its theory might be, was explicitly designed to provide a rule of life in a world for which older prescriptions were inadequate or irrelevant and the success of new ones directly dependent on their acknowledgement of contemporary needs. The chapters which follow discuss various positions which the Stoics adopted on these questions, and through them some of the essentials of Stoic moral theory can be seen.

In the sixth chapter S. G. Pembroke gives the first comprehensive account in English of *oikeiōsis*. This concept, one of the most original and difficult in Stoicism, has been inadequately discussed by most writers on Stoic ethics. Approximately translatable as 'a feeling of endearment' *oikeiosis* is a concept through which many of the Stoics' views of human and animal nature were expounded. Through a thoroughly documented analysis of the extant sources, many of them fragmentary and inaccessible, Pembroke argues for the central importance of *oikeiosis* in Stoicism. Among the main themes discussed in his chapter are the Stoic attitude to the family, the evolution of morality in the individual and the Stoic view of justice. Unlike those who have tried to make Theophrastus the source of Stoic *oikeiosis* Pembroke argues that a more likely line could be traced back to Socratic discussion.

In the Stoic concept of value all things are strictly either good, bad or indifferent. The class of good things comprises only virtue(s), vice alone is bad, but the category of 'indifferents' was a broad one which contained sub-divisions of value within itself. The relation of these intermediates to the goal of human action is complex; it was strongly criticised in antiquity and has been much discussed since. I. G. Kidd, in an important paper first published in 1955, examines some modern arguments which claim to find a change in Stoic attitudes on this relationship between Zeno and Posidonius, but finds the case unproven. Kidd argues that later Stoics did not deviate from orthodoxy in their view of the *summum bonum*, and in demonstrating this he examines the technical terms of value and the concept of moral action to which they refer. He also investigates the relation between ethics and physics. Thus his essay may be read as a synoptic treatment of Stoic views on man's moral nature and its connexion with nature as expressed in the external world.

A regular charge levelled against the Stoics by their ancient critics was double-talk. Their concept of indifferents which were 'preferred' but not good was held to invoke a double standard of value, and a similar criticism of having it both ways was directed against their attempts to combine determinism with some degree of human autonomy. Pantheism and divine omnipotence are further factors which complicate the Stoic theory of human action. I have tried, in the eighth chapter, to discuss the Stoic treatment of human action from different perspectives, for contemporary discussions place undue weight on particular aspects of their theory. While unable to rid the Stoics of some degree of incoherence I have also argued that their interpretation of freedom as self-determinism is quite compatible with a belief that all events, including choice, are determined. Character is the crucial factor here, to which moral responsibility is ascribed. But the Stoics failed to show how a character fully determined by antecedent causes can bear the weight of moral judgement attributable to it.

Among later Stoics Posidonius is an important but enigmatic figure. Fortunately through Galen we have fairly detailed evidence for his psychological theory which differed in important respects from that of earlier Stoics. I. G. Kidd, in the ninth chapter, examines a key feature of this theory, Posidonius' conception of emotions, and he also shows how this affected Posidonius' ethics. Posidonius was famous in antiquity for his scientific achievements, and Kidd points out how his interest in the emotions may be traced to a general concern with discovering the causes of phenomena and making theories square with facts. This chapter gives an interesting demonstration of the limits within which a Stoic could stray from orthodoxy on details and still remain true to the essentials.

Later Stoicism is also the main theme of the final chapter. Gerard Watson, in a discussion of 'the Natural Law and Stoicism', focuses attention on some of the problems which arise for Stoic ethics from their concept of natural law. He traces the origins of this concept and then gives a detailed treatment of its presentation in Cicero. Topics examined elsewhere in this book, including *oikeiosis* and determinism, are put together here, and Watson also discusses some of the practical applications of natural law and its later influence.

The absence of a chapter on the antecedents of Stoicism should not be taken to imply a belief in its discontinuity with earlier Greek philosophy. In fact, though scholars differ on the relative importance of specific influences, most now agree that Stoicism represents a continuation and development of much that went before. As I. G. Kidd observes (p. 213), the Stoics themselves were conscious of working within a tradition as well as breaking new ground. The dialogue between Stoics of the early period and the Sceptical Academy is one of the most interesting events in later Greek thought. Had it continued into the first century A.D. the Stoa might have been saved from fossilisation. But the growth of Roman imperialism coincided with a decline in all the schools of philosophy. Interest in logic and physics, where it existed at all, was confined to commentary on past theories, and when Plutarch or Galen come to discuss Stoicism in the first and second centuries A.D. they revive debates which were current three or four hundred years earlier. This is antiquarianism, but at least it attests to an interest in the theory of Stoicism. Even after the Stoa ceased to exist as a school many of its doctrines survived through the influence they exercised on Neoplatonism and the Christian fathers. Much later, Stoicism was to leave its mark on humanists of the Renaissance and rationalists of the Enlightenment.

I

Phantasia Kataleptike / 8qu... bouyous/

F. H. SANDBACH

When, sometime in the winter of 87–86 B.C., Antiochus of Ascalon received two books written recently by his aged former teacher Philo of Larisa, head of the Academy in Athens, he was very angry.[1] It seems that Philo had maintained that the sceptical Academy had not denied the possibility of knowledge, but only that there was such a thing as a *phantasia kataleptike* or 'cognitive presentation'. He had thereby abandoned the key position of Carneades' scepticism. To grasp the truth, Carneades had argued, if that phrase involves the consciousness that one is grasping it, is impossible unless there is in the mind a 'presentation' of the sort meant by those words. There are, however, no such presentations, and it is therefore never possible to know that one has hold of the truth. That there is truth, that there are objective facts or real things (*pragmata*) Carneades did not deny; he denied that any statements about those facts could be known to be true. Although most presentations, he said, probably correspond to the facts, there are none of such a kind that they can be recognised with certainty as corresponding. If there are no such presentations, knowledge cannot be possible.

The phrase *phantasia kataleptike* was taken by Carneades from the Stoics,[2] whom he was consciously attacking. Such a presentation was declared, at least by Chrysippus and his followers, to be a test of truth, and probably the basic test, on which the validity of any other tests depends. It must therefore, unless there is to be some superior test by which its credibility will be established, carry in itself the mark by which it can be recognised. The absence of such a mark from all presentations was maintained by the Academic sceptics: Cicero, *Acad. Prior.* II 101, neque tamen habere insignem illam et propriam percipiendi

B   L.P.S.

these do not contain a peculiar mark of truth and certainty which exists nowhere else

notam; 103, non inesse in eis propriam, quae numquam alibi esset, ueri et certi notam.

The rendering 'cognitive presentation' has been adopted after some hesitation.[3] The adjective *kataleptike* is ambiguous. It is formed from the verb *katalambanein*, which means 'grasp', 'apprehend', and may have an active or a passive sense. There is no English adjective with the same ambiguity. 'Cognitive' is always active. I shall argue later that the Stoics made use of the ambiguity of their word. *Phantasia* is a word that belongs to philosophical language, in which it functions as the noun of the verb *phainesthai*, 'appear', with a wide range of meaning. 'Presentation' is more technical, but it seems to indicate what the Stoics meant by the word.

typosis

A *phantasia* is, according to them, an impression (*typōsis*) or alteration (*heteroiōsis*) in the psyche, and in that part of it they called the *hēgemonikon*, or command-centre. It occurs when something 'becomes apparent', *phantazetai*. We should call it a mental event, and associate it with changes in the brain. For the Stoics the two things are one and the same: the psyche is material, and any mental event *is* a physical event. So presentation is a physical change in the psyche. The word was first used to give a name to what happens when sense-organs are turned to the outer world. Objects in that world make an impression on the percipient. But his psyche is aware not merely that it has undergone a change: it simultaneously *perceives* the external object, and part of the change is this perception. This is very clearly stated in Aetius (= Ps. Plut. *Placita*) IV 12, I (*SVF* II 54), who bases himself on the authority of Chrysippus.

mental change = physical

A presentation is a happening that occurs in the psyche, displaying both itself and[4] what has caused it. For example, when by vision we look upon what is white, what has occurred in the psyche through the act of seeing is an affect; and because of this affect we can say that there is a white object which it implies. *Phantasia* has its name from *phos* (light); for just as light makes itself visible and also the things it encompasses, so the presentation displays itself and also what has caused it.

Although in the example given the presentation correctly reveals the external object, it need perhaps not be supposed that it always does so. Certainly elsewhere we meet with 'false presentations' obtained by vision (*SVF* II 131, p. 40.34, perhaps Chrysippus). But clearly this passage does imply that there always is an external object, and that is explicitly stated in the sequel, where the affect that does not arise from an external object is called by another name, *phantastikon* or 'imaginative product'. Elsewhere this limitation of *phantasia* is not preserved, but the word is applied to dreams and the hallucinations of madmen (Sextus *Adv. math.* VIII 56, *SVF* II 88).

The passage of Aetius is obviously written with reference to those presentations that arise through the senses. Presentations that arise by mental activity, not through the stimulation of the sense organs, must usually be *about* external objects, although not immediately caused by them, e.g. presentations that the sun is larger than the earth, or that a providential God exists. But if one thinks that somewhere there are Centaurs or men with eyes in their chests, that corresponds to a hallucination, e.g. 'this is a dagger I see before me'. (See further below Chapter V pp. 82ff. on *logikai phantasiai*.)

II

Cicero reports a manual simile used by Zeno to illustrate the stages of cognition, and it has become famous. He started by holding out his open hand with fingers outstretched: 'a presentation', he said, 'is like that'. Then he contracted his fingers a little: 'assent is like that'. Then he closed his hand entirely, saying that was apprehension or cognition. The word he used was *katalepsis*, a new name. But when he had brought up his left hand and firmly clasped his fist with it, he said that knowledge was a thing like that.[5]

This image presents the first stage, *presentation*, as purely receptive. As Sextus Empiricus puts it, it does not lie with the subject, but with the object that causes the presentation, that he is affected as he is.[6] All that is required of the percipient is that he shall be ready to perceive. For example, to see he must open his eyes, and that corresponds to holding out the hand. This analysis is, however, inapplicable to presentations that arise not from the senses, but through the mind. A man who as the result of reflection has a presentation that the earth goes round the sun must create that presentation in himself.[7] It is no doubt a weakness of the Stoic scheme that they applied the same word to what 'appeared' through the senses and to what 'appeared' to the mind. What was said about the first was not always appropriate to the second. Mental presentations were of increasing importance, and Epictetus, who made 'the right use of presentations' his ideal of morality, had them more in view than those that came from the senses.[8] Nevertheless, the accounts that we have of presentations are almost all formed with reference to the latter sort; and similarly disputes about the existence of the cognitive presentation were often carried on in terms of sense-perception and used illustrations drawn above all from the sphere of vision. This was not only simpler, but also justified by the Stoic doctrine that the mind was at birth like a blank sheet of paper. It had powers but no content. Sensation supplied the first content, and unless some of that was known to be reliable, no development of it by the mind could deserve any greater credence.

In this paper I shall follow the precedent of the ancient world and concentrate on the presentations that come through the senses. Some, but not all, of what I say will apply also to mental presentations.

Assent is assent to a presentation. But if a presentation is nothing but a physical change in the psyche, a *typosis*, how can one assent to it? Assent should be to a proposition; it is *that* which is true or false. This criticism was made by Arcesilaus (Sextus *Adv. math.* VII 154). But something can be said for the Stoics.

Suppose I look at a round object. It will—at any rate for Chrysippus–lie at the base of a cone of air in tension, and in some way its roundness will be conveyed along that cone to my eyes and thence to the *hegemonikon*, which will be affected thereby. Now if I am aware of the affect in my *hegemonikon*, there can be no question of giving or withholding assent to that; only by a deliberate falsehood could I deny the awareness. But a presentation is something more. What 'appears' to me is not merely that there is a certain affect in my *hegemonikon*, but that there is an external round object. More than that, the object will normally be identified as belonging to some class of round object, as being an orange or a cricket-ball; or even as a particular member of a class, as when we say, not 'that appears to be a planet', but 'that appears to be Venus'. The presentation, the *phantasia*, 'what appears', is at once an impression made through the senses and an interpretation of that impression. So Plato at *Sophist* 264 a-b says that *phantasia* arises by way of sensation, but that 'what appears' is a combination of sensation and opinion. Similarly for Chrysippus the *phantasia* reveals not only itself but also that which caused it; that is to say it gives information about the external object. It is this information to which we can assent or refuse to assent. An anecdote about Zeno's pupil Sphaerus illustrates the point clearly. Ptolemy Philopator had a dish of wax pomegranates put before him and when the philosopher reached to take one exclaimed that he had assented to a false presentation. Sphaerus replied that his assent was not to 'those are pomegranates', but to 'it is probable those are pomegranates'.[9]

Admittedly Zeno's psychology was elementary. He correctly saw that perception is something more than awareness of a sensation. But this physical explanation of the activity as the reception of a kind of print[10] of the object perceived was clearly inadequate and even misleading. Even Chrysippus' modification, which substituted for the print the vague notion of an 'alteration' of the material psyche, was unsatisfactory, since he did not explain how one could assent to such a thing.[11]

Apprehension, or cognition, was said to be assent to cognitive presentation.[12] Hence Zeno's symbol, which suggests that assent and apprehension were succeeding stages, is misleading. Is it also misleading when it suggests that what is grasped by apprehension is the presentation, just as it is the presentation to which assent is given? I believe not, if trust can be put in Cicero and Augustine. The first writes of Zeno: quoniam esset quod percipi (=*katalambanesthai*) posset. quid ergo id est? uisum. The word uisum is in itself ambiguous. It could mean 'the thing seen', but it was also regularly used to translate *phantasia*, and that is how it is used here, for Cicero continues: quale igitur uisum? tum illum ita definisse: ex eo quod esset, sicut esset, impressum et signatum et effictum.[13]

But although grasp, apprehension, cognition, whatever we

call it, is primarily of the presentation, it is secondarily of the external object, because the presentation, as we have seen, declares or makes plain that object, and a cognitive presentation does so truthfully, being 'in accord with the object'. To apprehend the presentation is then also, and more importantly, to apprehend the object from which it originated.

There is, however, a difference in that whereas the whole of the presentation is grasped, it is not necessarily the whole of the object that is apprehended. The presentation does not of necessity reproduce all the characteristics and qualities of the object. To invent an example, the cognitive presentation of the moon given by sight will not provide any information about its far side, or its temperature, or whether it smells of green cheese. Hence Cicero writes that comprehensio (=*katalepsis*) was so called, non quod omnia quae essent in re comprehenderet, sed quia nihil quod cadere in eam posset relinqueret.[14]

If *katalepsis*, apprehension, is a grasp primarily of the presentation, but secondarily of the external object, it is easier to understand the phrase *kataleptike phantasia* and its opposite *akataleptos phantasia*. The first adjective belongs to a type that is usually, but by no means always, active in sense, the second to a type that is even more predominantly passive.[15] This distinction fits. The *akataleptos* is a presentation that cannot be grasped, and so no question arises of a secondary grasp of the object. The *kataleptike*, on the other hand, is so called in deliberate ambiguity. It is one which when grasped entails grasp of the object. Although strictly speaking the presentation is not itself the agent that grasps the object but the medium through which the mind grasps it, the adjective can be understood in an active sense, 'the presentation associated with the process of grasping'.

An explanation[16] of the word *kataleptike*, now rightly abandoned, was that it indicated that the presentation gripped the percipient and dragged him to give his assent. *Katalepsis* is in the ancient authorities always an activity in which the percipient is the agent. But the question remains open whether a cognitive presentation is one such that it is inevitably followed by assent. Here it seems to me that only one thing is certain: some people, whom Sextus calls 'younger Stoics', possibly Antipater or others of that time, gave examples of cognitive presentations which did not win assent; Admetus had a cognitive presentation of Alcestis when she returned from the dead, but he did not accept it, and Menelaus did not accept the presentation he had of Helen when he met her in Egypt.[17] I do not think there is any evidence to show what was the opinion of the older Stoics. No weight can be put on their insistence that assent was something for which we are responsible; the phrase used, ἐφ᾽ ἡμῖν, does not imply that it is possible that we should do the opposite of what we in fact do. Whether assent necessarily follows on a cognitive presentation or not, we are still responsible for giving or withholding it. Nor do I think that any conclusion can be drawn from Cicero, *Acad. Prior.* ii 38; there Antiochus' views are being put forward, and it is maintained controversially that the mind yields to *perspicua* as certainly as the scale to an imposed weight; but the supporters of *perspicua* do not accept their identity with cognitive presentations (ibid. 34).

III

Pohlenz maintained that for Zeno the test of truth was not, as for Chrysippus, the cognitive presentation, the *phantasia kataleptike*, but cognition itself, *katalepsis;* and that this difference was not a mere matter of words, but marked a change in psychological theory.[18] To abbreviate his argument and to maintain its force may be impossible, but I will attempt to summarise it as he put it in *Die Stoa*.

Zeno's position, according to Pohlenz, was this. Whether a presentation deserves credence is decided by Logos, which gives or withholds assent. *Katalepsis* takes place only when Logos has concluded that all the conditions for a cognitive presentation are fulfilled. But some presentations are so obviously plain that Logos will immediately accept it that the conditions are fulfilled. Now it is expressly recorded that Zeno found the criterion of truth not in the cognitive presentation but in *katalepsis*. This agrees with his basic position. The presentation has an external cause; assent to it first brings in an active element that ensures the autonomy of Logos. Posidonius tells us that many of the older Stoics held 'upright Logos' to be the criterion; and we can attach this view to Zeno. It does not mean that Logos can judge external things without a presentation; but only if the Logos is sound and 'stands upright', resisting misleading presentations, will its assent be correct. Soundness of Logos is a pre-condition for every act of cognition.

Chrysippus, he continues, did not recognize different powers in the 'soul', but temporary conditions of the *hegemonikon* or command-centre. That could make judgements, or it could be a presentation. For a presentation is 'the command-centre in such-and-such a state'. In Zeno's way of thinking the criterion had arisen from the co-operation of two independent factors both of which must function normally. For Chrysippus the two factors were replaced by a single process of cognition that was completed in two stages: a divorce between presentation and Logos was unthinkable, and a cognitive presentation necessarily induced assent. The natural result was to transfer the criterion to this presentation, which brought the objects of the outer world in a trustworthy manner before our consciousness. From Chrysippus' time it was not *katalepsis*, but the kataleptic or cognitive presentation that counted as the criterion. But he did not mean to depreciate the importance of Logos. It was fundamentally important that Logos should be autonomously opposed to the outer world, and possess the ability to accept or reject the presentations that arose.

I hope it is fair to say that Pohlenz' view is this. For Zeno the cognitive presentation brings the truth about the external world. But we do not know that any presentation is cognitive until it has been examined by Logos, which may establish that the conditions for a cognitive presentation are fulfilled. Those conditions are that the presentation should be (1) from an existent thing, (2) in accord with the existent thing, (3) impressed and ensealed, and (4) such as could not arise from a non-existent thing. If these are satisfied, then assent takes place, and is *katalepsis*. For Chrysippus the cognitive presentation necessitates assent, so that although an activity of Logos is still required, it is determined by the presentation; that presentation is therefore the test of truth. This view seems to me inadequately supported by the ancient evidence, and open to other objections.

(i) The test of truth of a presentation for Zeno seems to be,

according to Pohlenz' argument, not the *katalepsis* with which
he wishes to identify it, but the preceding activity of the Logos,
or the evidence (whatever that may be) used by the Logos to examine the presentation. Certainly *katalepsis* will follow upon this
activity, so that when there is *katalepsis* there will have been a true
presentation. It will be a proof of the presentation's truth, but
not a test of it. A degree certificate may be a proof of education,
but the test lay in the examination that preceded its award.

(ii) How can Logos decide that the presentation arose 'from
an existent thing' and therefore satisfied the first condition for
being cognitive? It is not known how or whether Zeno defined
'the existent', but later the orthodox definition was 'that which
causes a cognitive presentation'.[19] If by Logos discursive reason
is meant, then it cannot argue that a presentation is cognitive
because it arose from an existent thing; for an existent is only
known to be existent if it causes a cognitive presentation. There
would be a fatal *petitio principii*.

(iii) Diogenes Laertius records that 'certain others of the
older Stoics lay down correct reason as the criterion' (or 'a
criterion'), 'as Posidonius says in his book on the criterion'.[20]
Pohlenz slightly misrepresents this when he ascribes this view
to 'many' of the older Stoics, thereby making more plausible his
suggestion that Zeno is to be included among these anonymous
persons. To refer to the founder of your school by the phrase
'certain others of the older Stoics' would seem to me, I must
confess, a strange use of language. But it is more important that
the phrase 'correct reason' is elsewhere in our sources for
Stoicism particularly, perhaps uniquely, associated with the
ideal wise man or 'sage'.[21] Hence it is unlikely that Zeno would
have used it in this context alone to refer to the reason employed by all men to recognize cognitive presentations. I suspect that whoever it was who spoke of correct reason as a test
of truth did not do so with primary reference to the testing of
sense-data; rather they saw in correct reason a test of universal
applicability, but one which only the select few had the power
to use. It is to be noted that Diogenes (VII 47) defines the virtue
of ἀματαιότης, the possession of the wise, as 'a state that refers
presentations to correct reason'.

(iv) Is it true that Zeno made *katalepsis* and not the presenta-

tion the test of truth? No one in antiquity states that Zeno
differed from Chrysippus by not accepting the presentation as
a test. Pohlenz relies on Cicero, *Acad. Post.* I 42; inter scientiam
et inscientiam comprehensionem illam quam dixi collocabat
[sc. Zeno] eamque neque in rectis neque in prauis numerabat,
sed soli credendum esse dicebat. Cicero was following Antiochus,
and in the previous section wrote, again of Zeno: uisis non
omnibus adiungebat fidem sed eis solum quae propriam quandam haberent declarationem earum quae uiderentur. Can we
believe that when he wrote soli credendum esse he meant that
comprehensio (*katalepsis*) is the test of truth, but that by adiungebat fidem eis solum he did not mean that the cognitive presentations were such a test? The fact is that Cicero is not here in the
least concerned to state accurately what Zeno held to be ultimately the test of truth, but is arguing that there is in Zeno's
view a reliable method of cognition which is intermediate
between ignorance and perfect knowledge.[22]

Sextus (*Adv. math.* VII 152) gives it as Stoic doctrine that
knowledge exists only in the wise, opinion only in the bad,
while *katalepsis* belongs to both sorts and is the test of truth.
Since this opinion was, he says, attacked by Arcesilaus, it must
have been held by Zeno. But he gives no indication that it was
in any way inconsistent with orthodoxy. Later (ibid. VII 253) he
writes that the older Stoics say that the test of truth is the cognitive
presentation. He cannot intend to exclude Zeno, Cleanthes,
and all their contemporaries from the class of 'older Stoics'.

I conclude that there is no reason for seeing any difference of
substance between Zeno and Chrysippus over the question of
the test of truth. The former may, to be sure, have said that
katalepsis was the test. But if he did, he did not thereby intend
to deny that the ultimate evidence is the cognitive presentation,
recognized to be such by a kind of intuition.

IV

Pohlenz' account of Zeno's views is attractive because it seems
to give an answer to a question which must trouble many who
try to grasp the meaning of this doctrine of the cognitive
presentation. How are such presentations to be recognized?

How is a man to know that he is right to give them his assent?

Ancient sources fail to offer any help. There is no discussion of this problem in any author who expounds the Stoic doctrine, and the attacks of the critics are not directed against the use of any particular methods of recognition. Their charge is simply that men misjudge their presentations, taking false ones to be true and being unable to distinguish these false ones from that they claim to be cognitive. The Stoics claim that cognitive presentations have some peculiar quality that marks them out, but cannot indicate what that is except by the use of words like 'evident' (*enargēs*, Sextus *Adv. math.* VII 257, 403) or 'striking' (*plēktikē*, ibid. VII 257, 258, 403).

This ought not in fact to cause any surprise. How could the bona fides of a cognitive presentation be established? We may of course say that the percipient must be awake and sober and looking at the object in a good light and that the presentation must not be inconsistent with others, past or present, and so on. But this is simply to check one presentation by others. If the check is to be valid, those presentations must themselves be cognitive. And how are we to know that? We shall find ourselves involved in an endless regress, as is pointed out by Sextus *Adv. math.* VII 428–9. There must be a point to call a halt. There must be some presentations that are immediately acceptable, that are self-evidently true. That is what constitutes a cognitive presentation.

It is the attitude of common sense that most presentations are of this sort. In ordinary life every man has no doubt that what 'appears to him' is really there, that the sun *is* shining, that those objects are pomegranates, that a waggon and horses are bearing down on him. Only occasionally will he have doubts, so that (if he is a Stoic) he will say that he has a *phantasia akataleptos*. For the most part he will believe without reservation that his presentations give him a grasp of external reality.

NOTES

1. Cicero, *Acad. prior.* 11.
2. The fullest treatment of Stoic views on the subject is in Bonhöffer, *Epictet und die Stoa*, pp. 138–87, particularly 160–8. Later accounts that deserve attention are

to be found in Barth, *Die Stoa²*, pp. 104–5; Bréhier, *Chrysippe*, pp. 80–107, Hicks, *Stoic and Epicurean*, pp. 69–73, Pohlenz, *Die Stoa*, pp. 59–63, Watson, *The Stoic Theory of Knowledge*, pp. 34–7, Rist, *Stoic Philosophy*, pp. 133–47. My chapter was unfortunately with the printer before the last work was published.

3. It is used by Christensen, *An Essay on the Unity of Stoic Philosophy*, p. 59.

4. The text is doubtful. I have translated αὐτό τε καί; Diels in *Doxographi graeci* and von Arnim in *SVF* may be right to prefer ἐν αὐτῷ καί. Both readings have manuscript support.

5. *Acad. prior.* II 155 (*SVF* I 66).

6. *Adv. math.* VIII 397 (*SVF* II 91).

7. See Sextus, *Adv. math.* VIII 409 (*SVF* II 85). But the date of this doctrine is unknown. It may be an anachronism to attach it to Zeno; perhaps it is Chrysippean.

8. Bonhöffer, *Epictet und die Stoa*, pp. 141–5.

9. Diog. Laert. VII 177 (*SVF* I 625). Athenaeus 354e (*SVF* I 624), tells the same story, substituting birds for pomegranates.

10. Cleanthes, according to Sextus, interpreted the word literally, comparing the impress of a signet-ring. It is generally supposed that he was right in thinking that this was Zeno's meaning, especially in view of the words ἐναπομεμαγμένη and ἐναπεσφραγισμένη used in the definition of the φαντασία καταληπτική. I retain a lingering doubt whether it is right to ascribe such a simple-minded view to Zeno.

11. The difficulty of giving an adequate account of mental events in physical terms is notorious. I have wondered whether assent could be explained as preservation of the physical condition that constitutes φαντασία, and refusal of assent as allowing it to cease.

The Stoics underestimated the part played by the percipient in forming presentations. What we perceive depends upon past experience, and upon a selection from, and interpretation of, the stimuli that affect the organs of sense. I confess ignorance of the subject, which is difficult and complex. There is an interesting chapter in E. H. Gombrich, *Art and Illusion*, (London 1962) pp. 204–44, which deals with the perception both of drawings and of objects in the three-dimensional world of reality; see particularly the illustrations 220, 225, 232, 235 and 236. A stiffer work is M. D. Vernon, *A Further Study of Visual Perception* (Cambridge 1952).

12. The standard Greek definition of the cognitive presentation, which although nowhere explicitly ascribed to Zeno is undoubtedly his, runs as follows: ἡ ἀπὸ τοῦ ὑπάρχοντος καὶ κατ᾽ αὐτὸ τὸ ὑπάρχον ἐναπομεμαγμένη καὶ ἐναπεσφραγισμένη ὁποία οὐκ ἂν γένοιτο ἀπὸ μὴ ὑπάρχοντος.

13. *Acad. prior.* II 77. Augustine *Contra academicos* III 9, 18 gives as Zeno's doctrine: tale scilicet uisum comprehendi et percipi posse, quale cum falso non haberet signa communia. Another passage of Cicero seems to show that the presentation is grasped, but it contains two doubtful phrases that may detract from its authority. At *Acad. post.* I 41 he writes about Zeno as follows: uisis non omnibus adiungebat fidem sed eis solum quae propriam quandam haberent declarationem earum rerum quae uiderentur: id autem uisum (i.e. a presentation of this latter sort) cum ipsum per se cerneretur comprehendibile—(feretis hoc? nos uero, inquam: quonam enim alio modo καταληπτόν diceres?)—sed cum acceptum iam et approbatum esset comprehensionem appellabat. There can be no doubt that Cicero writes as if the uisum (φαντασία) is what is grasped. But can he be relied upon? There is no evidence that any Stoic gave the name of κατάληψις (*comprehensio*) to a καταληπτικὴ φαντασία that had received assent; it was the assent that they called κατάληψις. Then why does he suggest that the Greek term was φαντασία καταληπτός, not καταληπτική? It is this word καταληπτός, of necessarily passive meaning, which shows that

the presentation is grasped. Can Cicero have made a mistake, unlikely though that may seem? It has been argued that the word is confirmed by Epictetus *Diss.* IV 4, 13, where φαντασίαι καταληπτοί occur again. But since Schenkl's edition of 1916 it has been known that the Bodleian codex, from which all others are descended, had as its original text καταληπτικῶν; the letters ικ were erased by that ignorant busybody the second corrector, who was no doubt inspired to his mischief by the word ἀκαταλήπτων, which follows just after. But there is other support in a Herculaneum papyrus (*SVF* II 131) that sets out Stoic views as is reported to read εστι δ' ημεναπροπτωσιαδιαθεσισασυνκαταθετοσπροκαταληψεωσσυνκατιθετικηνκατανερ . . . . . αιφαντασιαικαταληπτωι.

Grumach, *Physis und Agathon* p. 74, argues that in so far as a presentation is grasped or not grasped by the mind it is called καταληπτός or ἀκατάληπτος, in so far as it allows the object to be grasped it is called καταληπτική. This may be right.

14. *Acad. post.* I 42 (*SVF* I 60). This is one of the surprisingly few passages that explicitly state κατάληψις to have external reality as its object. Diog. Laert VII 52, Cic. *Acad. prior.* II 23 Sextus VII 251 are, I think, others. But there are many where one may feel sure that this is meant. As Bréhier puts it, 'il ne s'agit pas seulement de juger des réprésentations mais d'atteindre des réalitiés' (p. 100 note).

With some hesitation I take *relinqueret* to mean 'pass over, neglect' rather than 'relinquish, take and then drop'. κατάληψις is not permanent until it has been converted into knowledge; unless one is a 'wise man', one can be argued out of it (*SVF* I 68). But perhaps a κατάληψις, so long as it exists, does not relinquish any element in the presentation.

15. For verbal adjectives in—τικός with a passive sense, see e.g. Plato *Timaeus* 55e, γῆ . . . τῶν σωμάτων πλαστικωτάτη, ibid. 58d, κινητικὸν . . . καὶ ὑπ' ἄλλου. Adjectives in—τός from transitive verbs are, if compounded with ἀ- privative, usually passive, but observe e.g. ἀνόητος, ἀνώμοτος. The ambiguity I see in καταληπτική is envisaged by Bréhier p. 95, but rejected. The view that a presentation is καταληπτική because it is one by means of which the percipient apprehends the external object is commonly held, e.g. by Hicks, Bréhier, Pohlenz, Watson.

16. It was that of Zeller, and so gained currency.

17. *Adv. math.* VII 254–7.

18. 'Zenon und Chrysipp', 175ff.; *Die Stoa* i pp. 60–2. His view is briefly criticised by Rieth, *Gnomon* xvi (1940) 106, to whom he replied in *Grundfragen*, pp. 105ff. It is accepted by de Vogel, *Greek Philosophy* iii p. 119, rejected by Rist, *Stoic Philosophy*, pp. 138ff.

19. Sextus *Adv. math.* VII 426, XI 183 (*SVF* II 70, 97). [See further Chapter V, p. 91. Ed.]

20. VII 54.

21. See *SVF* IV (index) p. 93, Pearson, *Zeno and Cleanthes*, pp. 8–9, Hicks, *Stoic and Epicurean*, pp. 70–1. [On *orthos logos* and the sage see further Chapter V, p. 102. Ed.]

22. This point is made by Rieth, loc. cit. Pohlenz must lay weight on the word *soli*. I do not share the doubts of Halm and Christ about the genuineness of the word, but also do not think that Cicero can have meant that *comprehensio* was the only thing we can trust. We must be able to trust knowledge also. And unless the presentation can be trusted, how can trust be put in *comprehensio*? Either Cicero, as so often, is not precise, or by *soli* he means *per se*: *comprehensio* is by itself sufficient for belief; we do not need its conversion into knowledge before it can be trusted.

II

Ennoia and Prolēpsis in the Stoic Theory of Knowledge

F. H. SANDBACH

The starting-point of Plutarch's dialogue *De communibus notitiis* is a claim made by the Stoics that Providence sent Chrysippus to remove the confusion surrounding the ideas of *ennoia* (ἔννοια, conception) and *prolēpsis* (πρόληψις, preconception) before the subtleties of Carneades were brought into play.[1] Unfortunately our surviving information on the subject is so much less full than could be desired that it has again returned to an obscurity from which there have been two really detailed attempts to remove it. The one, by L. Stein (*Erkenntnistheorie der Stoa* pp. 228–76), is most unsatisfactory;[2] the other, by A. Bonhöffer (*Epictet und die Stoa* pp. 187–232), though of the greatest value in many ways, is vitiated by the fact that it constructs a system from the use of the words by Epictetus and then attempts to attach this system to the old Stoa in the face of the evidence of the doxographers, which is emended or violently interpreted to suit Epictetus. Even if Epictetus were in general a good authority for the technicalities of Chrysippus—and in the opinion of J. von Arnim he is not[3]— this would not be a sound method of procedure. The only safe way is to take first the statements which can be attached to the old Stoa, and having obtained our results from these, to see whether Epictetus does in fact agree.

Bonhöffer contends that the term *koinē ennoia* (universal conception) is equivalent to *prolepsis*, though finally he restricts it to the most general part of a preconception, that actually brought to consciousness in the mind of every human being; and that *prolepseis*, which are 'spermatically' inborn and develop independently of any sense-impressions, only occur in a field

restricted to moral conceptions and conceptions of the divine.
The unsatisfactory nature of this scheme is most easily shown
by a piece of evidence with which he was not acquainted.[4]
This is from the work of Alexander *De mixtione* (p. 217 Bruns =
SVF II 473): 'he [sc. Chrysippus] tries to confirm the existence
of these varieties of mixture by means of our universal conceptions and says that we acquire these conceptions from nature
as excellent tests of truth' (τὸ δὲ ταύτας τὰς διαφόρας εἶναι τῆς
μίξεως πειρᾶται πιστοῦσθαι διὰ τῶν κοινῶν ἐννοιῶν, μάλιστα δὲ
κριτήρια τῆς ἀληθείας φησὶν ἡμᾶς παρὰ τῆς φύσεως λαβεῖν ταύτας).
If preconceptions and universal conceptions are equivalent,
then Chrysippus did not restrict them, whatever Epictetus may
have done,[5] to the moral and theological field.

There is need, therefore, for a new consideration of this part
of the Stoic theory of knowledge, namely the conception,
ennoia, and its subdivision, *prolepsis*.

I

The starting-point of the discussion must be the generally
accepted identity of *koine ennoia* and *prolepsis*.[6] The evidence
usually quoted consists of two passages which are supposed to
show that preconceptions are universal and therefore *koinai
ennoiai*. One is from Seneca, *Ep. mor.* 117, 6: 'we are accustomed
to give much weight to a preconception that belongs to all men,
and with us it is an indication of truth that something seems to
all men to be true' (multum dare solemus praesumptioni
(=προλήψει) omnium hominum et apud nos ueritatis argu-
mentum est aliquid omnibus uideri). The other is from
Plutarch, *Comm. not.* 1060A: 'to carry on philosophy in disregard
of conceptions and preconceptions that are universal' (τὸ παρὰ
τὰς ἐννοίας καὶ τὰς προλήψεις τὰς κοινὰς φιλοσοφεῖν).

The natural interpretation of these passages is that some
prolepseis are not universal. For if all *prolepseis* are universal, why
should anyone take the trouble to add 'that belongs to all men'
or 'that are universal'? But these additions are not uncommon;
Sextus, reproducing Stoic syllogisms, says 'according to the
universal conceptions and preconceptions of all men piety exists'
(*Adv. math.* IX 124=*SVF* II 1017). Plutarch regularly uses the

expression 'universal preconceptions' (*koinai prolepseis*, 1041F, 1073D, 1074F). Epictetus (*Diss.* IV 1, 42) speaks of 'preconceptions that are universal' (τὰς προλήψεις τὰς κοινάς.). Alexander *De mixtione* (p. 227 Bruns = *SVF* II 475) shows that the theory of 'total mixture' (κρᾶσις δι' ὅλων) is contrary to 'the universal preconceptions'. From such passages the natural inference is that just as of *ennoiai* some only were universal, so it was with *prolepseis*; the non-universal preconceptions whose existence we should infer we actually find in Plutarch (*Comm. not.* 1084D): 'in maintaining these things they do violence to universal preconceptions, but there are other doctrines by which they do violence to their own'. (ἀλλὰ ταῦτα μὲν παρὰ τὰς κοινὰς βιάζονται προλήψεις· ἐκεῖνα δ' ἤδη παρὰ τὰς ἰδίας)[7], and 1081B, 'so that in every way their preconceptions about non-corporeal things and bodies become confused' (ὥστε πάντῃ τὰς περὶ τῶν ἀσωμάτων καὶ σωμάτων αὐτοῖς ταράττεσθαι προλήψεις).

It might be objected that Plutarch used the word in a popular un-Stoical way. But it is just from Plutarch's use of it in 1060A and from a similar use in Seneca that the very idea has been drawn that for a Stoic all preconceptions were universal. Further, as far as I know, no ancient author ever suggests that there was any peculiarity in the meaning attached to the word by Chrysippus; if there had been, it would have been a likely ground for attack in *De communibus notitiis* (cf. 1084F, 'they suppose conception to have an essence that is contrary to our conceptions', ἐννοίας δ' οὐσίαν ... παρὰ τὰς ἐννοίας ὑποτίθενται, and 1073B–C, 'what else are we doing now but convicting their sect of perverting and doing violence to our universal conceptions by implausible 'facts' and incomprehensible vocabulary?').

But we still have to reckon with the evidence of Epictetus. *Diss.* I 22, opens with the statement: προλήψεις κοιναὶ πᾶσιν ἀνθρώποις εἰσίν ('preconceptions are common to all men'; the sequel confirms this rendering).[8] The context shows that he was thinking of the preconceptions of the good, the beautiful and other simple moral ideas. As an example he quotes: ὅτι τὸ δίκαιον καλόν ἐστι καὶ πρέπον.[9] That his phrase must be limited to such things he shows himself, for in other places he speaks of *prolepseis* which we cannot believe are universal, e.g. the *pro-*

lepsis of Cynicism (*Diss.* III,22, 1). Epictetus' statement is, then, inconsistent with his own use of the word; there is no reason for believing it to be consistent with that of the old Stoa.[10]

We thus see that the evidence by which it is sought to prove the identity of preconception and universal conception is quite insufficient, and that some of it points to a directly opposite conclusion. The interpretation of the doxographical evidence, which will be considered next, is greatly simplified by the abandoning of this supposed equivalence.[11]

II

Diocles Magnes (in Diog. Laert. VII 54) defines *prolepsis* as a 'natural conception of the general characteristics of a thing' (ἔννοια φυσικὴ τῶν καθόλου).[12] It is thus opposed to 'the state-ment of the characteristic property' (ἰδίου ἀπόδοσις), which was, according to the Stoics, the essence of a definition.[13] This, then, is one distinguishing mark of the preconception; it is an undeveloped conception, as opposed to the thought-out definition. For example the Stoics said that all men precon-ceived the gods as immortal and blessed and benevolent;[14] but their definition was a development of this: 'a living being, immortal, rational, perfect' (or 'intellectual'), 'in a state of happiness, unreceptive of all evil, exercising providence over the world and the things in the world' (Diog. Laert. VII 147 = *SVF* II 1021).

Preconception is limited by Diocles to conceptions that are natural. What these are we have to try to gather from a muti-lated passage of Aetius (*Plac.* IV 11 = *SVF* II 83):

When man is born, he has the commanding part of his soul like a sheet of paper serviceable for writing upon. On this he inscribes each one of his concepts. The first method of inscription is through the senses. For perceiving something, e.g. white, they have a memory of it when it has departed. And when many memories of a similar kind have arisen, then we say we have experience (*empeiria*). Experience is the mass of similar presentations. * * * of conceptions some come about naturally in the aforesaid ways and undesignedly, but others through our instruction and attention. The latter are called 'concep-tions' only, the former are called 'preconceptions'. Reason, for

C   L.P.S.

which we are called rational, is said to be completed from our preconceptions over the first seven years of life.

The plural, 'aforesaid ways', shows that something has fallen
out after the preceding sentence, and it is supposed that originally the passage resembled one in Diocles Magnes (Diog. Laert.
VII 52 = *SVF* II 87):

things conceived have been conceived some by direct experience,
some by resemblance, some by analogy, some by transposition, some
by composition, and some by contrariety [then follow examples] . . .
and some things are conceived by inference, like propositions and
space; and something just and good is conceived naturally; and by
privation, for instance a man without hands.

Here 'direct experience' (*periptōsis*) corresponds to 'experience'
(*empeiria*) in Aetius,[15] and the following modes to those there
omitted, but summarized by the phrase 'in the aforesaid ways'.[16]
The two passages together give a perfectly consistent account of
a preconception as the first conception of a thing, arrived at
without special mental attention, and derived either directly
or by some simple and unconscious mental operation from the
data given by the senses.

This straightforward interpretation could not be adopted by
anyone who believed preconceptions to be universally held.
There must be many conceptions that cannot possibly be
universal, yet arise naturally from experience, and ought therefore, according to Aetius, to be preconceptions. Thus the
champion of the rule that preconceptions are universal must
assume, as Bonhöffer does, that Aetius entirely misses the
difference between conception and preconception. On our
explanation no such assumption is required.

Can't we get universal conceptions arising naturally
from experience?

III

Bonhöffer had two other reasons for not accepting the evidence
of Aetius: he supposed preconceptions to have been limited to
fundamental ideas of morals and religion, and he thought they
were inborn in potentiality, or 'spermatically' as he put it.

There seems, as it happens, to be no case in which it can be
shown that a member of the old Stoa spoke of a preconception

of anything but the gods or moral terms. For preconceptions of natural objects we have to go to Epictetus, who speaks of a preconception of a philosopher, of a carpenter, of a musical man (iv 8, 10), or of what is healthy (ii 17, 9). But this is pure accident, due to the fact that in our fragments the word *ennoia* is used where the more definite term *prolepsis* might have been used if accuracy had been consulted. An example is supplied by the passage from Alexander *De mixtione* quoted in the second paragraph of this chapter. Here the *koinai ennoiai* concerned with mixture cannot be anything but preconceptions, since the words 'we acquire these conceptions from nature' show that they are 'natural conceptions' (*physikai ennoiai*), which on the undoubted evidence of Diocles (Diog. Laert. vii 54, quoted above) are equivalent to *prolepseis*.[17]

Plutarch not only says of many pieces of Stoic doctrine outside the field of moral conceptions that they are contrary to preconceptions,[18] but he also states that the Stoics attacked the Academy as philosophising against the preconceptions on a subject that lies outside that field—namely the problem of change and identity (*Comm. not.* 1083a–b).

Indirect evidence, too, speaks against the alleged restriction. Preconception, according to the Stoic theory of knowledge, made possible the search for and discovery of new knowledge.[19] That is, having a general idea of the characteristics of a thing, we have an indication of the lines to follow in a search for more definite knowledge. If preconceptions were limited in the way Bonhöffer suggests, they would be of restricted usefulness for this purpose. Again, a man's reason is said to be formed from his preconceptions.[20] Moral preconceptions would form a very insufficient basis. Bonhöffer realises this, and adds as a note (p. 193, n. 2), 'wobei jedoch nicht bloss die φυσικαί (sc. προλήψεις) gemeint sind', but he does not say what *is* meant.[21]

IV

A more difficult problem is presented by the origin and formation of those preconceptions which are universal. We may take as true in general the account gained by combining Aetius and Diocles, and yet doubt whether there was not behind *some*

universal preconceptions something more, something besides
the winning of an idea from the material provided by the senses.
These preconceptions are those of the moral sphere.

Chrysippus said of his account of good and evil that it 'had a
hold on our innate preconceptions' (Plut. *Stoic. rep.* 1041E = *SVF*
III 69, τῶν ἐμφύτων [sc. ἅπτεται] προλήψεων). All depends on
what meaning we are to give the word 'innate' (ἔμφυτος). The
orthodox view is that it cannot mean 'inborn', as this is contrary
to all the other evidence, and in particular inconsistent with the
image of the soul at birth as a sheet of paper ready to be in-
scribed with conceptions. Indeed, although ἔμφυτος does frequently mean 'inborn', there are some passages in which the
word is used of what is 'part of one's nature', as we say, without
any implication that it was there at one's birth. So in Euripides
frag. 776, τοῖς πλουτοῦσι τοῦτο δ' ἔμφυτον, σκαιοῖσιν εἶναι,
and Isocrates xi, 1, τοῖς πλείστοις τῶν νουθετουμένων
ἔμφυτόν ἐστι μὴ πρὸς τὰς ὠφελείας ἀποβλέπειν. See also
Dio Prusansis xii 39, quoted in note 24. It is not necessary,
then, to take ἐμφύτων to mean 'inborn'. Further, as the following paragraphs will show, what evidence we have on the origin
of ideas of good does not in any way suggest that anything
inborn played any part. In spite of this it is difficult to feel
confident that Chrysippus did not mean 'inborn' when he wrote
the word. But if he did, it was only a temporary aberration.

The other passage advanced in support of the idea that moral
preconceptions are in some way *a priori* and not derived from
experience is the sentence of Diocles (see above), 'and something just and good is conceived naturally' (φυσικῶς δὲ νοεῖται
δίκαιόν τι καὶ ἀγαθόν). Bonhöffer interprets this as opposing
to the preceding modes of conception, which are all ultimately
based on sense, a natural mode not so based. This explanation
leads at once to a contradiction with Cicero, *Fin.* III 33 (*SVF*
III 72): 'cumque rerum notiones[22] (= *ennoiai*) in animis fiant, si
aut usu (= κατὰ περίπτωσιν) aliquid cognitum sit aut coniunc-
tione (= κατὰ σύνθεσιν) aut similitudine (= καθ᾽ ὁμοιότητα)
aut collatione rationis (= κατ᾽ ἀναλογίαν), hoc quarto quod
extremum posui boni notitia facta est. cum enim ab iis rebus
quae sunt secundum naturam ascendit animus collatione
rationis, tum ad notionem boni peruenit. hoc autem ipsum

bonum non accessione neque crescendo ($=a\dot{v}\xi\eta\tau\iota\kappa\hat{\omega}s$) aut cum
ceteris comparando sed propria ui sua et sentimus et appellamus
bonum.' Bonhöffer explains that this passage of Cicero refers
not to the first conception of the good, to the *prolepsis* of the
good, but to a development of this conception. This is un-
convincing in itself, and made impossible by the similar passage
in Seneca, *Ep. mor.* 120, 4ff. Here on the question 'quomodo ad
nos prima boni honestique notitia peruenerit', Seneca says
'nobis uidetur obseruatio collegisse [sc. speciem uirtutis] et
rerum saepe factarum inter se collatio: per analogian nostri
intellectum et honestum et bonum iudicant.'[23] In point of fact
this passage of Cicero supplies the clue to the word $\phi\upsilon\sigma\iota\kappa\hat{\omega}s$
('naturally') in Diocles. First it must be noticed that the sentence
$\phi\upsilon\sigma\iota\kappa\hat{\omega}s$ $\delta\dot{\epsilon}$ $\nu o\epsilon\hat{\iota}\tau\alpha\iota$ $\delta\acute{\iota}\kappa\alpha\iota\acute{o}\nu$ $\tau\iota$ $\kappa\alpha\grave{\iota}$ $\dot{\alpha}\gamma\alpha\theta\acute{o}\nu$ is introduced as a kind of
postscript to the original list. Now the examples that Diocles
gives under the heading 'by analogy' are as follows: (1) Tityos
and the Cyclops, by increase; (2) the Pygmy, by diminution;
(3) the centre of the earth, by analogy from smaller spheres.
($\kappa\alpha\tau$' $\dot{\alpha}\nu\alpha\lambda o\gamma\acute{\iota}\alpha\nu$ $\delta\grave{\epsilon}$ $\alpha\dot{v}\xi\eta\tau\iota\kappa\hat{\omega}s$ $\mu\grave{\epsilon}\nu$ $\dot{\omega}s$ $\dot{o}$ $T\iota\tau\upsilon\grave{o}s$ $\kappa\alpha\grave{\iota}$ $K\acute{v}\kappa\lambda\omega\psi$,
$\mu\epsilon\iota\omega\tau\iota\kappa\hat{\omega}s$ $\delta\grave{\epsilon}$ $\dot{\omega}s$ $\dot{o}$ $\Pi\upsilon\gamma\mu\alpha\hat{\iota}os$, $\kappa\alpha\grave{\iota}$ $\tau\grave{o}$ $\kappa\acute{\epsilon}\nu\tau\rho o\nu$ $\delta\grave{\epsilon}$ $\tau\hat{\eta}s$ $\gamma\hat{\eta}s$ $\kappa\alpha\tau$' $\dot{\alpha}\nu\alpha$-
$\lambda o\gamma\acute{\iota}\alpha\nu$ $\dot{\epsilon}\nu o\acute{\eta}\theta\eta$ $\dot{\alpha}\pi\grave{o}$ $\tau\hat{\omega}\nu$ $\mu\iota\kappa\rho o\tau\acute{\epsilon}\rho\omega\nu$ $\sigma\phi\alpha\iota\rho\hat{\omega}\nu$). But Cicero expressly
guards against supposing that the good is conceived by any of
these methods ('crescendo' corresponds to the example of the
Cyclops, 'cum ceteris comparando' to the example of the earth's
centre, and no one would suppose that the good was conceived
by 'diminution'). Just so, whoever made the addition to the
original list in Diocles noticed that the good, though conceived
'by analogy', was not covered by any of the examples given;
accordingly he supplied the sentence under discussion, meaning
by $\phi\upsilon\sigma\iota\kappa\hat{\omega}s$ what Cicero calls 'propria ui sua' (and later
'genere non magnitudine'). We recognise the good through the
force of its own nature.[24]

It must be admitted that when we come to examine Epictetus he can hardly be interpreted otherwise than as believing
in 'inborn' preconceptions, but it is not justifiable to transfer
this to the orthodox Stoics of the third century. Between
Chrysippus and Epictetus lie the but half-charted waters of the
syncretism of the first century, the results of which we find in
Cicero. Stoicism affects Platonism, as in *Tusc.* 1 57, where Cicero

speaks in an account of the *Phaedo* of 'insitas et quasi consignatas in animis (= ἐναπεσφραγισμένας, a Stoic term) notiones, quas ἐννοίας uocant'; and Platonism gave to Stoicism a belief in inborn conceptions, as in *N.D.* II 12: 'omnibus enim innatum est et in animo quasi insculptum, esse deos ... Cleanthes quidem noster quattuor de causis dixit in animis informatas deorum esse notiones.' The four causes are various classes of natural phenomena, but the inconsistency between this and 'innatum' Cicero does not observe or else neglects.

The effect of Platonism on the mind of Cicero, or on that of the authors of his sources, is seen in the metaphors which he uses in speaking of conceptions, even where he purports to be reproducing Stoic ideas. To Chrysippus a preconception, though it might be incomplete as an account of a thing, was perfectly clear as far as it went.[25] But Cicero, with memories of Platonic *anamnēsis*, used metaphors which imply that the 'notio' contains the whole truth but is but dimly seen, through being in darkness or covered up; *Tusc.* IV 53: of all the Stoic definitions of bravery, 'quae non aperit notionem nostram quam habemus omnes de fortitudine, tectam atque inuolutam?' *Off.* III 76: 'complicatam notionem euoluere;' 81: 'explica atque excute intellegentiam tuam.'

V

So far *prolepsis* has been treated as if it were a technical term peculiar to the Stoic school. In point of fact we are told by Cicero that the word was invented by Epicurus for an idea which till then had no name (*N.D.* I 44). This has been unreasonably called into question, mainly on the ground that there is a difference in meaning between the Stoic and Epicurean terms which makes an independent origin probable.[26] The chief of these supposed differences are that the Stoic *prolepsis* is common to all mankind, and that it is confined to moral and religious conceptions, whereas the Epicurean may be individual and is in no way restricted in subject. From what has been said above, it will be seen that this rests on a misconception of the Stoic *prolepsis*. Also, had there been a difference in the meaning of the word as used by Stoics and Epicureans, some ancient would surely have mentioned it. As it is, the word is constantly used

in the disputes between all the schools, without any suggestion
that the parties meant different things by the term. What
difference there is lies not in the meaning of the word, but in the
accounts given of the origin of the thing denoted. For Epicurus
prolēpsis only arises by the way of memory, by the coincidence
of several presentations of the same object: the Stoics, while
retaining this method, also introduced as possible ways of
forming *prolepseis* the other simple mental operations, analogy
and the rest.

   In a passage already quoted Plutarch uses the phrase 'removing the confusion that surrounds preconceptions and conceptions' (*Comm. not.* 1059B). The nature of this confusion can only
be guessed, but the Epicurean origin of the word suggests that
its first use by the Stoics may have been in argument against
the Epicureans.[27] The latter used 'the preconception of all men'
to support their own views on the nature of the gods. The first
Stoics probably denied that it supported Epicureans, and
claimed that in fact it was in accordance with their own views.
If this line of argument is first attested for Chrysippus (Plutarch,
Stoic. rep. 1051E, *Comm. not.* 1075E = *SVF* II 1115, 1126), it is so
obvious that it must have presented itself to his predecessors. In
this way there would come into use a term, *prolēpsis*, for which
no place had been made in the Zenonian theory of knowledge.
We can imagine Arcesilaus and his followers turning on the
Stoics and demanding from them definitions of this new term,
distinctions between it and the familiar *ennoia*.

   A quotation from Cleanthes suggests another way in which
difficulty may have arisen. Among the causes which he gave to
account for the origin of the conception of the gods we find
'tertiam quae terreret animos fulminibus, tempestatibus,
nimbis, niuibus, grandinibus, uastitate, pestilentia', and by
many kinds of portents, 'quibus exterriti homines uim quandam
esse caelestem et diuinam suspicati sunt.' It seems that
Cleanthes is giving an historical account of the origin of the
conception of the gods without any idea that this primitive
conception may be used as evidence of their qualities. Thus
he allows that men should think of the gods as terrible and harmful.[28] It is significant that no parallel to this argument of
Cleanthes is found in any other Stoic writer.[29]

VI

This discussion of the word *prolepsis* may be concluded by a[30] consideration of an idea which has some points of similarity, namely, *enargeia*. In chapter 38 of *De Stoicorum repugnantiis*, side by side with the 'conception' of the gods, we find an *enargeia* appealed to. The fragment is from Antipater and runs as follows: 'We will give a brief account of the *enargeia* which we have about God. We conceive of a god as a blessed being, incorruptible and beneficent.' This *enargeia* tallies exactly with the *prolepsis* of a god.

The origin of the word appears to be, like that of *prolepsis*, Epicurean. Epicurus was of opinion that we must trust our *phantasiai* because of their clearness.[31] By a transference of meaning *enargeia* was used to mean a *phantasia* (presentation).[32] As far as I know, the word does not occur in any fragment of any Stoic earlier than Antipater,[33] and it is at least possible that he is using the word because he is attacking the Epicureans for denying beneficence to the gods.

But at some time or another the Stoics did adopt the word just as they had adopted *prolepsis*; Posidonius uses the adjective *enarges* (apud Galen *De plac*. p. 400, Müller), and in Plutarch *Comm. not.* 1083c the Stoics appear as 'these champions of *enargeia*'. It was easy enough for the Stoics to adopt the word, because by *enargeia* Epicurus meant to denote just that quality of a *phantasia* which Zeno denoted by the word *kataleptikē*, that quality which makes a man feel certain of its truth. Epicurus expressed this actively, making the presentation real enough to command belief; Zeno passively, making it real enough to be capable of being firmly grasped by the mind.[34]

The words *enarges, enargeia* provide a good example of the way the schools borrowed one another's vocabulary, for not only did the Stoics take them from the Epicureans, but the later Academy took them over also; Philo of Larisa agreed that some things had this clearness and were certainly true, though he denied that clearness implied comprehensibility, as the Stoics maintained.[35]

This chapter reproduces, with a few minor corrections, an article published in *Classical Quarterly* xxiv (1930) 44–51, but except in the notes Greek of the original version has mostly been transliterated or translated. Two further supplementary notes are needed.

(1) I have allowed Diocles Magnes to stand as the author of various passages quoted from Diogenes Laertius, although I am not now sure that the current view, which makes him the author of the whole of vii 50–82, is correct. There is no other evidence that Diocles' work, which was entitled Ἐπιδρομὴ τῶν φιλοσόφων, contained such detailed technical matter. Elsewhere he is quoted for personalities or biographical details. Secondly, I do not feel confident that the text of vii 48 is sound. It runs: καὶ ἵνα καὶ κατὰ μέρος εἴπωμεν καὶ τάδε ἅπερ αὐτῶν εἰς τὴν εἰσαγωγικὴν τείνει τέχνην, καὶ αὐτὰ ἐπὶ λέξεως τίθησι Διοκλῆς ὁ Μάγνης. 'I will quote what Diocles of Magnesia says' (Hicks), and 'nous citons à la lettre Dioclès' (Bréhier), are translations of the last clause that conceal the oddity of the Greek. Can there be a lacuna after the word τέχνην? The sense might be as follows. 'In order to give in detail their views that concern the introductory art [sc. of logic], ⟨let us begin with the subject of presentations. And that they do this⟩ themselves also [reading καὶ αὐτοί], is stated in so many words by Diocles.' The quotation from Diocles would then occupy merely vii 49. There would be a point in this apology for beginning with presentations. Properly speaking their treatment belongs not to logic, but to psychology, a branch of physics. Diocles would be cited to explain that since verbal expressions, the subject of logic, are subsequent to the formation of presentations, the Stoics thought fit to treat presentation and sensation first.

(2) The explanation advanced in Section iv of the phrase φυσικῶς δὲ νοεῖται δίκαιόν τι καὶ ἀγαθόν is inadequate and unsatisfactory. The nature referred to by the word φυσικῶς must be that of the man who forms the concept, not that of the concept itself. I do not think that any convincing account has been given of why Diogenes has νοεῖται δίκαιόν τι and not νοεῖται τὸ δίκαιον. Some take the point to be that natural concepts are imperfect, awaiting development by reason; if that is the intention, it could have been more clearly expressed. Can

the meaning be simply that a conception arises 'naturally' that there is something just and good? This would not include of necessity any developed ideas of what this is, nor indeed imply that any such thing actually exists. But it exists as an object of thought. This interpretation is in effect not much different from the other, but perhaps better renders the Greek. (Attempts to emend, δίκαιον τί (nescioquis) or δίκαιόν τε (Grumach), are not plausible.)

Neither in 'Grundfragen' pp. 82–99 nor in *Die Stoa* does Pohlenz examine the phrase. He attempts, however, to find a kind of compromise between those who strictly maintain that all concepts arise from experience of the outside world and those who believe that moral concepts have, to some extent at least, an internal origin. He argues that through its awareness of self and ability to form value judgements the child obtains the conception that the 'good' and the 'useful' are what promote its being.[36] This he suggests is what Chrysippus meant by ἔμφυτοι προλήψεις. The child sees its being as an animal being, but with the growth of reason the man comes to understand that the truly good is what promotes his rational life. I see no reason why this account should not have been welcomed by a Stoic, but also no evidence of its connexion with ἔμφυτοι προλήψεις. In any case Pohlenz makes no claim that it is relevant to the way in which the concept of 'just' is formed.

NOTES

1. 1059C: τὸν περὶ τὰς προλήψεις καὶ τὰς ἐννοίας τάραχον ἀφελὼν παντάπασι καὶ διορθώσας ἑκάστην καὶ θέμενος εἰς τὸ οἰκεῖον.

2. See e.g. the opinions of von Arnim, *Deutsche Litteraturzeitung* (1888), p. 16; Bonhöffer, *Epictet und die Stoa*, pp. iv–v; Bevan, *Stoics and Sceptics*, p. 6.

3. *SVF* p. xvii, Epictetus, Musonius, Seneca, 'ad Chrysippum restituendum nullum fere usum praebent'.

4. *SVF* was, of course, not available when he wrote.

5. Evidence given later will show that the restriction does not hold even for Epictetus.

6. E.g. Zeller, *Philosophie der Griechen*, III i, 76. (All following references to Zeller are to this volume.) Ueberweg-Praechter, *Grundriss der Geschichte der Philosophie*[12] p. 1418.

7. Cf. the parallel expression in 1062A: οὐ μόνον παρὰ τὰς κοινὰς ἐννοίας φιλο-σοφούντων ἀλλὰ καὶ τὰς ἰδίας κυκώντων.

8. The same thing is implied in II 11, 2 in a similar context. Bonhöffer also quotes, in a different connexion (p. 220), Nemesius 203 = *De anima hominis*, Migne, xl 661, φυσικὰς δὲ λέγομεν ἐννοίας τὰς ἀδιδάκτως πᾶσι προσούσας, ὡς τὸ εἶναι θεόν. But the thoughts here are not so much Stoic as Platonic; the point under discussion is ἀνάμνησις.

9. Cf. IV 1, 44.

10. Bonhöffer attempts (p. 198) to explain away the inconsistency. He is not very intelligible, but seems to be driven here as elsewhere to the assumption that Epictetus did not always use the word in its proper meaning.

11. We may notice that when the context makes the meaning clear ἡ πρόληψις is used to mean ἡ κοινὴ πρόληψις, e.g. Plutarch, *Comm. not.* 1075E: πρὸς τὸν Ἐπίκουρον οὐδὲν ἀπολείπουσι τῶν πραγμάτων (ἐν οὐδενὶ, γραμμάτων Wyttenbach) ἰού ἰού φεῦ φεῦ βοῶντες ὡς συγχέοντα τὴν τῶν θεῶν πρόληψιν (cf. 1075A). This is exactly paralleled by the very frequent use of ἡ ἔννοια = ἡ κοινὴ ἔννοια (παρὰ τὴν ἔννοιάν ἐστιν 1073D, 1077A, 1077E, etc., τῆς περὶ θεῶν ἐννοίας 1076A, σχέτλια ποιεῖν τὸν Ἐπίκουρον λέγουσι καὶ βιάζεσθαι τὰς ἐννοίας 1082E). It is probably this usage of πρόληψις that accounts for the persistence of the view that all preconceptions are universal.

12. A difficult phrase; Bonhöffer tries to connect τὰ καθόλου with conceptions not derived from experience, as being less definite than those that are. This is connected with his theory of the restriction of preconceptions to the moral field, which is, as we shall see, certainly false. Stein (p. 237 n. 511) gives the impossible rendering, 'die überall waltende Weltordnung'.

13. For the general idea of this distinction cf. Galen in *SVF* II 229: ἀρξώμεθ᾽ οὖν αὖθις ἀπὸ τῶν ἐννοηματικῶν ὅρων οὓς οὐδὲν ἔφαμεν ἑρμηνεύειν πλέον ὧν ἅπαντες ἄνθρωποι γινώσκουσιν . . . οὓς οἱ δεινοὶ περὶ τὰς προσηγορίας οὐδ᾽ ὅρους ἀξιοῦσιν ἀλλ᾽ ὑπογραφάς τε καὶ ὑποτυπώσεις ὀνομάζειν. On ἴδιον see Rieth, *Grundbegriffe* pp. 57ff.

14. Cf. Plutarch, *Comm. not.* 1075E and *Stoic. rep.* 1051E.

15. περίπτωσις is a word that did not remain the technical term of any one school. It occurs in Epicurean doctrine, Diog. Laert. x 32): ἐπίνοιαι πᾶσαι ἀπὸ τῶν αἰσθήσεων γεγόνασι κατά τε περίπτωσιν καὶ ἀναλογίαν καὶ ὁμοιότητα καὶ σύνθεσιν, συμβαλλομένου τι τοῦ λογισμοῦ, and Sextus uses it as if it were a generally accepted notion (*Adv. math.* VIII 56). Cicero appears to translate it by 'usu' (*Fin.* III 33, see below). It must be connected with περιπίπτω in the neutral sense 'meet with', and seems to have meant 'direct experience', as is now recognised by *LSJ*.

16. The plural τρόπους has also been explained as meaning μνήμην καὶ ἐμπειρίαν (Diels, *Doxographi Graeci* p. 400). Aetius is then committed to a statement of obvious incompleteness. The explanation given above supposes no inaccuracies, and is in accord, for what that may be worth, with Cicero, *Ac.* II 30 (=Antiochus, see Zeller, p. 619, n. 2): 'cetera (sc. uisa) autem similitudinibus (=καθ᾽ ὁμοιότητα) construit (sc. mens) quibus efficiuntur notitiae rerum quas Graeci tum ἐννοίας tum προλήψεις uocant.'

17. Cf. *SVF* II p. 32 note, 'φυσικαὶ ἔννοιαι apud Chrysippum eadem sunt quae προλήψεις'.

18. E.g. 1059E: πίστεως πρόληψιν and 1073D: τὸν φυσικὸν αὐτῶν λόγον οὐχ ἧττον τοῦ περὶ τελῶν διαταράττοντα τὰς κοινὰς προλήψεις.

19. Plutarch, frag. 216 (f) Sandbach, Bernardakis VII p. 29 = *SVF* II 104, under the heading ὅτι ἄπορον ὄντως εἰ οἷόν τε ζητεῖν καὶ εὑρίσκειν ὡς ἐν Μένωνι προβέβληται (the well-known problem, p. 80E), οἱ δὲ ἀπὸ τῆς στοᾶς τὰς φυσικὰς ἐννοίας αἰτιῶνται.

20. See the last sentence of Aetius quoted above. Chrysippus, *SVF* II 841, calls it an ἐννοιῶν τέ τινων καὶ προλήψεων ἄθροισμα.

21. The only other kind of πρόληψις he mentions is the πρόληψις διηθρωμένη, peculiar among Stoics to Epictetus, which is properly not a preconception at all, for it is obtained δι' ἡμετέρας διδασκαλίας καὶ ἐπιμελείας. Also if the field of pre-conception is restricted, so must be that of 'articulated' or developed preconceptions.

22. Whether called an ἔννοια or πρόληψις the thing meant is the same (cf. Aetius, ἐκεῖναι δὲ καὶ προλήψεις, quoted at the beginning of Section II). The trans-lations are those given by von Arnim. The index to SVF gives notitia = ἐπιστήμη: though it may sometimes bear this meaning, Cicero usually employs it as a synonym for notio.

23. It is true that Seneca says: 'natura semina scientiae dedit, scientiam non dedit.' But in all that follows no place is given to any inborn ideas in the formation of the conception of the good. The 'semina' seem to be the facts observed.

24. It may be noted that no trace of innate preconceptions is to be found in Panaetius' account of the formation of moral ideas, reproduced by Polybius VI 6 (Schmekel, Die Philosophie der mittleren Stoa, pp. 64ff.). This agrees with Cicero and Seneca in making them rest on the observation of good and evil actions, and ends αὕτη καλοῦ καὶ δικαίου πρώτη παρ' ἀνθρώποις κατὰ φύσιν ἔννοια. Innate precon-ceptions are equally lacking in the Posidonian passage in Aetius, Plac. I 6, headed πόθεν θεῶν ἔννοιαν ἔλαβον ἄνθρωποι (SVF II 1009). Panaetius and Posidonius were both Platonising Stoics who, had their predecessors believed in innate precon-ceptions, would scarcely have suppressed the notion. A very similar account of how early man won the conception of divinity is given by Dio Prus., XII 27ff. Though the observation of nature is the only method he mentions, he does not hesitate to call the resulting conception ἔμφυτος; cf. especially c. 39: τὴν ἔμφυτον ἅπασιν ἀνθρώποις ἐπίνοιαν ἐξ αὐτῶν γιγνομένην τῶν ἔργων. Plutarch, Comm. not. 1070C may perhaps be relevant to this question. There he enquires whether any theory has done greater outrage to normal feeling than that of the Stoics about the good, καὶ ταῦτα, he continues, ἐν τοῖς περὶ ἀγαθῶν καὶ κακῶν αἱρετῶν τε καὶ φευκτῶν οἰκείων τε καὶ ἀλλοτρίων ἃ μᾶλλον ἔδει θερμῶν [τε] καὶ ψυχρῶν λευκῶν τε καὶ μελάνων σαφέστερον ἔχειν τὴν ἐνάργειαν. ἐκείνων μὲν γὰρ ἔξωθέν εἰσιν αἱ φαντασίαι ταῖς αἰσθήσεσιν ἐπεισόδιοι, ταῦτα δ' ἐκ τῶν ἀγαθῶν τῶν ἐν ἡμῖν σύμφυτον ἔχει τὴν γένεσιν. But I am uncertain of the meaning of the last sentence, and uncertain whether Plutarch is here confuting the Stoics out of their own mouths or not.

25. It must have been a φαντασία καταληπτική: cf. Antipater's use of the word ἐνάργεια, considered below.

26. Stein, Erkenntnistheorie der Stoa, pp. 248–50. He also alleges that Cicero is an untrustworthy witness.

27. The idea that it was borrowed to meet the attacks of the Academy seems less likely; for they were concerned chiefly with the validity of sense-impressions, in support of which preconception, and particularly the Epicurean preconception, based only on the accumulation of sense-impressions, would have been of little or no use.

28. Cf. Plut. Stoic. rep. 1051E (SVF II 1115): πρὸς τὸν Ἐπίκουρον μάλιστα μάχεται (sc. Χρύσιππος) καὶ πρὸς τοὺς ἀναιροῦντας τὴν πρόνοιαν ἀπὸ τῶν ἐννοιῶν ἃς ἔχομεν περὶ θεῶν, εὐεργετικοὺς καὶ φιλανθρώπους ἐπινοοῦντες.

29. Pearson, Zeno and Cleanthes, p. 284.

30. I have nothing to say on the subject of πρόληψις as a test of truth. The correct interpretation seems to me to have been given by Bréhier, Chrysippe, p. 103.

31. Cf. Ep. ad Men. 123: θεοὶ μὲν γὰρ εἰσίν. ἐναργὴς γὰρ αὐτῶν ἐστιν ἡ γνῶσις.

32. Usener, Epicurea 247 = Sextus, Adv. math. VII 203: τὴν φαντασίαν ἣν καὶ ἐνάργειαν καλεῖ. Zeller, III i, 401, n. 3, calls this an 'eigentümliche Bezeich-nung'.

ENNOIA AND PROLEPSIS 37

33. It is not entered at all in the Index to *SVF*. Yet Bevan, *Stoics and Sceptics*, pp. 35, 37, talks of *enargeia* in explaining Zeno.

34. This interpretation of the word καταληπτική is well upheld by Bréhier, *Chrysippe*, pp. 80–100. The famous phrase μόνον οὐχὶ τῶν τριχῶν λαμβάνεται is definitely put down to *younger* Stoics by Sextus, *Adv. math.* VII 257, and is not applied to every φαντασία καταληπτική, but to such as 'contain no obstacle'.

35. Zeller, p. 616, n. 2: Cicero, *Ac.* II 34.

36. [Cf. S. G. Pembroke, Chapter VI, p. 37, Ed.]

III

Categories and their Uses

J. M. RIST

In his book *Stoic Logic*, first published in 1953, Benson Mates devotes something less than a page to the Stoic categories. His hesitation about saying more is explained as due to the fact that our best sources for Stoic logic, namely Sextus Empiricus, Diogenes Laertius and Galen, have little to tell us about categories, and that what information we have comes very largely from the Aristotelian commentators who are both late and 'relatively unreliable'.[1] Since Mates's book appeared, Miss Margaret Reesor has made two attempts to clarify the situation,[2] but despite her useful work much still remains unclear. In particular the category of quality, with its two subdivisions, specific and particular quality, provides considerable problems. Nor, despite the work of Phillip De Lacy,[3] is it at all clear what the categories were used for. Nor again do we yet fully understand how the categories fit into the materialist world-picture which the Stoics normally offer us.[4]

Zeno seems to have founded his physics on the thesis that everything that exists must be either active or passive, and that it can either act or be acted upon.[5] This necessitates that anything which can neither act nor be acted upon—if there is such a thing—is both 'non-existent' and, in the Stoic view, incorporeal. Hence the theory arose, subscribed to by most members of the school, that there are four kinds of immaterial 'things' which cannot properly be said to exist, but which can be thought of as 'subsistent'.[6] These are void, place, time, and what they called *lekta* or 'things meant'. A thing meant is described as 'the thing itself revealed by sound which we grasp as subsisting together with our thought'.[7] There were some Stoics who were worried about the status of *lekta*, but the evidence which we have about them—and they included a prominent but mysterious figure named Basileides—does not show with any kind of certainty what they actually said. Often the orthodox Stoics seem to have stated that the 'incorporeals' subsist,[8] but the word 'subsist' (*hyphistasthai*) does not appear in the report of Basileides,[9] although the other word sometimes used by the orthodox, namely *hyparchein*, does. We must conclude that we do not know how the argument ran in detail; we only know that there was an argument.[10]

Let us forget about the unorthodox. The normal Stoic view, formulated in detail by Chrysippus, is that there are four kinds of immaterial 'thing'.[11] How is this to be squared with the doctrine, for which there is a great deal of evidence, that according to the Stoics 'bodies alone are real'?[12] The phrase in Plutarch gives the position away. Plutarch writes ὄντα γὰρ μόνα τὰ σώματα; they call bodies alone existents (*onta*). This means that incorporeal things would be called something other than *onta*, namely subsistent things. Thus 'existence' (*ousia*) would not be the most general term the Stoics would be willing to predicate. First of all they speak of 'things'; then they divide these into two classes, (a) existent things, and (b) subsistent things like time as well as non-existent (i.e. fictional) things like centaurs. Our best evidence is a passage of Seneca, where it is pointed out that 'what is' (*quod est = to on*) is not the highest class; in the view of 'certain Stoics' there are 'in the nature of things' certain things which do not exist. Seneca gives examples of these: centaurs and giants and whatever else can be constructed by the mind but which has no reality (*substantia = ousia*).[13] The name given by Seneca to this highest grouping of all, which embraces both what exists and what does not, is 'something' (*quid*); other authorities give us the Greek name (*to ti*).[14] Confusion about this concept, wilful or otherwise, began early. Alexander of Aphrodisias tries to argue that whatever can be called 'something' (*ti*) must be an existent (*on*);[15] this is precisely what the orthodox Stoics were concerned to deny. It is noteworthy that Alexander does not mention the Centaurs and Giants which Seneca had used in his example. If he had, it might have been more obvious than he liked to admit that there is a category distinction between horses which exist and Centaurs which do not. But in this

Alexander is only typical of many Greek thinkers in ignoring problems, partly grasped by the Stoics, about fictional or otherwise non-existent nameables.

We have seen that incorporeal things include *lekta*. And the categories themselves are examples of one type of *lekton*; they are incomplete *lekta*.[16] By this is meant that they need to be combined with subjects to form propositions; they are in fact predicates.[17] In other words, if we put something into a category, we expect to be told something about it; we will understand that x is so and so. Now the Stoics posited four categories only. Passages listing the names of these four together are very late, but there is no reason to believe them to be inaccurate.[18] The usual names are substance (*hypokeimenon*), quality (*poion*), disposition (*pōs echon*) and relative disposition (*pros ti pōs echon*). Our first problem, therefore, is to determine what is meant by the term 'substance'. The answer to this has been hit upon, though perhaps inadvertently, by De Lacy, though, since in his article it is embedded in a good deal of argument which is not necessarily acceptable, it may not be apparent.[19] De Lacy writes as follows: 'The first category is enlarged somewhat to include not only the inquiry *what* a thing is, but also *that* it is.' As an example of this De Lacy cites Epictetus on the problem of learning 'that God exists', and a little later on 'what the universe is and who arranges it'.[20] But it might be argued that the questions 'What is God' and 'Does God exist?' are not as dissimilar to the Stoic as might at first be supposed. For the Stoics, as we have seen, if God exists, he would be material (and of course he is material). Hence the question 'Does God exist?' could (logically) appear as 'Is God an existent?' (ἔστιν ὁ θεὸς ἐν τοῖς οὖσιν). Similarly the question 'What is God?' would basically appear as 'Is God an existent or not?' If we now view this in terms of our previous discussion about 'things' and 'existent things', we should be able to conclude that, if God (or anything else) exists, that is, is a material object, he will fall under the scope of the categories. We shall be able to say more of him than simply that he is a 'thing' (*ti*): he will be an existent thing. He will be substantial (*substantia*) and, of course, material.

Our proposition is, therefore, that the test for membership

in the first category is simply whether the object exists, that is, is material or not. We observed that the name of the first category is usually 'substance' (*hypokeimenon*), but there is good evidence that the word 'being' (*ousia*), which must, as we have argued, have carried the sense of existing as opposed to not-existing, was used, among others, both by Chrysippus and by Posidonius. That Posidonius may not have understood Chrysippus' full meaning is not immediately relevant. The important point for our present purposes is that they both used the word to name the first category.[21]

At this point a slight objection must be considered. According to Zeller the earlier Stoics failed to draw the necessary distinctions; thus there is some justification for the confusion in the minds of their rivals as to the name of the highest possible grouping of things.[22] Zeller suggests that what we have called 'things' (*tina*) were sometimes called *onta* by the Stoics; thus, by implication, he provides a certain justification for those in antiquity who argued that every 'thing' must be an existent thing (*on ti*). According to Zeller the word 'thing' (*ti*) was probably introduced only by Chrysippus as the best term to describe not only existing things (*onta, ousiai*) but non-existing things like Centaurs.

There is a firm tradition, which our authorities refer to Zeno himself, that Platonic Forms have no independent existence, but are *ennoemata*, false concepts which arise in the mind; they are in themselves neither existing things nor qualified existing things, but likenesses of them (οὔτε τὶ ὂν οὔτε ποιόν, ὡσανεὶ δέ τι ὂν καὶ ὡσανεὶ ποιόν).[23] This evidence would suggest that there are some 'things' which are not existing things but likenesses of existing things. We should think of fictional characters as bearing obviously striking resemblances to existing characters. The evidence thus suggests that the Stoics would not like to call their most general class 'existents' (*onta*), because such a class could not include likenesses of existents. But even if we reject the *attribution* of the doctrine of likenesses of existents to Zeno, we have only proved that Chrysippus distinguished imitation existents from existents, not that Zeno did not distinguish them, What Zeller needs are passages to prove that some of the earlier Stoics did not make the distinction, or at least that they did not relate it to the categories. He offers two such passages, neither of which serves his turn.

The first passage is from Diogenes Laertius. The Stoics are made to say that the widest genus is that which, while being a genus, cannot be put into a genus, for instance *to on* (VII 61); but all that this proves is that the Stoics held that *to on* is unique. What would they have said of *to mē on*? It seems that Chrysippus (?) must have held that 'being' and 'non-being' cannot be said to have enough in common to warrant being put into the same genus. 'Being' therefore would be the only member of its genus; it is unique. In the next sentence of Diogenes the Stoics are said to have held that Socrates is *eidikōtaton*, because being an example of a most specific *eidos* (species) he cannot be subdivided into *eidē*. Like 'being' though for different reasons, Socrates is unique. But the fact that the Stoics said that *to on* cannot be put into a genus only means that there is no superior genus to *to on* (= *hypokeimenon*); and genus and category are frequently synonymous in Greek. We know that the Stoics never called 'things' (*tina*) a category. Only existing things have to do with categories directly. In the case of non-existents predication and classification can only be by analogy. So all the passage from Diogenes proves is that *on* is the widest category, that is, that it is a term equivalent to *hypokeimenon*.

Zeller's second (and only other) passage is from a letter of Seneca which we have already examined.[24] We read as follows:

There is something higher than body, for we say that some things are corporeal, others are incorporeal. What will this be . . .? That to which we just gave the rather inappropriate name 'that which is' (*quod est*). . . . That which is is either corporeal or incorporeal.

From the context, however, it appears that this view is not attributed to the Stoics but to Plato! The view of 'certain Stoics', as we outlined it above, is that 'things' form a more general class than 'existents'. But if this is the view of 'certain Stoics', what did the others hold? Did they hold that existents (*quod est*) form the highest class? That is not the most obvious interpretation of what Seneca says. His argument is: (1) *quod est* is the highest class for the Platonists; (2) the Stoics offer a higher class; (3) some Stoics say this highest class is 'things' (*quid*). It is hard to know how to interpret this evidence, but at least Seneca does not mean what Zeller makes him mean, namely that the earliest Stoics began their classification with *quod est* and that the wider grouping (*quid*) was added by Chrysippus. Perhaps the ambiguity in Seneca arises from the later controversy within the Stoic school, which we mentioned at the beginning of this chapter, about whether incorporeals should properly be designated 'things'. Perhaps some of the Stoics thought that 'things' must mean 'existent things' (*ti* must mean *on ti*), and were unwilling to accept any kind of classification broader than category one (*hypokeimenon*, *ousia*). These thinkers would find it impossible to classify anything other than material existents. Hence, perhaps, there could be no grouping more general than category one. But if this is the controversy to which Seneca alludes, he does not make his position very plain. Nevertheless, we may conclude that one thing we can be sure of is that there is no evidence for Zeller's claim that the earliest Stoics called their highest class *on*, and that they neglected what was later called *ti*. Zeller's attempt to solve the problem by alluding to the view of Ritter that the older Stoics 'must' have called their most general class 'being', is a desperate move, unsupported by the evidence. We may conclude that the distinction between 'things' and 'existents' goes back to Zeno and that Zeno regarded 'being' not as the most general class but as the most general category.

If a 'thing', therefore, is to be admitted into category one, it must be an existing thing. If it is in category one, it is an existing material object; it is a substance (*ousia*, *hypokeimenon*). A definition of substance (*ousia*) ascribed to Zeno himself should be mentioned here: 'substance is the prime matter (*prōtē hylē*) of all existing things'.[25] The sum total of substance is everlasting and neither grows nor diminishes. There are, of course, particulars, which are 'bits' of substance. These particulars, which the Stoics often call *ousiai*, admit of division and blending. The qualitative change of a particular is explained as a re-configuration of the substance; the 'first' configurations are said to be colours.[26] It is incorrect to say, as Miss Reesor does, that there is no evidence that Zeno distinguished between the substance and the quality of a particular in his treatment of

growth and change.[27] According to Galen the thesis that both
'substances' and 'qualities' are capable of total mixture (δι' ὅλων
κεραννῦσθαι) was that of Zeno himself.[28] And if qualities are
thus susceptible of this kind of material mixing, and are specifically separated in Zeno's sentence from substances, it is hard to
think that Zeno did not distinguish between them. Miss Reesor
argues that Zeno thought that the substance of the particular is
subject to qualitative change, but there is no evidence for that.
Two particulars can be compounded into a new unit by total
mixture, but their *ousia* does not change its quality as such.
Strictly speaking all *ousia* is one in any case; it is one existing
whole. It was only the view of Posidonius, who, as so frequently,
misunderstood the original Stoic doctrine, that *ousia* could
undergo qualitative change (*alloiōsis*).[29] This mistake presumably arose because Posidonius failed to grasp the implications
of the fact that having an *ousia* merely means being a material
object. *Qua* matter, matter *cannot* change; it *exists* as it is and no
other mode of existence is possible.

We have argued that, although Zeno spoke of colours as
configurations of substance, he must have regarded them, like
other qualities, as material causes capable of the physical act
of total mixture.[30] This doctrine was clearly formalized by
Chrysippus, as extant fragments make abundantly clear.[31] For
Chrysippus qualities are currents of air, and as such are capable
of total mixture both with one another and with 'substance'.[32]
This means that in any particular existing thing (*ousia*) there
are at least two kinds of material totally mixed together, the
'prime matter' and the quality. These can never exist apart; a
piece of iron, for example, cannot exist without being hard.[33]
Hardness is a quality and is therefore material.

In the world of the Stoics metaphysics concerns itself primarily with two things, the whole (*ousia* in general) and the
particular objects. Analysis of the world will therefore be an
analysis of particular objects. Each particular object will
consist of at least two material components, neither of which
can exist in isolation. We can thus understand a passage of
Plutarch where it is said that each of us is double and has two
substrates. As we should expect, the first substratum is called
substance (*ousia*); there is a lacuna in the text where the second

substratum should be named, but the gap has been correctly filled by von Arnim, who reads 'quality' (*poiotēs*).[34]

Our argument is that for the Stoics metaphysics is concerned with particulars. We should expect, therefore, that when we are dealing with existing things (category one), we should be told more about them, such as that they belong to a certain species and genus. But we should also expect the Stoics to emphasise those aspects of the particular which make it a particular, rather than those which make it a member of a class. Hence it is important that the word *poios* means in a Stoic context a qualified object (that is, a blend of two inseparable substances).[35] The Stoics talked about the general and the particular qualities of their qualified objects, but the emphasis on the particular qualities is so great that it has proved very difficult for students of Stoicism to understand what a general quality is. The term 'common quality' occurs first in Diogenes of Babylon, but this is probably due to the fragmentary nature of our sources.[36] There is no reason to suppose that Chrysippus at least did not use it. Certainly he used the phrase 'individually qualified' in passages quoted by Plutarch and Philo which will require detailed consideration.[37] The distinction between particularly and generally qualified objects is mentioned also by Simplicius[38] and Syrianus.[39] Syrianus makes the curious and questionable remark that according to the Stoics οἱ κοινῶς ποιοί are prior. It seems to be easier to understand what an 'individually qualified' entity is than a 'generally qualified' one, so we will start our further enquiries into quality there.

The most important text is provided by Philo in his treatise *On The Eternity Of The World* (48–9). It has been discussed at length by Miss Reesor and Colson and compared with a passage of Plutarch on the same theme.[40] Colson professes himself baffled by the problem of reconciling the passages, and Miss Reesor's solution, if I understand it, is not entirely satisfactory. Since the passage in Philo presents a paradox, it is not susceptible of clear and brief summary; it must, therefore, be quoted in full. Philo's text, as translated by Colson with a few modifications, runs as follows:

Chrysippus, in his treatise on 'increase' makes the following marvellous statement. Starting from the premiss that 'Two individually qualified entities (*duo idiōs poia*) cannot possibly exist in the same substance (*epi tēs autēs ousias*)', he continues, 'As an illustration, suppose that one person has all his members and that another has only one foot, and let us call the first Dion and the defective one Theon, and then suppose that Dion has one of his feet cut off.' Now if we ask which of the two has suffered destruction, he says that Theon is the more correct answer. This seems more of paradox than of truth. For how can one say that Theon the unmutilated is not destroyed? 'Quite rightly', he replies, 'for Dion who has had his foot amputated has passed over into the defective substance (*ousia*) of Theon. Two individually qualified entities (*duo idios poia*) cannot exist in the same substrate (*hypokeimenon*), and so Dion must remain and Theon has been destroyed.

Miss Reesor argues that the point of this is that when Chrysippus said that *duo idios poia* cannot exist in the same substrate he understood 'substrate' as quality. We recall that Plutarch tells us that each of us is double and has two substrates.

But although it seems possible that in the passage of Philo the word 'substrate' refers to quality, that is, to the air current, it cannot in fact do so, since according to Philo Chrysippus used the word 'substance' (*ousia*) to represent the substrate in which two qualified entities cannot exist.[41] What Chrysippus is saying is that in the case of every particular existing object, such as Theon, there is only one 'individually qualified entity'; in other words Theon is unique. The paradox arises, and is obviously regarded by Chrysippus as intolerable, because the uniqueness of Theon is being explained in terms of his having only one leg. If being one-legged is Theon's only claim to existence as Theon, then as soon as Dion becomes one-legged he takes on Theon's characteristic, that which makes Theon Theon; and therefore (obviously!) Theon ceases to exist. Presumably the absurd situation was concocted because Chrysippus found it difficult to explain the importance of individual qualities to a philosophical world used to talking only about universals.

There is a passage of Plutarch which seems to contradict the view of Chrysippus reported by Philo, but which does not in fact do so. What it does is make a single exception to the rule that 'two individually qualified entities' cannot be present in a single substance.[42] The context of the passage is an argument between the Stoics and the Academy. According to the Academy, says Plutarch, two doves are two substances (*ousiai*) with one quality, while the Stoics, he implies, hold that they are one substance (*ousia*) and two qualified entities (*poioi*). Plutarch would seem from the lines which follow to be speaking of 'individually qualified entities'. He regards the Stoic view as paradoxical.

In this passage Plutarch unwittingly brings out the weakness of the Academic position which Chrysippus had obviously grasped. He seems to think that the only difference between two doves is numerical. They are two objects, qualified in the same way by the single quality, doveness. As the passage from Philo makes clear, Chrysippus would have found this intolerable. He said that the two doves are both existents. *Qua* existents they are both one; they both exist and are material (category one). Hence they have one 'substance'. Nevertheless they are individually differentiated and not substitutable; hence they are 'two qualified entities'. There is, of course, a problem here. The problem is why we call them both doves. Have they nothing in common beyond the fact that they are existent material objects? We shall return to this, the question of 'common qualities', later.

What puzzles Plutarch about the Stoic position is how to square the thesis that two doves are two *poia* with the thesis which, he says, they are continually putting together, that there can be two individually qualified entities (*duo idios poious*) in *one* substance (*epi mias ousias*). And this is a statement which has puzzled modern scholars also, for it contradicts the dictum attributed to Chrysippus by Philo that two individually qualified entities can *not* exist in the same substrate. And we have argued that by substrate Chrysippus means substance (*ousia*). We must look at what Plutarch attributes to Chrysippus in more detail. Quoting Chrysippus, then, he tells us that, when the universe is destroyed by fire, Zeus, who alone of the gods cannot be destroyed, retires (*anachōrein*) into providence (*pronoia*),[43] and that Zeus and Providence, which are presumably qualified entities, will both continue to exist in the single substance aether (ἐπὶ μιᾶς τῆς τοῦ αἰθέρος οὐσίας). It is very unfortunate that we do not know the context of this passage, but something useful can be reconstructed. Clearly Chrysippus wanted to emphasise that Zeus *alone* of the gods survives. And yet he says that Providence also survives in aether. The obvious conclusion is that Zeus and Providence are identical; they are simply names for the same power in different aspects of its activity. This is in any case a well-known part of Old Stoic teaching.

But if Zeus and Providence are different aspects of the same divine power, why are they called 'individually qualified entities', both of which are present in a single substance? The answer to this depends on what the single substance is. It is in fact matter in general, the basic material reality of the world. Clearly every individually qualified entity is present in one substance in this sense of substance, where substance is the prime matter of all things.[44] All things can 'retire' into this substance. What distinguishes Zeus and Providence from ordinary particulars is that at the conflagration ordinary particulars lose their individuality as they pass into one another; Zeus, on the other hand, who seems to stand for the organising principle and seed of the world, does not disappear. It is true that he does no organising during the conflagration; he only 'foresees' what is to be—he has retired into Providence—but he will return to action with the next cycle of world events as the active force in the world. As all the Stoics held, the two basic principles of the world are god (Zeus) and matter.[45]

This seems to be the line on which the passage in Plutarch should be approached. It was almost certainly a misunderstanding on Plutarch's part to suggest that the relations of Zeus, Providence and the substance of the world as a whole can be applied usefully to the relations of particular qualified entities and particular substances. It is impossible to know precisely what Chrysippus wrote from Plutarch's paraphrase, but when Plutarch says that Zeus and Providence come together and continue to exist in the single substance of aether (ἐπὶ μιᾶς τῆς τοῦ αἰθέρος οὐσίας), could Chrysippus have meant that in aether alone two qualified entities can co-exist?

So much for the present for *idios poia*. We must now turn our attention to the more elusive problem of common qualities. If we think again of the passage of Plutarch, we shall recall that the difficulty of an analysis of two doves as one substance and two particularly qualified entities is that it seems to suggest that there is nothing more in common between them than that they are both existent material objects and that they cannot be substituted one for the other. The problem is: Why do we call them both doves? In other words, what do the Stoics make of species and genera? There is no doubt that it is this problem which they are trying to solve when they talk about common qualities. What we want to understand is the relationship between common qualities and substances (category one), and also between common qualities and individual qualities (category two).

We might expect that the answer to this is that common qualities also fall within category two, simply because they are qualities. The difficulty is that there is no doubt that common qualities are incorporeal, as we shall see. How then can they be classed with individually qualified entities? It would follow from their incorporeal nature that common qualities according to the Stoics cannot *exist* (that is, have an *ousia*-category one). This conclusion can be deduced from the Stoic attitude to Platonic Forms and to universals. According to the Stoics 'from Zeno on', what Plato calls Forms are simply our concepts; and concepts are images (*phantasmata*) arising in the mind, which are neither existents nor qualified entities,[46] but mere likenesses of these real material objects. A similar view is specifically attributed to Cleanthes,[47] and there is no reason to believe that it was not held by the whole school from the beginning. Chrysippus was prepared to distinguish genus from species by the argument that it is possible to recognise what is generically pleasant by the mind and what is specifically pleasant through the senses. An example would be that, although it makes sense to say that eating fruit is pleasant, strictly speaking one does not eat fruit but a type of fruit, such as an apple. When we eat a particular apple we obviously taste and enjoy the particular apple, and after eating an apple we say that we enjoy eating apples. It is the apple-flavour that we enjoy with our sense of taste, not, Chrysippus would say, the fruit-flavour. It is not possible to taste fruit-flavour and enjoy it, but only the flavour of kinds of fruit. There are obviously

difficulties about this suggestion. What, for example, would Chrysippus reply to a man who said that he had eaten many, or even all, kinds of fruit, and could in fact taste fruitiness whenever he ate an apple?

At any rate we know that the Stoics recognised common qualities, and that these common qualities, as *phantasmata* or *ennoiai*, are incorporeal. Further evidence that they are incorporeal has been assembled elsewhere and need not be reconsidered here.[48] Our problem is why the Stoics put these common qualities into the category of quality, into the category, that is, of material objects (the air currents) rather than with other incorporeals like time, void, place and the *lekta*. The answer to this is not easy to find. Part of the explanation may be that, whereas common qualities are classes of particular qualities, such things as time are not. Perhaps the Stoics supposed that it is methodologically helpful to bracket sets of qualities with the individual qualities of which they are composed.

It has recently been argued, at first sight very paradoxically, that 'the Stoics must have used the term substance to designate the common factor present in all members of the genus',[49] and that 'the two categories substratum (*hypokeimenon*) and qualified (*poios*) may go back to Chrysippus' distinction between the common and particular quality'.[50] We have suggested earlier, however, that the term substance (*ousia*) was not used by the Stoics to refer to anything other than category one. If this is correct, it must be wrong to associate it with the genus, which clearly is to be discussed in connexion with category two. Nevertheless we must still face the suggestion that what later Stoics call substrate (category one), Chrysippus thought of as common quality. There are two points against this. First, there is no evidence that the Stoic view of common qualities changed after the time of Chrysippus. Secondly, if 'the common quality was the unqualified substratum, which was usually the genus or species',[51] how could it be incorporeal, since the unqualified substratum is corporeal? And if the substratum is genus and species, how is it in fact unqualified? It cannot be unqualified since one genus must differ from another.

The whole attempt to think of common qualities as any kind of substrate must be dropped. Substrata for the Stoics are either substances (category one), elsewhere called prime matter, or individual qualities, which are air currents. Individual existents are material objects qualified in particular ways. The phrase 'common quality' is used to denote the common factor that groups of air-currents share. It is only a name and has no ontological importance. That does not mean that it has no importance whatever. It explains, however, why it has been difficult for students of Stoicism to understand common qualities. They have often wanted to make common qualities prior in some sense to particular qualities. Syrianus, doubtless for metaphysical reasons of his own, did the same in antiquity.[52] But precisely the opposite is the case. A passage of Simplicius makes the matter clear. According to the Stoics, says Simplicius,[53] 'the common aspect of quality is a differentiation of substance, not separable by itself, but ceasing in concept and character'.[54] This decisively refutes in advance the view that common quality is the unqualified substrate. Whatever the word 'substance' means in the passage of Simplicius, common quality is a differentiation (*diaphora*) of it.

When we turn to the last two categories, disposition (*pōs echon*) and relative disposition (*pros ti pōs echon*), we are faced with a different kind of problem from those we have so far considered, for despite the amount that has been written by Zeller, Rieth, Pohlenz, Miss Reesor and others, it is not easy to conceal the fact that we have very little evidence indeed; in particular we lack good information about what the two categories contain.

Dealing with disposition first, we find that we rely on Simplicius, Dexippus and Plotinus to give us examples of what falls within this category.[55] Apparently dispositions included times ('yesterday'), places ('in the Academy'), actions, lengths ('three cubits'), colours ('white'), and others. The category seems to include conditions or states of particulars. If this is so, disposition is a category dependent on the category of quality. Particular qualified entities, therefore, can be further described by a statement of their various dispositions. Furthermore, we recall that quality itself is a material substrate of a particular 'totally mixed with the substance (*ousia*) which is present in all actually existing things'. It seems from Stoic usage

that the category of disposition was used to describe conditions
of the qualitative substrate, not of the existential (category one)
substrate of the particular. According to Porphyry, whose
accuracy we have no reason to doubt, the soul was described by
the Stoics as an air-current in a certain disposition (πνεῦμα πὼς
ἔχον),[56] while in Sextus we read that virtue is the *hegemonikon*
(the ruling part of the soul) in a certain disposition.[57] To introduce the category of disposition is to tell the enquirer more
about the quality, the air-current, which marks the particular
individualisation of each existing thing. From this it would
follow that every qualified entity (*poios*) is also *pōs echōn;* everything must be in some kind of disposition at any particular time.

It has sometimes been held, for example by Zeller, that the
category of disposition provides us with 'accidental' qualities
but not essential ones, and that these latter would appear under
the category of quality itself. This view involves a misunderstanding of the relationship between 'qualities' and 'dispositions', and represents an attempt to view Stoicism through
Aristotelian eyes. Let us go through the process of placing a
particular object, say a man walking, in the categories. We first
decide whether he exists. If he does, he is a substance (category
one). But we need to know more than whether he is an existent
material object; and in any case all substances are qualified.
He is, then, a particular blend of prime matter with a series of
air-currents which form the material of his qualities. The man
walking is a particular qualified entity. But to say so much is to
speak of the man—let us call him Dion—in an abstract way. If
we wish to consider Dion as an object of thought unrelated to
any actual position in space and time, it might be enough to
employ only the categories of substance and quality. But when
we wish to talk about Dion's activities as an existent human
being, that is, when we make him the subject of propositions
referring to actual events in the world, we have to consider
Dion's 'disposition'. What happens when we wish to say 'Dion
is walking'? What we have to say, according to Chrysippus,[58]
is that Dion, or his *hegemonikon*, is disposed in a certain way. In
other words, if we wish to describe particular events or situations
in the world, and not limit ourselves to generalisations, we have
to introduce the category of disposition. Since every particular

at every time is in fact (necessarily) in some disposition or other, it is absurd to suggest that dispositions are only 'accidental qualities'. In brief then to introduce the category of disposition is to place the existing object (category one), which is an individual entity (category two), in a particular spatio-temporal situation (category three, disposition).[59]

It was argued by Rieth that the phrase *pōs echon* refers to something which produces a certain disposition in its substratum.[60] This is a possible, though less natural, way of translating the Greek words, but Rieth's interpretation cannot be correct. For, if dispositions were active powers, they would have to be material objects, that is, in Stoic terms, substrates. Yet there is not a scrap of evidence that they were so regarded. The easier translation of *pōs echon* as 'being in a certain state', is also the obvious philosophical sense required. Dispositions do not act on the substrate that is a qualified entity; they are states of that entity. To list in the category disposition is to describe the actual condition of an individual thing.

Our evidence about the fourth category, that of relative disposition, is a little easier to interpret. Examples of relative dispositions are rightness and leftness, fatherhood and sonship.[61] Simplicius, who is our principal source of information, devotes a great deal of time to the fact that the Stoics were concerned to point out that relative dispositions are not simply relations (τὰ πρὸς τί). Relation is not a Stoic category, and many relatives in the Aristotelian sense of the term would not fall under the head of relative dispositions. Presumably confusion occurred over this matter in antiquity and the Stoics tried to clarify it. Apparently 'sweet' and 'bitter' were regarded as relative terms, and the Stoics wanted to explain how they differed from, for example, 'right' and 'left'. The gist of the very difficult passage of Simplicius, where this is explained, is that sweet and bitter have a 'power in them' (ἡ περὶ αὐτὰ δύναμις) and that they are 'according to differentials' (κατὰ διαφοράν).[62] In the view of the Stoics this means that they are qualities. Apart from substances (*ousiai*) only qualities can be said to have power, power, that is, to act or be acted upon. They must, therefore, be material objects existing relatively to substance. Knowledge of an object's relative dispositions does not inform us about the object's existence as an object. Relative dispositions are the relations of an individual thing to other individual things which are associated with it in the world, but on which its continuing existence as an entity does not depend. For the Stoics such relationships are in some sense constructs of the mind, though they are not 'accidentals' in an Aristotelian sense. Relative dispositions, say the Stoics, are observed in accordance with bare disposition towards something else (κατὰ ψιλὴν δὲ τὴν πρὸς ἕτερον σχέσιν). We can recognise a man's existence without knowing that he is a father. If his children die, he ceases to be a father (fatherhood being a relative disposition). He does not cease to exist, but, instead of being a father, he is an ex-father.

We can now determine the similarities and differences between the categories of disposition and relative disposition. Disposition, we found, gives us information about the particular spatio-temporal situation of individuals, whose role in the cosmos we may wish to describe. Relative dispositions give us further information about that situation. However, in the case of relative dispositions we acquire information which can only be regarded as true if we have particular knowledge of other material objects beside the one we set out to describe. If walking is to be predicated of Dion, we can discuss Dion's walking activities without reference, according to the Stoics, to other material objects. Since fatherhood is a relative disposition, we cannot properly describe Socrates as a father without at least implicit reference to his son. Zeno, though not Chrysippus, seems to have approached the question of the virtues by way of the category of relative disposition, though possibly he did not use the term. Virtue is one—that is, presumably, a disposition of the personality—but it seems to be a plurality because it is operative in different areas of human life.[63]

In his article on the Stoic categories De Lacy claimed to have found the categories in use as methodological principles in the writings of men like Epictetus and Marcus Aurelius.[64] This claim has been received with some scepticism, and I must number myself among the sceptics. Nevertheless it has been the purpose of this chapter to argue that they are in fact methodological principles of some kind. They are meant to guide the enquirer into the status of particular things.[65] They give us the proper series of philosophical questions. The first question is: Does x exist? If the answer is Yes, x is in category one. Now all substances (category one) are qualified entities (category two). Therefore the next questions must be: What are the differentiating features of x? What are its generic, specific, and above all individual characteristics? Now all individual existing things exist in space and time. Therefore the next question is: What is the spatio-temporal situation of x? This question has two answers. The spatio-temporal situation of x in so far as that situation does not depend on y gives us category three. The spatio-temporal situation of x in so far as that situation does depend on y gives us category four.

Benson Mates has written that 'we are told that these four categories are so related to one another that every preceding category is contained in and more accurately determined by the next succeeding one', and cites Zeller as his authority.[66] A slightly disbelieving note can be detected, and the statement as it stands is, as we hope to have shown, incorrect. Nevertheless the view of writers like Plotinus that the Stoic categories follow upon one another in a fixed order is correct.[67] Category two cannot be understood without reference to category one, nor category three without reference to category two. Category four does not depend on category three, but it is natural to consider the non-relative dispositions of a qualified entity before its relative dispositions.

[handwritten Greek notes: Ἐνεστώς συντελικός / Παρατατικός / Παρῳχημένος συντελικός / Παρατατικός]

NOTES

1. *Stoic Logic*, p. 18.

2. 'The Stoic Concept of Quality', *AJPh* lxxv (1954) 40–58; and 'The Stoic Categories' ibid. lxxviii (1957) 63–82.

3. De Lacy, 'The Stoic Categories as Methodological Principles' *TAPhA* lxxvi (1945) 246–63.

4. Earlier work of importance on the categories is to be found in Rieth, *Grundbegriffe*, esp. pp. 22–9, 55–84, and Pohlenz, 'Die Begründung' and 'Zenon und Chrysipp'.

5. Diog. Laert. VII 134 etc. (*SVF* I 85).

6. Sextus, *Adv. math.* x 218 (*SVF* II 331).

7. Sextus, *Adv. math.* VIII 12. [See further Chapter V, pp. 76-7. Ed.]

8. Cf. Sextus, *Adv. math.* VIII 70 (*SVF* III 87), Diog. Laert. VII 63.

9. *Adv. math.* VIII 258 (*SVF* III Bas. 1). [These terms are discussed in Chapter V, pp. 89f. Ed.]

10. For other evidence about the status of incorporeals in the view of orthodox Stoics cf. *SVF* II 331, 521, 541.

11. The word *pragma* is used of *lekta* by Sextus (*Adv. math.* VIII 12). I do not think it is necessary to follow Mates (op. cit. 11) and translate this as 'entity', so long as we understand that 'things' for the Stoics are not to be identified with 'existents'. See below [and Chapter V, p. 107 n. 10. Ed.]

12. Plut., *Comm. not.* 1073E. Cf. Zeller III i, p. 119 for further references if needed.

13. Sen., *Ep. mor.* 58, 15. (*SVF* II 332). For Centaurs as examples of non-existent things see the learned note of A.S. Pease in his edition of Cicero's *De natura deorum* (Harvard 1955) p. 483.

14. *SVF* II 329–30, 333–5. Cf. Goldschmidt, *Le système stoicien* p. 25. [See further Chapter V, pp. 88f. Ed.]

15. Alex. Aphr., *In Top.* (*CAG* 2 II) p. 301, 19 = *SVF* II 329.

16. Diog. Laert. VII 63 (*SVF* II 183). [Grammatical implications of this are discussed in Chapter IV by A. C. Lloyd. Ed.]

17. Cf. Mates, pp. 16–17.

18. Simp., *In Cat.* (*CAG* VIII p. 67, 1f. = *SVF* II 369); Plot., *Enn.* VI 1, 25 (*SVF* II 371).

19. De Lacy, op. cit., esp. p. 255.

20. *Diss.* II 14, 11; II 14, 25.

21. For Chrysippus, Philo, *De aet. mundi* 48–51 (*SVF* II 397); for Posidonius (*ap.* Ar. Did.) Stob., *Ecl.* I, p. 178 W. A possible Aristotelian background for the Stoic category one (existence) may be provided by *Anal. post.* II 89b 31–5.

22. Cf. Zeller, op. cit. 94, note 2.

23. *SVF* I 65. Cf. Diog. Laert. VII 50 (*SVF* II 55) for the distinction between φαντασία and φάντασμα.

24. Sen., *Ep. mor.* 58, 11.

25. Stob., *Ecl.* I p. 132, 26 W. (*SVF* I 87).

26. Aetius, *Plac.* I 15, 6 (*SVF* I 91).

27. Reesor, *AJPh* lxxv (1954) 41, note 5.

28. Galen, *In Hipp. De hum.* I (16, 32 K. = *SVF* I 92).

29. Stob., *Ecl.* I p. 178 W.

30. Other evidence that qualities were already material for Zeno is provided by Reesor, op. cit. 41–2 and *AJPh* lxxviii (1957) 63–5, though her conclusion is offered with unnecessary hesitation.

31. *SVF* II 449, 463 etc.

32. Cf. *SVF* I 85.

33. Cf. *SVF* II 449.

34. Von Arnim's reading is printed by Pohlenz in the new Teubner (*Comm. not.* 1083D = *SVF* II 762). Zeller read ποιόν, but, as Miss Reesor has observed, (*AJPh* lxxviii, 81) ποιός denotes not 'quality' but 'a particular qualified entity'.

35. See note 34.

36. Diog. Laert. VII 58 (*SVF* II 22 Diogenes). [A. C. Lloyd, Chapter IV, p. 66, relates the term to the grammatical category of 'general name'. Ed.]

37. *SVF* II 396, 397.

38. *In De anima* (*CAG* XI) p. 217, 36 (*SVF* II 395).

39. *In Met.* (*CAG* VI) p. 28, 18 (*SVF* II 398).

40. For Colson, see appendix to Loeb *Philo* IX, pp. 528–9, and for Miss Reesor, *AJPh* lxxv 46–7.

41. It is true that Plutarch calls qualities οὐσίαι at *Comm. not.* 1085E (*SVF* II 380) but this is Plutarch's argument against Chrysippus, not Chrysippus himself. I have been unable to find any passages where the Stoics themselves call qualities *ousiai*. Usually, on the contrary, the two are distinguished, as at *SVF* I 92.

42. Plut., *Comm. not.* 1077CD (*SVF* II 396 and 1064).

43. Cf. ἀναδεδράμηκε in Philo (49).

44. Cf. *SVF* I 87 discussed above.

45. *SVF* I 85.

46. *SVF* I 65.

47. *SVF* I 494.

48. Miss Reesor, *AJPh* lxxv 50–2; Zeller, 102 etc.

49. Miss Reesor, op. cit., 46. This view has been accepted by Watson, *The Stoic Theory of Knowledge*, p. 49.

50. Miss Reesor, *AJPh* lxxviii 81.

51. Ibid.

52. *SVF* II 598.

53. *In Cat.* (*CAG* VIII) p. 222, 30 (*SVF* II 378). Cf. Rieth, *Grundbegriffe*, pp. 64–9, 79.

54. I read (with Kalbfleisch) ἐννόημα for ἐν νόημα. The emendation is Peterson's and is wrongly rejected by Zeller.

55. Simp., *In Cat.* (*CAG* VIII) p. 66, 32ff. (*SVF* II 369); Dexippus, *In Cat.* (*CAG* IV, 2) p. 34, 19ff. (*SVF* II 399); Plot., *Enn.* VI 1, 30 (*SVF* II 400).

56. Cf. Eus., *Praep. ev.* XV 11, 4 (*SVF* II 806).

57. *Adv. math.* XI 23.

58. Sen., *Ep. mor.* 113, 18 (*SVF* I 525).

59. The importance of the metaphysics of the individual in Stoicism is illuminated by Edelstein, *The Meaning of Stoicism* (Camb. Mass. 1966) pp. 19–28.

60. Rieth, *Grundbegriffe*, pp. 77–84.

61. Cf. Simp., *In Cat.* (*CAG* VIII) p. 165, 32–166, 29 (*SVF* II 403). Cf. Chrysippus as quoted by Varro, *De Lingua Latina* 10, 59 (*SVF* II 155), though the phrase 'relative disposition' does not occur here. Father, son, right and left are given as examples of πρός τι ἔχοντα by Dionysius Thrax (p. 35, 3 Uhlig). Cf. Pohlenz, 'Die Begründung', 185–8. Chrysippus apparently also regarded 'part' as denoting a relative disposition, since it has no meaning apart from 'whole' (Plut., *Stoic rep.* 1054E ff. =*SVF* II 550).

62. For detailed but faulty discussion of this long passage cf. Rieth, *Grundbegriffe*, pp. 70–84.

63. Plut., *Stoic. rep.* 1034C (*SVF* I 200). Cleanthes seems to have held a similar view to Zeno (*Stoic. rep.* 1034D (*SVF* I 563)), as also did Ariston (*SVF* I 351, 374, 375; III 259). The view of Chrysippus seems to be that relative disposition should not be invoked to account for the plurality of virtue (cf. Miss Reesor, *AJPh* lxxv, 41–3).

64. De Lacy, *TAPhA* lxxvi, 18.

65. Cf. Christensen (*An Essay on the Unity of Stoic Philosophy*, 51) for an interpretation of the categories which has certain similarities with the one offered here.

66. *Stoic Logic*, p. 18.

67. *Enn.* VI, 1, 30 (*SVF* II 400).

IV

Grammar and Metaphysics
in the Stoa

A. C. LLOYD

Stoics divided what they called dialectic into the study of the utterance (language as sound) and the study of the utterance as meaningful (language as what is said, the *lekton*). Because dialectic was the science of the true and false, study of the *lekton* covered questions both of epistemology and of logic. Because on the other hand language was based according to Stoics on natural, not conventional signs, the study of the utterance covered questions not only of etymology, formal grammar, metre and so on, but questions of parts of speech and of rhetoric that we should have expected to fall under the *lekton*.[1] Diogenes Laertius has a seemingly casual list of subjects that fall under the 'topic' of the utterance (VII 44): but some features of it may perhaps not have been noticed.

In the order of this list, 'the utterance composed of letters' includes of course the primary sounds which are the basis of etymology; 'parts of speech' was a subject in its own right; 'solecism', which is the 'incongruity' or wrong order of words in a composite expression, represents the subject of *syntaxis* (*ordinatio*), while 'barbarism', which is the use of a single word contrary to its customary meaning, could represent among other subjects amphiboly.[2] 'Poems', 'metrical utterance' and 'music' were also commonly regarded as subjects within this topic; Chrysippus wrote a book on poetry and another on how to read poetry, which Diogenes classed under logic. In fact if we recognise the way in which regular subjects under the first study of language, language as utterance, are represented by Diogenes' list we find that the only obvious omission is that of inflection (*declinatio*). But while this is a glaring omission it is the one subject which may not have been known to the Old Stoa.

Traditional grammar distinguishes between the *derivation* of one word from another, like 'fathead' from 'fat', and the *inflection* of one word, like 'fatter' instead of 'fat'; the first kind of change was *paragōgē* and regarded as generating a new word, the second was *klisis* or an 'inflection' of the same word—and confined in the case of nouns and adjectives originally to gender, number, case and comparison. Clearly this begs questions about the inadequate concept of a word. It does not tell us unequivocally how to class adjectives formed from nouns, like 'Roman' from 'Rome'. They were classed by the earliest grammarians with inflections.[3] But Karl Barwick has shown how this can be traced back to a distinction between what was called 'extrinsic' and 'intrinsic' word-change, that is, a change, or derivation, which respectively does and does not signify a new concept, as he calls it.[4] The Latin *'vis'* signifies force and so in some sense does its adjectival derivative *'violens'*; *'vitis'* and *'via'* and *'vincio'* were also thought to derive from *'vis'*, but extrinsically since they do not signify force but vine, path and fastening. What made the distinction possible was the survival of the doctrine of terms from Aristotle's *Categories*. For according to that doctrine 'Socrates is wise' means that wisdom inheres in Socrates, so that 'wise' means (*signifies*) there the same as 'wisdom' in 'wisdom is a virtue'. It enabled Diogenes of Babylon to use the philosophical word 'accidents' for the classes of *intrinsic* change or derivation; the thing, or term, that is 'signified' by 'Rome', 'Roman', 'Romans' is the same, namely Rome, so that the inflections do not represent essential but nonessential change.[5] Hence the branch of grammar called 'accidence'. The *extrinsic* changes—from *'vis'* to *'vitis'* or 'fat' to 'fathead'— were regularly held to follow one or other of three principles: the new word was related to the old by the similarity or by the nearness or by the contrariety of what they signified. (The proverbial *lucus a non lucendo* is an allusion to the third of these principles.) But these principles seem to be unknown to Chrysippus and may well have been the invention of Diogenes of Babylon. It is true that the distinction which the early grammarians recognised between inflection and other word derivation partly cuts across the distinction between intrinsic and extrinsic derivation. But if it was Diogenes who first looked for distinct sets of rules or, what comes to the same thing, subdivisions of inflected and non-inflected derivations, this would suggest that the early Stoa did not recognise inflection as a scientific topic. Diogenes Laertius' list would thus be altogether less casual than it may have seemed.

The study of language as meaningful—according to the Stoics what is signified as distinct from the sign—is covered by the other half of Diogenes Laertius' list.[6] This comprises the subjects of presentations (*phantasiai*), of the *lekton*, with its subclasses of propositions and predicates, and of arguments and fallacies. The bulk of it is thus what we call logic, while what we call grammar belongs to the study of the utterance. But it must be repeated that the division between the two halves of dialectic is an unstable one, and was recognised as such by the Stoics, on account of their belief that there was a natural, that is intrinsic, connexion between the sound or utterance and what it signified. There is a further reason why the division should be unstable: it is cut across by the distinction between *lexis* and *logos*. *Lexis* was defined as 'utterance (or sound) composed of letters', *logos* as 'significant utterance (or sound)', for 'blityri' is articulated into letters but has no significance.[7] Certainly *logos* could be, and was, classed in the first half of dialectic since it is a sign (or signs) not what is signified. But to examine what is signified, or the meaning of the utterance, when this meaning is again distinguished from the thing or fact it refers to, is just to examine the utterance as a significant one. The meaning of the utterance 'Dion is walking' is that Dion is walking; the utterance is a saying, so that to study what it says, the *lekton*, is to study what it is, the *logos*. It was not therefore inadvertent, and certainly not un-Stoic, to have described (at the outset of this paper) the second half of dialectic as the study of the utterance as meaningful. The 'utterance' however, *is* also a *lexis*; and one might say that the concept of *logos* straddles the two halves of dialectic inasmuch as it involves the two aspects, the sound and the meaning possessed by the sound.

If we reduce the *lexis* 'Dion is walking' to its elements, we have 'd', 'i', 'o' and so on, that is, letters of the alphabet. As a *logos* its elements are noun, verb, participle—or whatever *parts of speech* we recognise. This is Stoic doctrine.[8] Porphyry, who in such matters often stands midway between the Lyceum and the Stoa, said that nouns and verbs were elements of *logos*, while the remaining parts of speech were elements of *lexis*, presumably on the grounds that these have no meaning in themselves but depend for it on the nouns and verbs. This had philosophical implications which were re-inforced by its acceptance in the commentaries of Boëthius and in the classical grammar of Priscian.[9] It is clearly influenced by an Aristotelian—and ultimately Platonic—doctrine of terms, the interchangeable subjects and predicates of a syllogistic premiss, and by an Aristotelian doctrine of categories as the meanings of non-complex utterances. The combination of these doctrines made the meaningfulness of 'wise' depend logically on the meaningfulness of 'wisdom'; both doctrines were reflected, if vaguely, in the opening chapters of *De interpretatione*. But Porphyry had in mind the Stoic division of dialectic when he claimed that Aristotle's categories belonged to the utterance *qua* significant but parts of speech (like rhetoric and even formal logic) to the utterance *qua lexis*.[10] If there is inconsistency here it is likely to be caused by the fact of the Stoics having two distinctions which were connected but not thought to coincide, that between utterance and *lekton* and that between *lexis* and *logos*.

What Stoics themselves thought about parts of speech and categories must be largely a matter of inference, if not speculation. But it is of more importance to the understanding of their philosophical position than has perhaps been realised. Aristotle regularly spoke of his categories as though they were *summa genera*, which makes their existence facts of nature, not just facts of our language. Were the Stoic categories facts of nature?

Zeno and Cleanthes appear to have recognised four parts of speech: the name, the verb, the article and the conjunction.[11] These are the literal translations, which we have inherited by way of the Roman grammars. But the 'conjunction' included prepositions, the 'article' included pronouns and demonstratives; the division of the 'name' into proper names and general names ('appellations') may have been due to Chrysippus; a fifth part, the adverb, may have been added by Antipater.[12]

As for categories, although we have practically no Stoic

information, the Stoa was dogmatic that there were four: subject, quality, disposition, relative disposition.[13]

A number of writers have followed Schmidt's original work on Stoic grammar in noticing a correspondence, and claiming that it cannot be an accidental one, between these categories and the four parts of speech. They have done little more than notice it.[14] But it is possible to see good reasons for expecting such a correspondence before we consider its details.

The first must be the fact which has already been emphasised that a language as a system of phonetic signs bears, according to the Stoics' flat contradiction of Aristotle, a natural, not an arbitrary or conventional relation to what these are signs of. Etymology was an important branch of dialectic. It was taken over from the Stoa by the Alexandrian grammarians, for whom its importance was chiefly as a key to unlock the meanings hidden in the words of poets. For the first Stoics it had been (as the etymology of 'etymology' witnesses) a means to discover the truth in the plain sense of fact, not what someone wrote or said was fact.[15]

They defined dialectic—and not just rhetoric—as the science of speaking 'well', which meant 'truthfully or appropriately', that is in conforming with the relevant facts.[16] (So too, a lesson in 'orthography' was as objective as a lesson in nature study: the letters of a word are sounds, which if misspelt will misrepresent the word, just as the word is a sound which may or may not represent what it is supposed to signify.) A striking example of the quasi-scientific use of etymology, in what was then a familiar controversy of the philosophical schools, can be seen in one of Chrysippus's arguments for the seat of the ruling principle, or reason, being the heart not the brain: voicing the first syllable of 'ego', which indicates the self, makes the lower lip and the chin point to the chest.[17] I have no doubt that the 'right *logos*' which was a fundamental criterion in their moral theory was understood by Stoics far more literally than by Aristotle—or at least by some translators of the *Nicomachaean Ethics*.

This kind of 'natural' relationship between names and things had direct application only to those sounds or linguistic signs which were logically and genetically primitive.[18] Other words

were formed from these by different principles. Barwick specu-
lates that Diogenes of Babylon formulated the standard three
principles of *similitudo, vicinitas* and *contrarium* in order to extend
a defective theory of the naturalness of language;[19] the old
Stoa had appealed, for example, to merely aesthetic considera-
tions to explain word changes. But according to Chrysippus
language itself would have been defective since it was shot
through with 'anomaly' and 'ambiguity'.[20]

It would be desirable for this natural relation of language to
be identified much more precisely. Unfortunately this can
hardly be done; and the obstacle seems in this case to be as much
philosophical incoherence of the theory as lack of testimony to
it. In the traditional controversy (as in the *Cratylus*) it was taken
for granted that naturalness as opposed to conventionality of
language meant *similarity* between spoken words and the things
they stood for or named.[21] The difficulty is now this. Two
things can be similar only in respect of (one or more) properties;
the properties of a sound are very limited in comparison with
those of most other things—basically they are not much more
than loudness, pitch, timbre, length and one or two secondary
ones like agreeableness. At worst then a 'natural' explanation
will hold only for those words that name sounds, like 'do', 're',
'mi' or 'bang', at best for those also that name things which
have sounds, like 'peewit' or 'puffer'. In either case the class is
too small to make a general theory of language; in the second
case while no doubt a wider class than in the first it suffers other
limitations which are obvious from reflection on our examples.
The difficulty escaped notice partly by ill-defined extensions of
the theory beyond the actual sound of the word—for instance to
a gesture which normally accompanies it—but for the most
part by the theory being taken to refer to the *meaning* of the
word instead of the thing it named. The instinct to take it that
way is correct enough, for unless the word happens to be a
proper name (e.g. 'Thames') there is no thing, except something abstract called a universal or a sense or what not, which
the word (e.g. 'river') does name. But it destroys the theory by
making it circular. The properties of a sound such as 'Thames'
and of a thing such as the river Thames can be observed
independently and compared: but what 'river' means cannot

be identified in order to be compared with the sound except by pre-supposing some other, 'conventional', relation between it and the sound. This difficulty in turn escaped notice whenever the theory was applied, as we should expect it to be applied, within the class of things named which have sounds; here the meaning of, say, 'river' could be taken as any river, which could then be confused with all rivers as a closed class (all the rivers). But then it fails to avoid the original difficulty of how it is to be applied to things that neither are nor have sounds. An actual example from a Stoic or Stoicising source will make this clear.

The *Principia dialecticae* traditionally attributed to Augustine makes room for the extended application by the fact that objects of senses other than hearing share properties with sounds; honey tastes smooth and the name of it, *mel*, sounds smooth.[22] Apart from any objection to the lack of specificity or the arbitrariness of selecting the relevant property (since more words than *mel* sound smooth and more things than honey are smooth) the theory still needs to be extended again to words that do not name what we might call sense data. The *Principia dialecticae* mentions the need and contrives to meet it by claiming that *crux* is the natural word for cross because it sounds rough— unlike the smooth *voluptas* which stands for pleasure—and a cross is the cause of pain.

It is clear that however ill-chosen the example may be, the principle involved in extending the theory beyond sense data, if not beyond sounds, will be equally objectionable. By and large the word's meaning which is to be similar to the word's sound will have to be the thought evoked by the word or the thought of the thing.

The thought of the thing, or the thing as thought of, was what the Aristotelians identified with the meaning or significatum of a general word.[23] For the purpose of extending the theory of language as natural beyond names of simple sense-data the Stoa had in effect to accept this identification. But that belonged (as the examples from Chrysippus and the *Principia dialecticae* illustrate) to their theory of etymology which explained the historical origin of the actual signs present. They had also a purely philosophical theory about significance as such, and this theory did not accept the identification. What an expression signified was the *lekton*, and this was certainly not, according to Stoics, a thought—or certainly not what Aristotle and his followers meant by a thought, which was an act of thinking. One may view the *lekton* as something whose place is taken in Aristotle by the thought or concept; this would mean that the work of the *lekton* was done in Aristotle by the thought or concept. It is true, there is an alternative to this, for one may view the *lekton* as something which escaped recognition by Aristotle. Both would seem to be valid historical viewpoints. But each may appear to the other to be question-begging; and this would be because the choice between them depends on the historian's own presuppositions about meaning.[24]

There is a second difference from Aristotle. For Aristotle there is no relation or similarity between the expression and what it signifies: but there is between what is signified and the thing referred to.[25] He does not however explain the nature of the similarity. Nor can it be denied that there is no clear distinction between sense and reference—witness his ambiguous use of the term 'signify' (σημαίνω).[26]

For the Stoics there is no question, in this context, of similarity betwen the *lekton* and the thing, but there is a similarity which is in fact isomorphism between the *lekton* and the expression.

I have suggested however that there is a latent and unacknowledged conflict between the Stoic theory of meaning and the Stoic theory of etymology. It is to the latter theory that the doctrine of the naturalness of language really belonged. This is confusing because Aristotle's doctrine of the conventionality of language belonged to his theory of meaning. [27] But the effect should be to make us all the more ready to expect a correspondence between categories and parts of speech, which are classes of expression, since they belong to the study of the utterance. If categories were kinds of things or *summa genera*, belonging to the study of nature, their correspondence with parts of speech would follow from the simple, and presumably earliest though inadequate, theory of etymology. If they were kinds of things meant, belonging to the study of the *lekton*, their correspondence would follow from the isomorphism involved in the theory of meaning. In fact, I shall argue, the proper place of Stoic categories was with the *lekton*.

Two further pieces of evidence suggest more straightforwardly that Stoic categories and parts of speech are to be connected. The category of quality was divided into 'common' and 'particular' quality, or that which could belong to many individuals and that which could belong only to one individual. This division was used by Diogenes of Babylon to define 'appellation' and 'name' respectively.[28]

Secondly, one of the criticisms raised in the early Empire against Aristotle's categories was that they failed to account for conjunctions and prepositions. The critics in this case are known to have been in or connected with Stoic circles.[29]

Turning to the details of the correspondence we find little difficulty in the *name*. Once this had been divided into the proper name and the general or common name (appellation) Diogenes of Babylon's definitions would appear self-evident: 'appellation is a part of speech signifying common quality: e.g., "man", "horse"; name is a part of speech indicating particular property: e.g., "Diogenes", "Socrates".' Each such particular property is presumably complex (a conjunction of properties) since it was thought capable of definition. In Stoic thinking the designation of each of the four categories was the designation of some object such as Diogenes, from four points of view—or five when we divide quality into two. *We* name categories by the names, as it were, of the points of view and so regard them as properties of the object. For the Stoics the category that we prefer to call the particular quality was just Dion himself, and the common quality was man ('man' is of course a general name or common noun in traditional grammar), which is still Dion, but no longer as he is uniquely or indeed properly.[30]

We are dealing of course with parts of speech recognised in Stoic grammar. These varied, so that without affecting the principle there would be variations in the allotting of the later more settled parts of speech to the categories. Modern writers on Stoic grammar and logic make too little allowance for this.

For example, it is unclear whether the original general names, or 'appellations', included adjectives such as 'pink' and 'soft' or, under the influence of Aristotle's distinctions, only such words as 'man' and 'river' which indicated kinds of things. But this was probably not clear or agreed among the early Stoics themselves. There is a similar difficulty over the meaning of *rhēma*, which in the days of Plato and the Sophists had no doubt meant 'predicate' in a pretty vague way that distinguished neither between logic and grammar, nor within grammar between adjectives and verbs. Grammar itself has always suffered from a conflict between the semantic or lexical approach represented by the Stoic definitions of common and proper nouns, and the syntactic or formal approach represented by the Stoic definition, or partial definition, of a conjunction as an uninflected part of speech.[31] From the semantic point of view, the *verb* belongs undoubtedly with the category called disposition, whether or not some Stoics said the same also of adjectives such as 'pink' and 'soft'. The participle merely draws attention to the conflict facing the grammarians; for it satisfies the semantic definition of a verb as 'signifying something predicated of one or more things' but not the formal property, of having no cases, that belonged to its alternative (but alike Stoic) definition.[32] According to Priscian it was in fact classed by the Stoics with the verb.[33]

We are left with two categories, subject and relative disposition. The so-called subject is what is referred to by the subject of a normal sentence; it is therefore that which is claimed to exist; and there is a word-class whose job it is to make this claim, namely the definite article and demonstratives.[34] The part of speech which according to the Stoics included this class included too much. But it has a sub-division called by them, but not by us, the definite article; and by putting a passage of Sextus Empiricus alongside the grammarians' evidence we can see how this sub-division corresponds exactly to the category of subject.

Priscian tells us not only that early grammarians had called pronouns 'articles' but that Stoics had divided the part of speech they called 'article' into 'indefinite' and 'definite'.[35] Stoic *indefinite articles* were the indefinite pronouns (and pronominal adjectives) including relative and interrogative pronouns, like 'someone', 'some', 'who' and 'who?', and also what we call the definite article; their *definite articles* were the personal

and demonstrative pronouns like 'I', 'mine' and 'this'.[36] It is
fairly clear that what they were trying to distinguish was
definiteness and indefiniteness of reference, or so called designating and non-designating expressions. (A necessary condition of
a designating expression is the existence of what it purports to
name.)

We are told by Sextus Empiricus that non-complex expressions were classed by Stoics as 'definite', 'indefinite' and 'intermediate'. Definite propositions were those which were 'expressed demonstratively: e.g. "this (man) is walking", "this
(man) is sitting" (for I indicate some particular man)';
indefinite propositions are 'governed by an indefinite expression: e.g. "someone is sitting" '; intermediate propositions are
those like "a man is sitting" or "Socrates is walking", for here
'the kind is distinguished' but 'the individual person is not
pointed to'.[37] The condition, 'expressed demonstratively', has
perhaps to be taken rather exactly. It is true that the Stoa
normally identified types of proposition by the presence of a
type of word in its expression; that is how indefinite propositions are identified here, without regard for the obvious complaint of circularity. But 'expressed demonstratively' cannot
define a purely formal category; it is not the word which
indicates or points, but (as Sextus says) I who point. The fact
that a word belongs formally—that is, when restricted to its
narrowly linguistic environment—to the same class as 'this'
does not suffice to make it 'definite'; and this is illustrated by
what would otherwise be a serious difficulty, Diogenes Laertius'
example of an indefinite proposition.[38] Conversely personal
pronouns could be counted 'definite articles' because although
lexically more like variables, when used—in other words, as
parts of the utterance—they are accompanied by some sort of
gesture. The etymology of *ego* that has already been mentioned
shows at least in this instance how inseparable the Stoics thought
the word, the meaning and the gesture.

The upshot is that the Stoics had a sub-class of 'definite
articles' which we may call 'true demonstratives', and that
these correspond to their category of subject. They are like
Russell's logically proper names.

What we call the definite article was excluded: but that is

probably of less philosophical importance. The chief reason—
others appear confused—for excluding it seems to have been
that its connexion with gesture is less assured than in the case of
personal pronouns.[39] Apollonius Dyscolus was able to argue
that since its function is to refer to something previously mentioned or implied by the context it is as definite as the pronouns.[40]
But I suspect that the Stoics were attending as much to the
literal or physical notion of indicating as to the semantic and
syntactic notion of referring; the first is the standpoint of
epistemology, the second of grammar and logic, and they perhaps fell between the two stools. None the less they were the
only ancient philosophers who would have been at home in the
modern discussions about proper names, definite descriptions
and referring expressions, to say nothing of meaning and truth
conditions. The grammarians' proper name could not correspond to the category of subject and did not even belong to the
part of speech called 'article', because it was (in the modern
sense) connotative. 'Dion' signified the *logos* which was unique
to Dion. 'This' and 'that' signified by indicating, i.e. pointing
to something. Hence the Stoic doctrine that the truth of a proposition of the form 'Dion is walking' entails one of the form
'this (man) is walking'.[41] And Chrysippus drew a consequence
for modal logic—namely that a possible p could imply an
impossible q—from the fact that if Dion is dead, this (man) is
dead; for 'Dion is dead' may be true, but this (man) is dead can
never be true.[42]

Relative disposition has been assigned by modern writers
alternatively to the *conjunction* (which included the preposition)
or to a subdivision of the verb, viz. the *transitive verb*.[43] The
objection to the second alternative is that it would leave conjunctions out when that was a complaint apparently made
against Aristotle's categories by Stoics themselves. But it seems
to make the better sense; and Stoics did distinguish the transitive verb as being relational or a two place predicate, for they
had a name for it.[44]

Stoics named categories after the qualified subject rather than
the quality. So far from being an abstraction a quality was
material according to the Stoics. This is not the place to go into
their difficult distinction between that and the qualified subject.

But since the differently qualified, disposed, related subjects represent different categories only by differing in respect of, or from the point of view of, a quality, disposition or relation, we must often translate the Stoic category-names as though they were these qualities etc. rather than the subjects. (The same of course goes for Aristotle's account of the category, quality.) We can then understand how there was an order in the categories; for Plotinus tells us in effect that individual dispositions are dispositions of qualities and qualities are dispositions of matter, so that all properties are properties of matter.[45] The 'of' here is 'about' in the Greek. So a standard subject-predicate sentence, exemplified for the Stoa (like some Megarians and Cynics before them) by a noun and a verb rather than a noun, copula and adjective, would be attributing a disposition to a particular quality or qualified subject: e.g. 'Dion walks'.[46]

At the same time Plotinus's argument that all the categories except subject reduce to states of a single subject, matter, is not one which the Stoa would have rejected. In nature their co-presence consists in mixture; and that leaves no room for an order of priority—nature is, so to speak, monolithic. In themselves, however, they are in an order, which is a matter of super-imposition, not just of co-presence. (Running is superimposed on Dion and being in front may be superimposed on him running.) But this is possible only in *logos*. The 'about' of Plotinus's text thus takes on added significance.[47] And it follows that the study of the categories properly belongs to the study of the *lekton*, that is, a branch of dialectic. They have been mistakenly placed under physics by von Arnim and others.

A comparison with a similar class of objects may make the matter simpler. *Opposites* were all dealt with among the *lekta* by Stoics;[48] and that is where they are to be found in von Arnim's collection. Heat and cold, wisdom and folly are four opposites which are alike in being material: but considered as opposites they are two types. This is discovered by the dialectician.

Certain philosophical consequences for the understanding of Stoicism will also follow. Aristotle's categories underlay his logic, which underlay his metaphysics. But they belonged to a doctrine of terms; and this was one fundamental difference from Stoic categories. It was noticed by Simplicius who had to remind his readers that for an Aristotelian 'justice, just, justly and unjust' all belonged to one category;[49] and it is to be explained by the dependence of Stoic categories on traditional grammar.

The significance of their being classes of *lekta*, not *onta* is more difficult. It does not imply a kind of idealism in which nature as we know it is 'fashioned by mind': but it implies, I think, a kind of rationalism in which *logos* is both objective and non-relative.[50] This is possibly the deeper meaning of the theory according to which language was natural not conventional, but which they failed to separate from a shallow theory of etymology and onomatopoea. Most philosophers have found it easier to start from the assumption that there is one world but more than one way of describing it, so that the choice of the description depends on, or is relative to, the describer while its truth or falsity depends on the world or state of affairs. The Stoics shared Heraclitus's belief that *logos* was part of nature, not something imposed on it by a human convention; they also shared his belief that it pervaded all nature, with the result that everything natural possessed some properties which it possessed. But they interpreted *logos* more plainly, as sounds which signified by describing. Features of description therefore were features of nature, so that their categories were, like Aristotle's, facts of nature. This however would hold only in the last analysis. The reason why the categories belonged properly, as I suggested, to dialectic and not to physics, is that though features of reality they are in the first place features of a sub-class of reality, namely descriptions; and descriptions themselves are of course a sub-class of significant sounds, the science of which is dialectic. More important, the notion of a description implies of itself a further division, that between the vehicle and what it conveys, which is the Stoic distinction between the utterance and the *lekton*. To the *lekton* belong the categories: but even at this level of abstraction the features of nature which were entailed by the pervasiveness of *logos* are not lost to sight. For the *lekton* corresponds isomorphically to the utterance, and in the utterance they are represented, save for anomaly, by the grammatical parts of speech.

NOTES

1. It must be borne in mind that Stoics did not have an agreed classification of dialectic, logic and rhetoric.

2. *Syntaxis* is strictly short for 'syntax of the parts of speech' (on which Chrysippus wrote (*SVF* II 206a)). The Stoic definition of 'solecism' was λόγος ἀκαταλλήλως συντεταγμένος (Diog. Laert. VII 59 (*SVF* III 24)); and the grammarian's maxim, *oratio est ordinatio dictionum congrua* (Priscian *Inst.* II 15 (*Gramm. lat.*, ed. Keil, ii p. 53. 28)) is pure Stoicism. See further Barwick's invaluable *Probleme der stoischen Sprachlehre und Rhetorik* pp. 21, 25, 26. But syntax itself was ignored by the Stoics as it was by the earliest surviving grammarian, Dionysius Thrax (contemporary with the Middle Stoa); in its place they might be said to have put logic.

3. Cf. Dion. Thrax p. 25 Hilgard (*Gramm. graec.* iii).

4. Loc. cit. pp. 46ff.

5. For the attribution of these συμβεβηκότα (=παρεπόμενα in Dion. Thrax) to Diogenes see Barwick *Remmius Palaemon*, pp. 92ff., 107ff.

6. VII 43.

7. Diog. Laert. VII 56 (*SVF* III p. 213). *Logos* may be a single word or a sentence or a succession of sentences.

8. Diog. Laert. VII 56, 57 (*SVF* III p. 213, 13; 24–6).

9. Porph. *ap.* Simpl. *In Cat.* (*CAG* VIII) pp. 10, 20; 11, 6.

10. Porph. loc. cit. The minor parts of speech *consignificant* (=προσσημαίνει, Aristotle *De int.* c. 3) and are *syncategorēmata* (Priscian *Inst.* II 15 (*Gramm. lat.* ii p. 54)). For Boëthius see, e.g. *De int.*² pp. 73–4 Meiser (on the verb).

11. On Stoic parts of speech there are many points open to question. But who first recognised each, and what exactly was included in it, are questions that, except for the place of demonstratives, do not affect my thesis. I therefore refer the reader to the evidence that is found best in R. Schmidt *Stoicorum grammatica* and L. Lersch *Sprachphilosophie der Alten*, Pt. II.

12. Proper name (*nomen proprium*) =ὄνομα κύριον; general name (*appellatio*, B. Mates (*Stoic logic*) 'class name') =προσηγορία; verb commonly =ἀσύνθετον κατηγόρημα (possibly in the infinitive =ῥῆμα, while in other moods =κατηγόρημα or σύμβαμα); adverb probably =μεσότης.

13. ὑποκείμενον, ποιός, πῶς ἔχων, πρός τί πως ἔχων.

14. Schmidt, op cit. 37. Cf. Haller 'Untersuchungen zum Bedeutungsproblem', *Archiv für Begriffsgeschichte* vii (1962) 84; Christensen (who has more to say) *Essay on the unity of Stoic philosophy*. Lersch, op. cit., Pt. II 28–9, is equally laconic on the other side.

15. Cf. Dahlmann *Varro u. die hellenistische Sprachtheorie*, pp. 10–14.

16. Alex. Aphr. *In Top.* (*CAG* II 2) p. 1 (*SVF* II 124); *cf. SVF* II 293.

17. Galen *Plac.* II 2, pp. 213, 12–216, 4; 327, 14–328, 6 Kühn (*Med. graec.*v).

18. πρῶται φωναί—of which there were 1000 according to one expert (Varro *De ling. lat.* VI 36)!

19. *Probl. der stoischen Sprachlehre* pp. 77–8.

20. 'Anomaly' = the grammarians' 'irregularity' as opposed to 'analogy' defined as ὁμοίου παράθεσις (Sextus, *Adv. math.* I 236). Later, there was a long controversy whether 'language', or 'correct language', was based on usage (συνήθεια, consuetudo) or analogy (similitudo). Its echo has survived: the teaching of Latin to the young is still recommended on the ground that 'Latin is a more logical language than English'.

21. Cf. Augustine *Princ. dialecticae* c. 6 (*Patr. lat.* XXXII 1412). The dependence of this tract on a Stoic source is self-evident.

22. Loc. cit. Similarly with wool (*lana*) and bramble (*vepres*), *ut audiuntur verba sic illa tanguntur.*

23. Aristotle *De int.* 16a 3–7; *An. post.* 77a 5–12 (predicates as universals); *De an.* 417b 23–25 (universals as thoughts; cf. *Met.* 1073a 1–3).

24. The second, alternative view is perhaps that of Dr Long, if I understand his impressive treatment of the *lekton* [see Chapter V, pp. 79ff]. Certainly, too, what one means is one's thought: the question which that begs is the philosophical one, what else one is going to *say* about thinking. [Professor Lloyd is right to attribute his 'second view' to me. But I don't think his alternatives are exclusive. I have argued that Aristotle does use *noema* for purposes analogous to those served by *lekta*, but that does not, in my view, entail a recognition by Aristotle of the same *kind* of semantic theory. Ed.]

25. *De. int.* 16a 7.

26. [See further Chapter V, pp. 79–81. Ed.]

27. This difference is obscured by the otherwise penetrating remarks and diagram on pp. 46–7 of Christensen's *Essay on the unity of Stoic philosophy.*

28. Diog. Laert. VII 58 (*SVF* III 213.)

29. Simpl. *In Cat.* (*CAG* VIII) p. 64. 18–19.

30. R. H. Robins, *Ancient and mediaeval grammatical theory in Europe* (London 1951) p. 27, is misleading here.

31. Diog. Laert. VII 58 (*SVF* III p. 214, 1).

32. Ibid. (*SVF* III p. 213, 1).

33. *Inst.* II 16 (*Gramm. lat.* ii p. 54).

34. Subject referred to $= \mathring{v}\pi o\kappa\epsilon\acute{\iota}\mu\epsilon\nu o\nu$. Subject of the sentence which refers to it $= \pi\tau\hat{\omega}\sigma\iota\varsigma$. Universal propositions, which do not necessarily have existential import, were analysed as hypotheticals.

35. *Inst.* XI 1 (*Gramm. lat.* ii p. 548); cf. Apollon. Dysc. *De pronom.* pp. 5ff. Schneider (*Gramm. graec.* i).

36. Prisc. *Inst.* II 30 (*Gramm. lat.* ii p. 61). See further Lersch Pt. II pp. 41–3. Grammarians seem to have made relative, interrogative and indefinite pronouns co-ordinate species (e.g. Dionys. Thrax p. 39, 1 Schneider). But my suggestion of an exhaustive division into definite and indefinite is supported by Varro *De ling. lat.* VIII 44–5, which was overlooked by Lersch and Schmidt. Indeed the whole of Varro's *pars appellandi* is covered by the division, for proper names are '*ut finita*' and general names '*ut infinita*'. For demonstratives cf. VIII 45.

37. *Adv. math.* VIII 96–7 (*SVF* II 205).

38. VII 70 where $\epsilon\kappa\epsilon\hat{\iota}\nu o\varsigma$ $\kappa\iota\nu\epsilon\hat{\iota}\tau\alpha\iota$ is classed with $\tau\grave{\iota}\varsigma$ $\pi\epsilon\rho\iota\pi\alpha\tau\epsilon\hat{\iota}$ and contrasted with $o\mathring{v}\tau o\varsigma$ $\pi\epsilon\rho\iota\pi\alpha\tau\epsilon\hat{\iota}$.

39. Apollon. Dysc. *De pronom.* pp. 6, 30–7, 7.

40. Ibid. 7, 1–6.

41. Alex. Aphr. *In An. pr.* (*CAG* II 1) p. 177, 28–33 (*SVF* II 202a, p. 65, 8–13).

42. *Ibid.* pp. 177, 25–178, 5 (*SVF* II 202a). [See further Chapter V, p. 97 Ed.]

43. Conjunction: Schmidt p. 37, Haller p. 84. Transitive verb: Christensen p. 50.

44. $\mathring{o}\rho\theta\grave{o}\nu$ $\kappa\alpha\tau\eta\gamma\acute{o}\rho\eta\mu\alpha$ (Diog. Laert. VII 64 (*SVF* II 183)). According to Ammonius *In De int.* (*CAG* IV 5) pp. 44, 16–45, 3 (*SVF* II 184) it would be called $\mathring{\epsilon}\lambda\alpha\tau\tau o\nu$ $\mathring{\eta}$ $\kappa\alpha\tau\eta\gamma\acute{o}\rho\eta\mu\alpha$: but his account is questionable; *cf.* Lersch Pt. II pp. 34–5; Zeller *Stoics, Epicureans and Sceptics* (Engl. transl. 1880) p. 95 n. 3.

45. VI 1, 30, 3–7 (*SVF* II 400); cf. Porph. *Sent.* p. 2, 1–2 Mommert. O. Rieth (*Grundbegriffe* p. 190), who denied this kind of order, mistook the meaning of

Simplicius' denial that πρός τί πως ἔχοντα were κατὰ διαφοράν, *In cat.* (*CAG* VIII) pp. 165, 33–166, 29. [On qualities as material see J. M. Rist, Chapter III, p. 44 Ed.]

46. Cf. κατηγόρημα as Stoics' name for verb. The fact is probably to be connected with their dynamic view of the external world as a moving continuum.

47. Seneca *Ep. mor.* 117, 13 is a valuable text here: Sunt, inquit, naturae corporum, tamquam hic homo est, hic equus. Has deinde sequuntur motus animorum enuntiativi corporum. Hi habent proprium quiddam et a corporibus seductum, tamquam video Catonem ambulantem. Hoc sensus ostendit, animus credidit. Corpus est, quod video, cui et oculos intendi et animum. Dico deinde: Cato ambulat. Non corpus, inquit, est quod nunc loquor, sed enuntiativum quiddam de corpore, quod alii effatum vocant, alii enuntiatum, alii dictum. Sic cum dicimus sapientiam, corporale quiddam intellegimus; cum dicimus sapit, de corpore loquimur. Plurimum autem interest, utrum illum dicas an de illo. [This text is translated on p. 77. Ed.]

48. Simpl. *In Cat.* (*CAG* VIII) p. 388 (*SVF* II 173).

49. *Ibid.* p. 208, 17–21.

50. Thus Watson's *Stoic Theory of Knowledge* makes Stoicism to my mind look too Kantian.

V

Language and thought in Stoicism

A. A. LONG

This chapter is an essay on Stoic metaphysics. It considers two inter-related topics: the theory of *lekton*, so far as this deals with the connexion between language and reality; and the theory of truth. For the Stoics, these were not subjects of 'metaphysics' but of physics and logic, with some ramification into ethics. Such were the three branches of philosophy which they recognised. But within them an important place was given to describing the structure of our thinking about the world, and it would be pedantic and misleading not to call this metaphysics.[1] The point needs stressing because it is rarely appreciated in accounts of Stoic logic. A firm barrier in Stoicism cannot be set between the analysis of arguments or propositions and the grounds for their verification. The latter require reference to a view of the world's structure and what can be said about it. Our problem then broadly is to find the context of logic and language in Stoicism as a whole.

I STATEMENT AND REFERENCE

Stoic ontology comprises 'objective particulars'. I borrow Strawson's phrase because, like Strawson, the Stoics take 'three-dimensional objects with some endurance through time' as their fundamental existents.[2] What these possess in common is 'body', and the test for something's existence is whether it can act or be acted upon.[3] This test is satisfied not only by material objects as we would understand that term today, but also by qualities; these too are 'matter in a certain state'. My state of health and even my moral character are dispositions of matter. But, for all that, they depend upon my existence as an individual, and the Stoics placed such 'spatio-temporal situations' in categories dependent upon the categories of 'existence' as a 'particular'.[4] Apart from the 'individuating quality' (*idiōs poion*) which persists throughout the history of any particular man, stone, table etc., the properties of a particular are states or ways of its being and they depend on it for their existence.[5] The individuating quality is not a quality at all in any normal sense of quality. It is that which allows us to say that this three-dimensional object is not the same as that one. The concept has been discussed in detail in the third chapter of this book, and I would only add here that, in physical terms, 'individuating quality' seems to be the name for the persistent form imposed by the universal stock of shaping material (*pneuma*) on some part of unshaped matter.[6] A particular in Stoic ontology is a material object which has definite shape as the sufficient and necessary condition of its existence.[7] 'Shape' here means the characteristic of a particular which makes it identifiable as such. Given such an ontology it is natural that the Stoics were much exercised about 'images' produced in the mind by external objects. For it is on such images, when they reproduce exactly the configuration of external objects, that they based the criterion of true perception.[8] And images, as we shall see, have a basic part to play in the Stoic theory of significant discourse.

There are various ways in which a person might indicate his ability to identify a particular. But the one which concerns us here is linguistic identification: that is, the ability of A to communicate that he is talking about P to B, and B's ability to indicate that he understands A to be talking about P. The fact that the Stoics were concerned with this problem is proved by a passage in Sextus Empiricus (*Adv. math.* VIII 11–12). Sextus is discussing conflicting opinions about truth, and he opens this book by pointing out a lack of agreement among philosophers concerning the status of sensibles and intelligibles as candidates for the predicate 'true'. Now he passes to a 'second controversy':

True and false have been variously located in what is signified (*to sēmainomenon*), in speech (*phōnē*), and in the motion of thought. The Stoics opted for the first of these, claiming that three things are linked together, what is signified, that which signifies (*to semainon*) and the object of reference (*to tynchanon*).[9] That which signifies is speech ('Dion'), what is signified is the specific state of affairs (*auto to pragma*)[10] indicated by the spoken word and which we grasp as co-existent with (*paryphistamenon*) our thought but which the barbarians do not understand although they hear the sound; the object of reference is the external existent, that is, Dion himself. Of these, two are bodies, speech and the object of reference. But the state of affairs signified is not a body but a *lekton*, which is true or false.

Sextus' final remark, if it refers to his example, suggests that applying to Dion his proper name is equivalent to asserting the true proposition 'this man is Dion'.[11] But the truth or falsity of *lekta*, though Sextus' ostensible concern, is not ours at this moment. His most interesting point arises from the reference to 'barbarians', that is, 'non-Greek speakers'.[12] What they are unable to do is to recognise the state of affairs signified by the spoken word 'Dion'. They might see Dion and they certainly hear 'Dion', but they are unable to connect the sound with its object of reference. To understand, as the Greek speakers do, is to perceive the connexion between the spoken word and its object of reference. And it is this reference of an utterance to some object which is 'what is signified' and *lekton*. The Stoics distinguished between 'merely uttering a noise' (*propheresthai*) and *legein*, which is to do this in such a way as to signify (*semaninein*) the state of affairs in mind (Sextus *Adv. math.* VIII 80). It is 'being significant' which distinguishes *logos* from *lexis*, and the subjects of significant discourse are 'states of affairs' (*pragmata*) which are actually *lekta* (Diog. Laert. VII 57). On the basis of these passages it is clearly proper to translate *lekton* by 'what is said' where 'what is said' covers 'statement' or 'state of affairs' (λέγεται πράγματα) signified by a word or set of words.[13] This translation I believe to be more accurate than 'what is meant' because *lekton* has logical and grammatical functions which make the most general rendering preferable.

The three distinctions drawn by Sextus are repeated in a letter of Seneca, who cites them in the third person (*Ep. mor.* 117, 13):

There are material natures, such as this man, this horse, and they are accompanied by movements of thought (*motus animorum*) which make affirmations about them. These movements contain something peculiar to themselves which is separate from material objects. For instance, I see Cato walking; the sense of sight reveals this to me and the mind believes it. What I see is a material object and it is to a

material object that I direct my eyes and my mind. Then I say
'Cato is walking'. It is not a material object which I now state, but a
certain affirmation about a material object. . . . Thus if we say
'wisdom' we take this to refer to something material; but if we say
'he is wise' we make an assertion about a material object. It makes
a very great difference whether you *refer* to the person directly, or
speak about him. [For the Latin text see p. 74 n. 47.]

In the course of this illuminating discussion Seneca observes
that 'affirmations about objects' are *lekta* (to be precise he offers
three Latin translations of *lekton*). We are to distinguish between the object of reference, Cato, and the assertion about
him 'that he walks'. And this assertion in turn is something
different from the utterance 'Cato ambulat'. The assertion or
lekton is 'what is said by "Cato ambulat" about Cato'. 'Cato is
walking' according to Stoic theory is an *autoteles axiōma*, which
means approximately that it is a proposition. Since the predicates true and false pertain to these but not to uncompounded
subjects and predicates Sextus would have done better to take
Seneca's example instead of 'Dion'.[14]

It is interesting none the less to learn that *lekta* embrace the
content of some separate words as well as sentences. 'Deficient
lekta', as the former type is called, appear to be signified by
verbs which lack a subject, e.g. 'writes', for we ask 'who?'
(Diog. Laert. VII 63). These are, of course, radically different
from the *lekta* expressed by sentences such as *Cato ambulat*.
Ambulat is defective because it lacks a reference; it is, in Frege's
terminology, a *Funktionname* 'used to talk about an object'. The
semantic content of isolated nouns is less clear. They are not
cited as 'signifying deficient *lekta*' but seem to have the role of
supplying such *lekta* with a subject (*ptōsis*) or reference (see
Postscript p. 104). In confining truth and falsity to the 'complete *lekta*', 'Cato is walking' etc., the Stoics follow Aristotle
(*De int*. 16a 13–16): 'thus names and verbs by themselves . . . are
like the thoughts that are without combination and separation;
for so far they are neither true nor false'. But the Stoic 'proposition' is not a combination of words (which are material
objects) but what the words assert (which is incorporeal).[15] The
parts combined in a Stoic statement are subject (*ptōsis*) and
predicate (*katēgorēma*).[16]

Lekta then, at least in their complete form, mediate between words considered as significant utterances and things.[17] (I say 'at least in their complete form' since it is difficult to see how the Stoics could take isolated predicates as referring expressions.) Combined with a subject they are the usage of words to say something meaningful about, or simply to refer to, things, and for the purpose of linguistic identification the speaker's *lekton* and the auditor's *lekton* must be the same. The fact that *lekta* are incorporeal and thus fail the test of existence is a problem to which we will return.

Before proceeding to further evidence about *lekta* in Stoic sources it is worth comparing more closely what Sextus and Seneca have to say with Aristotle's discussion of the relation between language and thought in the *De interpretatione* (16a 3–18). Aristotle there claims that utterances (τὰ ἐν τῇ φωνῇ) are symbols of mental states (παθήματα ἐν τῇ ψυχῇ), later called 'thoughts' (νοήματα), which are likenesses of actual things. The utterances (or written words) used as symbols are not the same for all men, but the mental states which they symbolise are the same. The notorious difficulties in this laconic discussion do not all concern us here.[18] The relevant point is Aristotle's view that there is a correspondence between spoken or written symbols and thoughts, both of which are sometimes true, sometimes false, and sometimes neither true nor false. We have to ask whether Aristotle's παθήματα ἐν τῇ ψυχῇ or νοήματα are similar in nature and/or function to Stoic *lekta*.

That they function as the same is clear enough. Both *lekton* and *noēma* are distinguished from the *significans* as its *significatum*. Both again, under appropriate conditions, can serve as propositions and therefore be true or false. But the theories of meaning which they provide are radically different. As Mates has shown, the Stoic theory may aptly be compared with the referential theories of Frege and Carnap.[19] Aristotle, perhaps owing to his metaphysical concern with distinguishing accidents and attributes from substances and essences, lacks a clear distinction between sense and reference. In the *De interpretatione* the relation between his *noemata*, acts of thought (which he elsewhere distinguishes from mental images), and the things of which they are likenesses, is one of copy to original. If such a

theory is adequate to explain the meaning of 'cat', it is certainly
not adequate to explain the meaning of 'sits', for of what thing
is the thought 'sits' a likeness? The problems become even
greater when the meaning of sentences has to be explained.
Elsewhere Aristotle generally operates simply with the distinction between *onoma* and *pragma*, where *pragma* is the 'thing'
to which the name is used to refer. Thus in *Topics* 108a 18ff. he
notes the value of distinguishing the various ways in which a
term is said (ποσαχῶς λέγεται): 'this ensures that reasoning is
directed at the thing itself (*auto to pragma*) and not at the name
which signifies it (*onoma*). For if the various ways in which a term
is said are not clear it is possible that the answerer and the
questioner are not applying their minds to the same thing'
(similarly *Soph. el.* 165a 6–14). Thought or thing? If thoughts
are likenesses of things it is all one, though Aristotle recognises
that 'goat-stag' signifies something of which no corresponding
thing (or referent) *exists*. But there are times when it is necessary
to distinguish clearly between some common object of reference,
say Cicero, and such expressions as 'writer of the *De Finibus*'
and 'consular opponent of Catiline'. Each expression is significant and different, but they do not pick out different 'things'.
In Stoic theory they are different *lekta*, asserted of one object.
Aristotle, in his more careful statements of how *noemata* are
related to *phantasmata* (e.g. *De mem.* 1 450a 30–b6), no doubt
allows that one and the same thought may be thought via
different images. But images can hardly be treated as equivalent or even analogous to the sense or content of all descriptive
expressions.

According to Simplicius the Stoics regarded 'things said'
(*ta legomena*) *and* 'thoughts' (*noemata*) as *lekta*.[20] This is clearly
incorrect, and later contradicted by Simplicius himself when
he distinguishes between not only *phonai* and *lekta* but also
between διανοήματα and τὰ παρυφιστάμενα ἀσώματα λεκτά,
which agrees with Sextus (*Adv. math.* VIII 12):[21] *lekta* are not
thoughts but 'what are coexistent with (or 'subsistent upon',
paryphistamena) thoughts'. This fact is partially grasped by
Ammonius, whose discussion is worth quoting in full:

Aristotle tells us what [things] are expressed primarily and immediately by nouns and verbs; his answer is 'thoughts', but through them

as intermediate 'things' [are expressed], and it is not necessary to conceive of anything, additional to them, intermediate between the thought and the thing which the Stoics, by positing *lekton*, have thought fit to nominate.[22]

Ammonius' account of the *lekton* is misleading. But it is sufficiently accurate to point an important difference between the Stoic and Aristotelian theories of meaning. Ammonius can only find the *lekton* redundant by failing to see, as we suspected independently, that Aristotle does not distinguish adequately between thought-content and reference.[23] On his interpretation of the *De interpretatione* spoken words signify things via the medium of mental events. And the interpretation seems a valid inference from the fact that 'thoughts' are 'likenesses of things'. In regarding *noemata* as true or false (under certain conditions) Aristotle implies that they are judgements, but in suggesting that they are likenesses he also implies that they call to mind or refer to things. Hence *noema* has to play the double role of mental picture and judgement. The two roles are not necessarily incompatible, but Aristotle's own account cannot be called satisfactory. In the *De anima* (III 432a 10ff.) to which he (or an editor) refers the reader of the *De interpretatione* Aristotle distinguishes clearly between *phantasmata*, the images which thought requires, and the thoughts themselves which constitute truth or falsehood when combined. But that passage has nothing to say on the relation between language and thought.

It may seem unfair to dwell at such length on the first chapter of the *De interpretatione*. Aristotle clearly regards what he says there as consistent with the *De anima* and his brevity may in part explain the confusions. But there is no doubt that Aristotle does lack a clear distinction between 'what the words say' and the mental picture of their reference. It is a garbled version of this distinction which the Stoics introduce, in Ammonius' words, by 'positing *lekton* between the thought and the thing'. (Fortunately we have evidence to show that his statement needs modification.)

To suggest that the Stoics came to approximate a distinction between meaning and reference by meditating upon Aristotle would be inappropriate. It is a distinction which their propositional calculus requires. But in a discussion of Stoic metaphysics it is necessary to inquire into the relation between *lekton* and thought. We have already seen that *lekta* and thought are intimately associated by Sextus, and an examination of the definition of *lekton* will, I hope, show that comparison with Aristotle is not misguided.

II   THINKING AND MEANING

Identical definitions of *lekton* are given by Sextus and Diogenes Laertius.[24] Sextus' context needs to be quoted in full:

ἠξίουν οἱ στωικοὶ κοινῶς ἐν λεκτῷ τὸ ἀληθὲς εἶναι καὶ τὸ ψεῦδος. λεκτὸν δὲ ὑπάρχειν φασὶ τὸ κατὰ λογικὴν φαντασίαν ὑφιστάμενον, λογικὴν δὲ εἶναι φαντασίαν καθ' ἣν τὸ φαντασθὲν ἔστι λόγῳ παραστῆσαι.

The Stoics held as a common view that true and false are in the *lekton*. And they say that *lekton* is that which is (subsists, *hyphistamenon*) correspondent to a rational presentation, and a rational presentation is one in which what is presented can be shown forth in speech.[25]

I take this difficult passage to mean that *lekton* is defined as the objective content of acts of thinking (*noēseis*) or, what comes to the same thing in Stoicism, the sense of significant discourse. This interpretation seems to follow from a passage in Diogenes Laertius (VII 49–50). There we are told that the generic criterion of 'things' is 'presentation' (*phantasia*), where criterion means the standard of truth or falsehood. Diogenes explains the *phantasia* is accorded this high status because no account of assent (*synkatathesis*), apprehension (*katalēpsis*) or thinking (*noesis*) can be given independently of *phantasia*: 'for this comes first, then thought, which is able to speak, expresses in speech what it experiences as a result of the presentation'.

The concept of thinking as internal discourse goes back to Plato.[26] In Stoicism it seems to mean that the processes of thought and the processes of linguistic communication are essentially the same. Whether a man is thinking to himself, speaking aloud or listening to speech he requires a *phantasia*: that is to say, his mind must be affected by something, have something presented to it. A *phantasia* is this affection, 'something which reveals itself and its cause'.[27] The term covers both impressions of material objects presented through the senses and concepts (impressions of immaterial objects) presented via the mind itself.[28] In revealing itself, we may interpret, a *phantasia* also reveals to men of normal health whether it is a product of the external world or a construct of reason or imagination. Perception and thought alike depend upon *phantasia*, for perception entails assenting to and apprehending a presentation, and it is perception which provides the material for building up ideas (*ennoiai*).[29] Assent is an activity of the *logos* which probably involves, as Watson argues, some comparison with previous experience.[30] But the process of perception, though dependent on a mental act, does not tell us what we are perceiving any more than matching a particular colour against a second colour tells us what the colour under observation is. To distinguish the mere presentations of sense from those also required for linguistic acts and discursive reason the Stoics appended to the latter set the adjective *logikai*. 'Rational presentations' are thoughts (*noeseis*) and peculiar to men, though it is not, I think, implied that every species of human *phantasia* is *logike*.[31]

The specific character of a *logike phantasia* is its ability to say something, *lekton*: 'it can reveal by speech what is presented' (i.e. its object). *Logikai phantasiai* (unlike some olfactory and tactile impressions) are expressible; they are impressions convertible into (or perhaps received as) words. A man might indicate his awareness of something by gestures and inarticulate cries; but *logos* enables him to express this in meaningful, communicable form.[32] The connexion between *logike phantasia*, *lekton* and 'the presented object' (*to phantasthen*) seems to be the same in fact as the connexion between sign, *lekton* and (external) object.[33] For the words which an auditor receives must be the utterance of the speaker's rational presentation.

If this is correct *lekta* are relevant not only to the Stoic theory of language but also to the Stoic theory of mind. We can now see that none of the Aristotelian commentators has given a completely accurate account. The Stoics do not like Aristotle identify the mind with what it thinks.[34] This accounts for Simplicius' mistaken equation of *lekta* with thoughts. In Stoic theory acts of thought are private (physical modifications of the *hegemonikon*) but the sense of the words in which they are expressed is immaterial, objective and something which others can grasp.[35] But *lekta* are not intermediate between thoughts and things if, as Ammonius implies, that scheme is taken to require speech as a fourth, additional entity. Words and thoughts are not strictly distinguishable here. *Logos* is both speech and reason. In Stoicism thinking requires the presentation of an object to the mind (*to phantasthen*) and the means of referring to (*ptosis*) and saying something about it (*lekton*). The two requirements are brought together in *logike phantasia*.

III   SIGNS AND SIGNALS: DO *lekta* EXIST?

It is necessary now to inquire more closely into the ontological status of *lekta*. At the beginning of this discussion I observed that only material objects are existents in Stoic theory. *Lekta* are incorporeal (*asōmata*). This would seem to settle the matter at once: *lekta* are not existents. But the position is not quite so simple. We have already encountered the terms *hyphistasthai* and *paryphistasthai* in reference to *lekta*. Moreover, Sextus, who offers arguments against the existence of *lekta*, certainly takes it that they do exist for most Stoics.[36] He also tells us that Basileides, a Stoic teacher of Marcus Aurelius?, denied the 'existence' (*hyparxis*) of *lekta*, which implies an exception to the normal position, and that battles concerning this problem are unending.[37]

There appears to be a serious contradiction here. Do *lekta* exist or not? If they exist does this invalidate the claim that only material objects exist? If they do not exist, what is their status? Did the Stoics themselves differ seriously in their opinions about *lekta*? As a preliminary to answering these questions a 'radical difficulty' discovered by Mates requires some mention.[38]

In Sextus' discussion of *lekton* (*Adv. math.* VIII 11–12) 'that which signifies' is identified with φωνή, 'voice'. *Phōnē* is 'vibrating air', a material object, and under it are classified 'speech' (*phone sēmantikē*) and the parts of speech.[39] A noun or a verb is a *meros logou semainon* . . . but in nature it is a species of *logos*, under the *summum genus* 'voice'.[40] This usage of *semainon* presents no problems, but according to Sextus the Stoics also employed a seemingly synonymous term, *sēmeion*, in a quite different sense: the *semeion* is not a material object but 'a true antecedent proposition in a valid conditional which serves to reveal the consequent'.[41]

Mates' problem is the fact that a *semeion*, on this definition, would be a *lekton*, since hypothetical propositions are a species of *lekta*, and therefore incorporeal. But 'things which signify' (*semainonta*), qua *phonai*, are material objects. Hence there is an incompatibility between such *semainonta* and *semeia*. The solution to this problem has been ably demonstrated by the Kneales, but the space devoted to it by Mates makes further discussion desirable.[42]

The evidence for *semeia* is largely derived from Sextus, but there is no reason to impugn his reliability on essentials and Zeno wrote a work 'on signals'. (I follow Mates in adopting this translation of *semeia*.) For a general understanding of what the Stoics meant by 'signal' we go to an argument which makes use of the premise 'signal is of the form "if this, then that" '.[43] Signal is thus a method of 'inference', as its application in another passage of Sextus clearly shows. There are two categories of signal: objects which are 'temporarily unseen' are revealed by a 'commemorative' signal which observation has shown to have a connexion with it.[44] Thus, we frequently observe that smoke and fire occur in conjunction and therefore smoke serves as a commemorative signal of fire. (This method of inference from actual states of affairs appears to be invoked by Chrysippus in his criterion for the truth of a conditional proposition. The logical significance of this has been well treated elsewhere, but it also has a bearing on Stoic metaphysics, as we shall see.)[45] Objects which are 'naturally unseen' require a different category of signal since they can never be observed in conjunction with anything else.[46] For them an 'indicative' signal is required. Thus, the soul is never perceived but bodily movements serve to reveal it. In such cases the signal 'at once by its own nature and constitution, practically sending forth voice (*phone*), is said to signify (*semainein*) that of which it is indicative'.

As this last remark shows the language used to describe signals can come very close to that used to describe the relation between utterances and what is said. But the similarity is purely verbal. Bodily movements do not *express* soul; they are material for inferring its existence. Mates argues that this discussion of signals is compatible with the view that they are physical objects. But this is incorrect. It is no more suggested that signals are physical objects than that *lekta* are utterances. 'If smoke, ...' not smoke as such is the signal. Sextus' criticism of signals is based on the claim, as Mates himself observes, that *lekta* do not exist, and therefore signals, as propositions, do not exist.[47] But Mates still finds a contradiction between this view of signals and Sextus' assertion (*Adv. math.* VIII 264) that 'sounds signify (*semainousi*), *lekta* are signified, including propositions, and since propositions are signified not "things which signify" (*semainonta*) the signal (*semeion*) will not be a proposition'.[48]

Now there is certainly a formal contradiction here if *semeion* is meant to denote both 'signal' (incorporeal) and 'that which signifies' (corporeal). But Sextus has caused the confusion himself by using *semeion* to refer back to *semainonta*. Given that he is out to criticise it is easy, though dishonest, to overlook the vital distinction between these terms, which are normally synonymous in Greek. Mates suggests this as a hypothesis but it is a fact for which Sextus elsewhere is evidence.[49] As the Kneales observe, the different terminologies belong to different theories.[50] Every proposition needs to be 'signified' by language; a *lekton* must be expressed in words. But this is quite compatible with its serving, under appropriate conditions, to signify a further proposition. *Semainonta* in Stoicism denote significant sounds (bodies), and are not substitutable for *semeia*. When Sextus discusses commemorative and indicative signals he does not refer to them by the former term.

Since signals are a species of *lekta* what applies to *lekta* in general should apply to them. Sextus himself argues that *lekta* and signals stand or fall together (*Adv. math.* VIII 261) and clearly thinks that his arguments against *lekta* are equally valid against *semeia*. Part of this refutation, which is thoroughly specious, turns upon showing that if there are signals they must be either perceptible (corporeal) or intelligible (incorporeal).[51] The Stoics deny the former possibility and Sextus claims that the latter would make signals ineffective since in Stoic theory the incorporeal cannot effect or suffer anything. The conclusion is that there is no such thing as a signal since it is neither *aisthēton* nor *noēton* and *tertium non datur*. At this point however Sextus cites arguments of the 'dogmatists' (i.e. Stoics) in favour of signals.[52] The first of these needs particular attention:

The Stoics 'say that man differs from irrational animals by reason of internal speech (*endiathetoi logoi*) not uttered speech (*prophorikoi logoi*), for crows and parrots and jays utter articulate sounds.[53]

Nor does he differ from other creatures in virtue of simple presentations (*haplei phantasiai*)—for they too receive these—but in virtue of presentations produced by inference and combination (*phantasiai metabatikei kai synthetikei*).[54] This amounts to man's possessing an idea of logical consequence (*akolouthia*), and he grasps the concept of signal because of this. For signal itself is of the following form: "if this, then that". Therefore the existence (*hyparchein*) of signal follows from the nature and constitution of man.

We may postpone for the moment consideration of the important word *akolouthia* in order to explain other matters arising from this passage. The ability to think (to discourse with oneself), to frame concepts and to draw inferences is part of man's nature. So much Sextus himself attributes to the Stoics and other texts show that these abilities are qualities, physical states of the soul, embraced under the terms *phōnētikon* and *dianoētikon*.[55] Making statements and drawing inferences are what we should call the activities of these soul-faculties. But the Stoics equated activity (*energeia*) with body and animal following the assumption that only (vital) bodies can act.[56] They regarded actions or dispositions expressed by means of verbs as predicates, assertions made about bodies, and incorporeal.[57] Thus 'being temperate' (*to sōphronein*) and 'being prudent' (*to phronein*) are *asōmata* and *kategoremata*, though temperance (*sōphrosynē*) and prudence (*phronēsis*) are material.[58] Hence we may conclude that making statements and drawing inferences are incorporeal predicates of the corporeal *logos* or *dianoia*.

None of this is mentioned by Sextus, but it is obviously highly relevant. If it is the case that statements (*lekta*) and inferences (*semeia*) do not exist in Stoic theory as independent entities it is also the case that the capacity to perform such actions and the activity of performing them exist as material objects, that is, as capacities or activities of men.

It should also be observed that Sextus says man grasps the

semeiou noēsin, the 'way of thinking inferentially'. *Noesis* (like *ennoia*) is no incorporeal abstraction in Stoic theory but a physical modification or activity of the mind.[59] It seems highly probable that the Stoics would have argued that signal as such is the same as *metabasis*, 'a capacity to frame inferences', and as corporeal and real as any other human power. The same applies to *endiathetos logos*, 'the ability to make statements to oneself'. Particular signals or inferences and statements would thus be related to the mind, a mate.ial object, as *phronein* is related to *phronesis*, a material quality. They are not existents in their own right but coexistent with or dependent upon thought.

Now the latter assertion is supported by texts already cited.[60] Did the Stoics in fact claim more than this for *lekta*? According to Sextus the debates concerned the *hyparxis*, the existence or reality of *lekta*, and *prima facie*, *hyparxis* carries no implication of 'derivative existence'. Yet quite counter to this we have the repeated assertion that 'existence' (*to on*) is predicated only of bodies.

First, a possible source of confusion needs mention. Although the Stoics declared only bodies to be existing things they also nominated a genus called *genikōtaton* 'most universal' embracing both bodies (*somata*) and incorporeals (*asomata*).[61] Evidence about the nature and function of this genus is tantalising, but we do know that its precise name was 'the something' and *lekta* were included under it. Alexander also implies by his criticism that *somata* and *asomata* mean *onta* and *ouk onta*. Hence a *lekton*, even if non-existent, is still something (*ti*). Sextus introduces his criticism of the *lekton* (*Adv. math.* VIII 74ff.) with the words 'how can we establish τὸ εἶναί τι λεκτὸν ἀσώματον which is separate from the sound and the object of reference?' Bury translates the Greek words 'that there exists any incorporeal expression' and this is a correct translation. But it is possible that Sextus had in mind a different Stoic assertion 'that an incorporeal *lekton* is something'.[62] The words τὸ εἶναί τι occur again a few lines later and elsewhere, and *hyparchein* is also found, but *esti*, which Sextus uses as synonymous with these terms, does not occur in passages which look like quotations from the Stoics. If Sextus took 'being something' and 'existing' as synonyms he could at once accuse the Stoics of inconsistency.[63]

But the Stoics, like Plato and Aristotle, seem to have maintained that there is no necessary connexion between objects of thought and existence.[64] Failure to recognise the fact that *lekta* are both *tina* and at the same time *ouk onta* might well produce contradictory accounts about their existence in polemical sources.

Second, we have to ask what the Stoics meant by the *hyparxis-hyparchein* of *lekta*, assuming that Sextus is correct in referring these words to them. I mentioned above that *hyparchein* does not naturally imply 'derivative existence', but it is a highly ambiguous word. In philosophical Greek it can mean: (1) 'exist' in contrast with appear or seem; (2) 'be the case' (be true); (3) 'be present in' or 'be predicated of' a subject; (4) 'be real' or 'be genuine'. All these uses of *hyparchein* occur in Stoic texts, and the first two are particularly important in their discussion and definition of truth.[65] In the passage of Sextus just cited the second and third senses are clearly excluded. As propositions complete *lekta* can certainly 'be the case' and deficient *lekta* can be predicated of a subject, but Sextus is not here concerned with these points.

In view of the fact that it is not *hyparchein* but *hyphistasthai* which occurs in definitions of *lekta* it is significant that the Stoics drew a distinction between *hyparchein* and *hyphestanai*. According to Stobaeus 'Chrysippus says only the present *hyparchein*; the future and the past *hyphestanai* but do not *hyparchein*, just as accidents (*ta symbebēkota*) are said to *hyparchein* as predicates, e.g. 'walking' *hyparchei moi* when I am walking, but it does not *hyparchei* when I am lying down or sitting'.[66] Chrysippus seems to be saying here that only the present is real just as verbs expressing continuous action can only *be truly predicated* of a subject at the time when the subject is performing the particular action. To say that the future or the past *hyparchein* would thus be as false as to say that walking is true of me when I am sitting down. Now it might be maintained that this distinction is intended to apply only to the theory of time. To be sure it is spelled out so precisely in only one other passage which repeats the substance of Stobaeus.[67] And there are summaries of Stoic doctrine in which *hyphestanai* simply means 'to exist'. But Galen confirms a distinction, which he calls a generic one, between *to hyphestos* and *to on*;[68] and in criticising it as pettyfogging he does not imply that the Stoics confined it to theories of time. Moreover time shares much with *lekta*; it is *asomaton* and some sources say that it is non-existent (*ouk on*) or exists only in thought.[69] Yet *hyparchein* can be applied to present time. It seems then that *hyphestanai/hyphistasthai* expresses a state subordinate to that denoted by *hyparchein* or *einai* where the terms occur together, or where one of the latter may be mentally supplied because the relation is between *to hyphistamenon* etc. and something which exists. Past and future underly the present since time is continuous, but they are not valid *now*.[70] Similarly *lekta* underlie an 'expressible presentation' since what is presented can only be articulated in a statement; but this entails nothing about their existence as such. Sextus' definition of *lekton* is τὸ κατὰ λογικὴν φαντασίαν ὑφιστάμενον (*Adv. math.* VIII 70) and his earlier phrase παρυφισταμένου τῇ διανοίᾳ (ibid. 12) must possess a parallel sense.[71] Given the distinction between *hyparchein* and *hyphestanai* it cannot be coincidence that the former word does not occur in definitions of *lekta*. To *lekta* which state what is the case or true *hyparchein* is readily applied, as we shall see, but the Stoics certainly distinguish in practice between 'existence' and other senses of *hyparchein* since no existential claim is made for 'the present' when it is said to *hyparchein*. It seems probable that here again failure to recognise an admittedly obscure linguistic distinction has led Sextus to attribute more to *lekta* than the Stoics themselves claimed. Even Basileides' denial of the *hyparxis* of *lekta* may be no more than a clarification of the orthodox position: *lekta* 'subsist' and may be true (*hyparchein*) but they are not *onta*. Our sources do not imply that *lekta* are independent entities. Just as 'walking' entails the existence of a walker, so *lekta* would appear to entail the existence of a mind. Whether this has the further consequence that *lekta* persist only so long as the expressions in which they are asserted is a question which may be postponed for the moment. But far from any text's asserting that *lekta* are *onta* there is unanimous evidence to the contrary. It is only possible to conclude that no Stoic to our knowledge asserted their independent existence.

IV   TRUE AND FALSE STATEMENT

Unfortunately we are not yet done with *hyparchein*. I have argued that *lekta* are not said to *hyparchein* where this word means 'exist'. But I also asserted that *hyparchein* in the sense 'be the case' ('be true') is applied to certain *lekta*. It is necessary therefore to consider how the Stoics came to apply the same word to existents and to statements. They were ready enough to coin a technical term to avoid ambiguity. The investigation of this problem brings us to the Stoic theory of true and false.

According to Sextus (*Adv. math.* VIII 10) 'the true is *to hyparchon* and is the contradictory of something'. Similar definitions are given of true and false propositions: φασὶ γὰρ ἀληθὲς μὲν εἶναι ἀξίωμα ὃ ὑπάρχει τε καὶ ἀντίκειταί τινι, ψεῦδος δὲ ὃ οὐχ ὑπάρχει μὲν ἀντίκειται δέ τινι (Sextus ibid. 85). In the second passage Sextus goes on to say that when asked what is *to hyparchon* the Stoics reply τὸ καταληπτικὴν κινοῦν φαντασίαν, 'that which excites an apprehensive presentation'. Now, what excites an apprehensive presentation must be a material object, for only bodies can excite anything and apprehension requires a presentation from a real object 'stamped and moulded in accordance with the object'.[72] Sextus however does not make this point here since he is out to convict the Stoics of circular reasoning. 'If asked about the *kataleptikē phantasia*, he says, 'the Stoics have recourse to the equally unknown *hyparchon*, saying "it is that derived ἀπὸ ὑπάρχοντος κατ᾽ αὐτὸ τὸ ὑπάρχον. . ."' Since *to hyparchon* and the *kataleptike phantasia* are explained in terms of each other we cannot know either of them nor the true and false propositions which are expounded by means of them.'

Sextus' complaints here are not justified in fact. The Stoics' basic metaphysical assumption is the existence of material objects none of which is identical to any other. These are not defined in terms of *kataleptike phantasia*; the latter is defined in terms of them. What makes a *kataleptike phantasia* the guarantor of valid perception is the fact that it enables a man to grasp the particular character of the object which prompts it.[73] I suggest then, or rather I am convinced, that the basic sense of *hyparchein* in Stoicism is 'exist' and in this sense it applies strictly only to material objects. This is what *to hyparchon* means when Sextus cites it as 'that which excites an apprehensive presentation'. When Sextus also says that true and false propositions were expounded by means of *to hyparchon* and the *kataleptike phantasia* he may be referring to a Stoic claim that the account of truth takes as its starting-point the fact that there are material objects and that men possess a means of accurately perceiving them. Our clue to the connexion between material objects and true statements is the common term *hyparchein*. It begins to seem likely that the *hyparxis* of statements depends upon the *hyparxis* of objects.

The Stoics applied the predicates true and false to different things, propositions (*axiomata* or complete *lekta*), presentations (*phantasiai*) and arguments (*logoi*), but the basic application was probably to propositions.[74] It has been convincingly argued by the Kneales that a passage in Sextus corroborates the view that the truth of presentations is secondary to that of propositions:[75] 'The Stoics say that some sensibles and some intelligibles are true, but the sensibles not directly (ἐξ εὐθείας) but by reference to their corresponding intelligibles (κατ' ἀναφορὰν τὴν ὡς ἐπὶ τὰ παρακείμενα τούτοις νοητά). For the true is *to hyparchon* and is the contradictory of something. . . '.

If 'having a contradictory' is a defining characteristic of true or false then presentations and other material objects are strictly excluded. It seems that a presentation can only be called true or false after it has been expressed in a *lekton*, or thought. But what about the first term in the definitions? It will not do to say with the Kneales that *to hyparchon* in the definition of true is 'used simply as a means of indicating in a convenient way the difference between truth and falsehood' . . . 'that anything which can be called true or false must have a contradictory'.[76] This is only part of the definition. The fact that true is the contradictory of false does not give us a use for the predicates until we know the situations which make each of them appropriate. And this the Stoics denoted by *to hyparchon* and *to mē hyparchon*. Let us translate these provisionally by 'what is the case' and 'what is not the case'. Then the true is 'that which is the case and is the contradictory of what is not the case'. There are many sets of contradictories. The differentia of the pair true/false is that both cannot be applied simultaneously to 'what is the case' or to 'what is not the case'. And now we must ask 'what is it that makes something the case?' The answer to this is the answer fastened on by Sextus, *to hyparchon*, now in the sense 'the prompter of an apprehensive presentation' or 'that which exists'. This is proved by the criterion for a true proposition: 'the simple definite *axioma* is true (*alēthes hyparchein*) when the predicate, e.g. walking, belongs to the thing falling under the demonstrative' (ὅταν τῷ ὑπὸ τὴν δεῖξιν πίπτοντι συμβεβήκῃ τὸ κατηγόρημα).[77] The passage is reminiscent of Chrysippus' discussion of the 'reality' of present time (see p. 89). The predicate asserted of the subject must correspond both in sense and time to the state of the object described. And it can only so correspond if the object is in that state. In physical terms the object and its state cannot be dissociated. 'Walking' is a disposition of the *hegemonikon*.[78] But in a statement Cato's walking (though not an existent in itself) can be picked out and truly asserted of Cato, if he is walking, because it correctly describes the state of an object.

What exist at any time are material objects in certain states. Men experience presentations accurately reproducing some of these, and the expression of such presentations will state what is the case or true, perhaps even what exists. Equally, some presentations are vacuous or inaccurate images of objects, and these, when expressed in *lekta*, will state what is false. In Stoic terms the whole theory may be summed up thus: a statement or *lekton hyparchei* (is the case) if what it describes *hyparchei* (exists) and what is described is true if the statement describing it is true. Just as the truth or falsity of sensibles appears to depend on the truth or falsity of *lekta*, so the *hyparxis* or non-*hyparxis* of *lekta* depends on the *hyparxis* or non-*hyparxis* of sensibles.[79] This does not mean that true statements are different from false statements ontologically. The *hyparxis* of a *lekton* indicates its truth-value, not its ontological status; whether true or false *lekta* 'co-exist with a rational presentation', and this definition is not confined to veridical *phantasiai*. It seems certain that the Stoics did not distinguish as precisely as we would think desirable between 'existing' and 'being the case'. Their theories of language, 'etymology' in particular, imply a much too crude and literal form of 'correspondence theory'. But the *hyparxis* of sensibles, material objects, is logically prior to that of *lekta*, and no *lekton* can 'be the case' unless what it describes exists. In short, we have further confirmation for the claim that no *lekta* have independent existence.

V   THE *lekton* AND REALITY

It should now be clear that the theory of *lekton* concerns more in Stoicism than technicalities of logic. Poor though our evidence is it gives good reason for thinking that the coherence of Stoicism as a whole finds its basis in the necessary connexion between *logos* and reality. How we interpret this connexion must affect any detailed consideration of Stoic physics and ethics.

The major difficulty is always to know what to take as a starting-point. Hence the very different assessments of Stoicism which have been given. In a recent book to which I am much indebted, Gerard Watson observes that 'there is, of course, no body corresponding to our statements in reality . . . *lekta* are the patterns which the mind tends naturally to impose on reality'.[80] On the other hand the Kneales suggest that 'the true proposition has a structure corresponding to a similar structure in the object described',[81] and I have argued along much the same lines.

If assertions about the incorporeal nature of *lekta* and time are isolated from texts which place *lekta* in relation to thought and material objects it is easy to arrive at Watson's position: 'strictly the relations and divisions between events are superimposed by our minds' (p. 38). Sextus, as he notes, claims that for the Stoics whole and part are in our consciousness, whereas material objects are neither whole nor part.[82] Similarly Proclus says that the Stoics regard the limits of bodies as 'subsisting purely in thought'.[83] Yet it cannot be correct to say that all *lekta* are impositions on reality by us. The Stoics did not hold such a view when they said 'It is day' is true 'if it is day',[84] 'It is day' is a statement which *describes* an empirical situation, not a mental construct.[85] Perhaps the Stoics would not have wanted to claim that 'the apple is a whole' or 'the table is bounded by limits' state things as they are; but there is no reason to think that 'half

the apple is green' or 'the table is square' are anything but
statements which can describe certain material objects as they
are. The passages from Sextus and Proclus imply a thoroughly
common-sense view: wholes, parts and limits are not existents.
Indeed, no predicates exist. But the fact that 'walking' does not
exist in itself does not entail that 'Cato is walking' is an imposi-
tion on reality by us. For unless Cato is walking the statement
is false. Statements themselves do not exist as material objects,
but the bodies which true statements describe instantiate the
causal, shaping power of cosmic *logos* which can express itself in
lekta[86].

The term *hyparchein* connects significant discourse with
material objects. A similar, perhaps even more important,
connexion is made by the term *akolouthia*. The human power
of drawing inferences from empirical data presupposes an *ennoia
akolouthias*, an idea of succession or consequence (see p. 87).
Indeed, *akolouthia* belongs to all three divisions of Stoic philosophy. In logic the fact that B follows from A is expressed as
$\dot{\alpha}\kappa o\lambda o\upsilon\theta\epsilon\hat{\iota}\ \tau\hat{\omega}\ A\ \tau\dot{o}\ B$.[87] The impossibility of a falsehood following
from a truth is expressed in the form $\dot{\alpha}\lambda\eta\theta\epsilon\hat{\iota}\ \psi\epsilon\hat{\upsilon}\delta o\varsigma\ o\dot{\upsilon}\kappa$
$\dot{\alpha}\kappa o\lambda o\upsilon\theta\epsilon\hat{\iota}$.[88] And *endiathetos logos*, internal speech (reason), is
described as 'that by which we recognise consequences and
contradictions' ($\tau\dot{\alpha}\ \dot{\alpha}\kappa\dot{o}\lambda o\upsilon\theta\alpha\ \kappa\alpha\dot{\iota}\ \tau\dot{\alpha}\ \mu\alpha\chi\dot{o}\mu\epsilon\nu\alpha$). But *akolouthia*
is not confined to what we would call 'logical consequence'.
The sequence of cause and effect is explained by reference to it,
for fated events occur $\kappa\alpha\tau\dot{\alpha}\ \tau\dot{\alpha}\xi\iota\nu\ \kappa\alpha\dot{\iota}\ \dot{\alpha}\kappa o\lambda o\upsilon\theta\dot{\iota}\alpha\nu$ or $\kappa\alpha\tau\dot{\alpha}\ \tau\dot{\eta}\nu$
$\tau\hat{\omega}\nu\ \alpha\dot{\iota}\tau\dot{\iota}\omega\nu\ \dot{\alpha}\kappa o\lambda o\upsilon\theta\dot{\iota}\alpha\nu$.[89] This use of a common term is exactly
what we should expect in view of Chrysippus' methods of
inference from actual states of affairs.

Given that the world operates according to a strict causal
nexus one of the roles of logic, perhaps its major role in Stoicism,
is to make possible predictions about the future by drawing out
consequences from the present. The cardinal assumption of the
Stoics is that man can put himself in touch with the rational
course of events and effect a correspondence between them and
his own actions and intentions. This assumption provides the
ethical aim of living *homologoumenōs*.[90] More particularly, ethics
is connected with logic and physics by *akolouthia* and its related
words. Man, we read, has an obligation to live $\dot{\alpha}\kappa o\lambda o\dot{\upsilon}\theta\omega\varsigma\ \tau\hat{\eta}$

φύσει; the good man is ἀκολουθητικὸς τῷ νόμῳ (=ὀρθῷ λόγῳ) and ἄρχοντι.[91] The words have no narrow political sense, nor should *akolouthia* etc. be translated by any expression which implies a sense different from that indicated for physics and logic. The good man's life is a consequence of or follows from nature and law. No wonder the Stoics accorded such ethical importance to physics and logic for the good man has to follow the natural sequence of cause and effect. He does this by virtuously performing *to kathēkon*, defined as an act ἀκόλουθον ἐν ζωῇ.[92] All the actions of the good man are ἀκολούθως τῇ ἑαυτοῦ φύσει, that is, they are completely consistent with his nature:[93] *kathekonta follow from* a creature's nature, hence the fact that self-preservation is the primary appropriate act and man's specific *kathekon* is 'living according to *logos*'.

Living rationally involves for the Stoic both understanding nature and acting in accordance with nature. Experience of events demonstrates their inter-connexion and man is able to grasp this connexion and express it to himself by means of *logos*. *Lekta*, the statements which he makes, bridge the gap between himself and the external world. They also provide the content of the imperatives which he issues to himself and obeys on the basis of his experience of nature.[94] Were there no possibility of expressing external reality, as it really is, 'live according to nature' would be a vacuous and impossible command. But the Stoics do not claim, with Kant, that the order in nature is imposed by us. There is no necessary incompatibility between reality and the content of sentences or thoughts. On the contrary, in a true statement the two must correspond precisely. To be sure *lekta* are incorporeal, but this entails that they have no independent existence, not that they are unreal *tout court*. The existing thing, my black cat, and the statement, 'my cat is black' are different ontologically, but they share the common category of being 'something'. The distinction between corporeal and incorporeal is no paradox, as some have alleged, but self-consistent and fundamental to Stoic metaphysics. Without it no exposition of the world would be possible.

Nothing illustrates the Stoics' passion for coherence better than the connexion they maintained between truth and the sage. But before discussing this it will be as well to dispose of a problem about *lekta* which was postponed. We have seen that every species of *lekton* requires the utterance of some expressible object present to the mind. Does this entail that *lekta* only persist as long as the sentences which express them? Most modern scholars have taken this view, and Sextus also adopts it for polemical purposes.[95] But the Kneales come to a different conclusion. In a discussion of the ways in which Stoic *axiomata* differ from and resemble modern propositions they write:[96] 'they exist in some sense whether we think of them or not . . . According to the theory of natural signs considered above,[97] an *axioma* which is a sign reveals another *axioma* which is its significate. The latter must therefore exist in order to be revealed.' This claim of the Kneales is not borne out by the evidence. The doctrine of signs or signals is a doctrine about connexions in nature, and such connexions hold or do not hold quite independently of thought. But what validates the inference from smoke to fire is not the independent existence of a *lekton*, 'there is fire', but the empirical fact that smoke is not observed to exist independently of fire: smoke can serve to 'remind' us of fire. Chrysippus seems to have equated logical and empirical compatibility and this points to the dependence of true or false statements on facts. *Lekta* are defined in terms of language and presentations and this points to their temporal dependence on the duration of thoughts and sentences. *Lekta* do not denote a world of propositions but the content of thought and significant discourse. Nor does the distinction between truth and the true imply anything to the contrary, as we shall see.

There is one further point raised by the Kneales which is of interest.[98] It appears that the Stoics talked of the 'death' of certain *axiomata*.[99] Thus 'this man is dead', where 'this' refers to Dion, is 'destroyed' after Dion's death, seemingly because the state of affairs referred to by 'this' has ceased to exist. The same statement is also impossible as a reference to Dion when he is alive, because contradictory. This is a difficult discussion related to a specific problem, an argument by Chrysippus against Diodorus to show that the impossible can follow from the possible. From 'Dion is dead' 'this man is dead' follows, yet 'this man is dead' is impossible because 'this' cannot refer. To call such a paradox the 'destruction' of a proposition entails nothing about the independent existence of *axiomata* in general. 'This man is dead' is destroyed even at the moment of utterance because its subject has perished. Such an example confirms the dependence of *lekta* on objects of reference; it does not show that if *lekta* are expressible they therefore exist. For any definite statement there must be a demonstrable subject.[100] Otherwise no truth or falsity is possible. But there is no evidence to show that *lekta*, as distinct from the speaker and his reference, persist outside acts of thought and communication.

VI.   TRUTH AND THE TRUE

I have already alluded to the fact that the Stoics drew a distinction between the noun *alētheia* (truth) and the hypostatized adjective *to alēthes* (the true). The final part of this chapter offers an attempt to elucidate the meaning of this distinction and to relate it to the previous discussion concerning language and thought.[101]

The evidence is contained in two passages of Sextus Empiricus the more detailed of which runs as follows:[102]

It is held by some, particularly the Stoics, that truth differs from the true in three ways: (1) in substance (*ousiāi*) since truth is corporeal but the true is incorporeal ... (2) in composition (*systasei*) since the true is regarded as uniform and simple in its nature ... whereas truth, as comprising knowledge, is on the contrary assumed to be something compound and a collection of many things ... (3) in meaning (*dynamei*), since the true does not belong to knowledge in all respects, but truth is thought to subsume knowledge.

The passages omitted from this translation extend the discussion of each differentia, and will be considered shortly. But at the outset it will be useful to remember that *aletheia* is ambiguous between 'reality', the object of knowledge, and 'truth', the quality contained in knowledge of facts or accurate statements about reality.[103] In Sextus' discussion the second sense of *aletheia* is paramount; but a reconciliation with the first is both possible and required by other evidence. Of which more below.

The distinction between truth and the true *qua* substance (*ousia*) turns on the fact that the true is a 'statement' (*axioma*), that is a *lekton*, and *lekta* are *asomata*. (Sextus himself gives similar definitions of 'the true' and 'the true proposition'.)[104] Truth, on the other hand, 'seems to be knowledge assertive of all that is true, and all knowledge is a particular disposition of the *hegemonikon* (a body), just as the fist is a particular disposition of the hand'. Distinguishing truth and the true in terms of 'substance' means finding a place for truth in the category of existents and rejecting the true from this, for in Stoic theory all *ousia* is corporeal.[105] The relation between truth and knowledge gets further clarification in Sextus' second point.

The 'structural' distinction between truth and the true is illustrated by the difference between a single citizen and the body politic. Whereas the true corresponds to the former, truth resembles the body politic in being 'a collection (*athroisma*) of many elements'. Truth is compound by nature, unlike the true. The same term occurs in a definition of the human *logos*: this is 'an *athroisma* of certain general notions (*ennoiai*) and conceptions (*prolēpseis*)'.[106] Knowledge itself is a disposition of the *logos*, and further commentary on its relation to truth is given in passages which make use of the term *systēma*, a synonym for *athroisma*.[107] Among four definitions of 'knowledge' (*epistēmē*) offered by Stobaeus two include this word:[108] *episteme* is a '*systema* of specific items like the rational apprehension of particulars present in the good man';[109] and, *episteme* 'is a *systema* consisting of skills pertaining to conduct, possessing its own stability, such as the virtues have'.

Like the previous two distinctions the third difference between truth and the true throws light on the Stoic concept of *episteme*. Truth and the true differ in meaning (*dynamis*) because a true statement may be made by someone who lacks knowledge. The types of speaker mentioned by Sextus are the bad man, the lunatic and the young child. Since only the sage possesses knowledge truth too is confined among men to him. Truth, it appears, is not judged merely by the correspondence of statements with facts. On the contrary, the sage can state what is false without forfeiting his claim to possession of truth. This assertion seems reasonable enough since the logic of lying entails misstatement by the speaker of what he knows (or believes) to be the case. But the queer thing about false state-

ments by the Stoic sage is that they are not (even) white lies.[110]
'If the sage speaks what is false', says Sextus, 'he does not lie
since he speaks from a cultivated disposition'; he does not
assent internally to the falsehood. This is compared with a
doctor saying something false for the good of his patient, a
general concocting a false message to encourage his men, and
a grammarian uttering a solecisim to exemplify linguistic
usage.

The point is elaborated elsewhere. Lying, according to
Stobaeus, is not just false statement, but that made with the
intention of cheating and deceiving the auditor.[111] Plutarch too
quotes Chrysippus as saying that 'God and the sage implant
false presentations, not demanding our assent or compliance
but merely that we should act and be prompted towards the
appearance'.[112] It appears then that if the good man can achieve
his purpose (only) by stating what he knows to be false he may
do so, since the purpose of his utterances is not to deceive but,
say, to encourage his troops.

The difficulty of this distinction is not so much its ethical
assumptions but the implications it seems to have for Sextus'
discussion of truth and the true. If truth consists of a body of
true propositions and these comprise the sage's knowledge how
can the sage stand as the human guarantor of what is true when
stating what is false?

An attempt to answer this question shows again how difficult
it is in Stoicism to separate logic too sharply from physics and
ethics. A distinction, similar to that between false statement and
lying, is recorded by Stobaeus concerning oaths:[113]

Chrysippus said that swearing truly differs from swearing well; and
perjury differs from swearing falsely. For with respect to the time at
which a man takes an oath he swears wholly truly or falsely. For
what is sworn by him is either true or false, since it is a proposition.
But there is no absolute distinction according to the time an oath is
taken between swearing well and perjury since the time is not present with reference to which the oaths were made. Just as someone is
said to keep or break faith not when he makes a contract but when
the time specified for the agreement is present; so too a man will be
said to swear well or ill when the time has arrived at which he has
agreed to perform what he swore.

Pseudes or *alethes* are words which fix the truth or falsity of state-ments made at a particular time. If the sage says 'reinforce-ments will arrive in an hour' when he knows that the enemy have recaptured the garrison he states what is false; and if he made this statement on oath he would swear falsely. But if, with the help of this statement, he swears that he will lead his troops to victory and succeeds he will prove to have sworn well. Similarly perhaps, possession of truth entails both knowing what is the case *and* the appropriate moral action, knowing that *p* (which is right) will follow if *q*. In order to secure *q*, the necessary condition, the sage may utter a falsehood which is justified by his intention to obtain *p*. The sage of course is neither omni-potent nor omniscient. But the quality of his knowledge is such that it can be equated with truth, and this must mean that he mirrors in his disposition and actions the cosmic law of cause and effect.[114] Since moral action is necessarily based upon the understanding of natural events the sage's possession of truth will enable him to draw out consequences from the present and act accordingly. Seen in this light a false statement, 'reinforce-ments are coming', may prove to have a consequence which meets future facts, 'the troops fight better', and thus find an honourable place in the sequence of cause and effect.

The notion of the good man as one whose knowledge and relation to reality is conspicuously different from others' goes back at least to Plato. But what precisely does it mean in Stoicism? A rehearsal of the sage's characteristics will reveal that he never assents to what is false, never opines, never forgets and is ignorant of nothing (meaning 'never makes weak or changeable assents').[115] But these characteristics, though strongly suggesting that the sage is in some way the criterion of truth or reality, fail to show what his knowledge consists in. Accounts of Stoic epistemology tend, quite correctly, to con-centrate on explaining the term *katalepsis*. But it is significant that Sextus, when relating truth to knowledge, describes the latter not as *katalepsis* but as an *athroisma* ('collection') of true propositions.[116] And we have seen that Stobaeus also offers two definitions of *episteme* which employ the similar word, *systema*. The conclusion to this must, I think, be that the collection or system of truths possessed by the good man is the source of his *katalepsis asphalēs*: his *logos*, consisting of a comprehensive set of true judgements, guarantees and secures his grasp of presentations.

All men exercise *katalepsis*, and as Sandbach points out, this involves interpretation or judgement.[117] But the good man's *logos* is stable while that of other men is characterised by *ptoia*, vacillation.[118] The good man never misinterprets what is presented to his senses. But how is his perception converted into knowing? Can we draw this distinction?

Some of the evidence suggests that knowing is nothing more than absolutely clear perception. But Cicero states that *comprehensio* in itself does not grasp all that is involved in its particular object, and that one of its functions is to provide the evidence from which *ennoiai* (concepts) are derived.[119] This ties in with Chrysippus' description of the *logos* as an ἐννοιῶν τέ τινων καὶ προλήψεων ἄθροισμα (see p. 99).[120] It is difficult to avoid the conclusion that what stabilises the sage's *katalepsis* is the possession of memory images and valid concepts against which he can test each *phantasia* as it presents itself in order to establish how it relates and whether or not it is true. If this is correct it helps to explain why some sources cite *orthos logos* (right reason) as the criterion. The sage possesses a disposition which may be termed, indifferently, *orthos logos*, *episteme* or *aletheia*. We may conjecture that his grasp of truth enables him to fit any new presentation into the ordered structure of his own mind, and this ability to place it constitutes not only perceiving but knowing—knowing, that is, how it *akolouthei* (follows) and what follows from it.[121] Compared with this ability, stating what is true appears as a purely contingent matter of matching the right words to the object of reference. It does not necessarily involve the 'why' (τὸ διότι) any more than perceiving correctly entails seeing why something is the case. But accurate perception and correct statement may be presumed as the material which the capacity of the mind for inference (*akolouthia*) uses, in order to establish connexions in nature and arrive by analogy at the *notio boni*.[122]

In this chapter we have seen something of the coherence which the Stoics tried to give to their system as a whole. It was a quality on which they prided themselves, as we learn from

Cato's peroration in *De finibus* iii 74: 'What can be found in the world . . . or among works of craftsmanship which is so well-arranged, so unified, so tightly connected? . . . What consequence does not agree with its antecedent? . . . What feature is not so attached to something else that if you removed a single letter, the whole would collapse? Yet there is nothing which could be removed'. It is easy to smile at this grand claim. But the Stoics, with their belief in a unified world which develops by rational principles, had to aim at a theory which was as coherent as the structure it represented.

'Universal nature', according to Chrysippus, is the only proper starting-point for moral philosophy, and the sole reason for studying physics is to establish the difference between right and wrong (Plut. *Stoic. rep.* 1035c–d). It follows that no clear distinction can be drawn in Stoicism between physics and ethics, between factual and moral statements. The virtues are physical states of the *hegemonikon*, and statements about them are objective: they refer to actual or possible states of affairs, the mind of God or the mind of a sage. The command to a bad man, 'become good' is a command to effect a physical alteration of his disposition, to become healthy instead of sick, stable instead of vacillating. In the pre-Roman Stoa deontological statements are very rare; and the reason is not hard to seek. What matters to the Stoic is not duty as such but ontology. If he is fully in touch with reality and of sound reason, then he acts rightly, that is, according to nature. A *kathekon* is not something performed *strictly from duty* (Kant's requirement of a moral action) but, what Kant deplored, an act chosen by reason on empirical principles and grounded in human nature and physical laws. The Stoics took man's life to be causally connected at any moment with cosmic events, and the sage is one who sees what policies and actions follow from this conjuncture.[123] Logic is thus a central feature of the system, providing, as it does, an analytical framework in which to place the relations between events and the propositions which express them. Without logic the Stoic could have no guarantee that his aims to live in accordance with the facts of nature are based upon valid inference. We do certainly find prescriptive language in Stoicism, particularly in references to law, and the status of such expressions requires further investigation. But though there is an important formal resemblance between the categorical imperative and *orthos logos*, the Stoic sage has acquired or derived 'right reason' from finding manifestations of it in the world at large. We may perhaps talk of his acting out of 'moral obligation' or of his performing 'duties'; but if so we refer not to an a priori concept of right action, but to the internal or external results which follow when a man has grasped that self-fulfilment (*eudaimonia*) can only be attained by a disposition which consistently matches human nature or reason to their cosmic counterparts.

In Stoicism *physis* and *logos* are the key concepts of moral discourse, and for man they are interchangeable. Nature of course is not a univocal term: what is natural for pigs qua pigs is not natural for men. But the ordered sequence of cause and effect in the external world is paralleled internally by the human 'concept of consequence'.[124] Things go wrong when men become alienated from reality and make false assumptions about it or draw invalid inferences. For thought and action are causally linked. Assent entails impulse, and what we assent to depends on our beliefs and grasps of situations.[125] The implications of this are seen in the Stoic account of moral corruption; misjudgements of value are faulty assessments of facts, and men so disposed fall into moral errors.[126] These can only be avoided by the use of *logos* for its proper purpose. 'Only the sage is a true logician' (μόνος ὁ σοφὸς διαλεκτικός).[127]

POSTSCRIPT

In discussing 'deficient *lekta*' (p. 78) I noted that these are not said to include the semantic content of isolated nouns such as 'Dion'. But some recent works state the view that the *ptosis* or grammatical subject which such nouns supply is a species of 'deficient *lekton*' (Mates, *Stoic Logic* pp. 16–17; Kneale, *Development of Logic* p. 144 (cf. 149); Watson, *Stoic Theory of Knowledge* pp. 47–9). To this view several qualifications must be made.

The only examples of ἐλλιπὲς λεκτόν cited as such are 'predicates', cf. Diog. Laert. VII 63, ἐν μὲν οὖν τοῖς ἐλλιπέσι λεκτοῖς τέτακται τὰ κατηγορήματα. None of the texts selected by von Arnim, *SVF* II 181–5, or others that I have consulted, gives 'Dion' or 'Socrates' or any other noun as words which exemplify deficient *lekta*. An ἐλλιπὲς λεκτόν is said to be a predicate which requires the nominative or certain other cases (*ptoseis*) of some noun(s) in order to make a complete statement, e.g. (Πλάτων) φιλεῖ; (Πλάτων Δίωνα) φιλεῖ; μέλει (Σωκράτει), Porphyry ap. Ammon. *In De int.* (*SVF* II 184). Furthermore, nouns whether proper names (ὄνομα) or common nouns (προσηγορία) are not defined as 'signifying *lekta* (or *ptoseis*)' but they signify 'individual or common properties' (Diog. Laert. VII 58). The properties of material objects are themselves material in Stoic theory, and thus belong to a different ontological status from *lekta*. A verb (ῥῆμα) on the other hand 'signifies an uncompounded predicate' (Diog. Laert. ibid.), which is a *lekton* and incorporeal.[128]

Are we then to conclude that the Stoics regarded the meaning of nouns, or certain types of noun, as something categorically different from that of verbs? This may be the wrong question. The evidence suggests rather that they thought of nouns and verbs as fulfilling semantic roles corresponding to their grammatical functions. Nouns, in virtue of their cases (*ptoseis*), enable *reference* to be made to things. Verbs signify predicates or *lekta* which must be combined with a *ptosis* or reference if a *lekton* or *axioma* is to be 'complete'. This point confirms the correctness of Benson Mates' application to the Stoics of a distinction between sense and reference (or denotation). But in Stoicism it is basic to this distinction that *ptoseis* are not 'deficient *lekta*' but the means of referring these to a subject or actual thing.

The position I have outlined has only one piece of evidence known to me against it. Sextus' example of *lekton* at *Adv. math.* VIII 12 is the single *semainomenon*, Dion. Since however Sextus seems to regard this as exemplifying something true or false it is possible that we should take Dion to be equivalent to some proposition, see n. 11 p. 107. On the other hand, at *Adv. math.* XI 29 Sextus refers to the fact that the same word may have several 'meanings', e.g. dog. 'By this word', he writes, 'is signified a *ptosis* under which fall the barking animal, and also the sea-animal, and the [*Cynic*] philosopher, and also the [dog-] star. But these *ptoseis* have nothing in common'. This statement by

H

Sextus is probably based on Stoic doctrine, though he uses it to illustrate Academic theories about the meanings of 'good' in contrast to Stoic theories. He appears to be saying that the word 'dog' signifies a grammatical function which classifies a plurality of different items. We have no specific information about the status of *ptoseis*. But it should follow from the fact that they are a necessary part of an *axioma* that its incorporeal nature also applies to them. Moreover, in the analysis of an *axioma*, the relation of a noun to its *ptosis* seems to be regarded as parallel to that of a verb to what it predicates (Plutarch *Quaest. Plat.* x 1009c).

We are on very uncertain ground here. But on the whole the evidence suggests that the meaning of an isolated noun like 'Dion' or 'man' is not a *lekton* but the thing ('property') to which it refers. The meaning of an isolated verb, 'writes', is not a reference to any thing (i.e. external object) but a *lekton*, an assertion parasitic on our thought. And in the complete sentence, 'Dion writes', what is signified is 'the attachment of an assertion to a nominative case' (λεκτὸν ἐλλιπὲς συντακτὸν ὀρθῇ πτώσει πρὸς ἀξιώματος γένεσιν Diog. Laert. VII 64). We can only make sense of this, I think, by taking 'nominative case' to denote the 'means of referring to' Dion. Whether that involves a fundamental confusion between grammar and semantics is a problem which cannot be examined here.

NOTES

1. An interesting and rather different attempt to discuss the 'metaphysics' of Stoicism is Christensen's *An Essay on the unity of Stoic philosophy*.

2. P. F. Strawson, *Individuals* (London 1959) pp. 15, 38. ὄντα ... μόνα τὰ σώματα καλοῦσιν, Plutarch *Comm. not.* 1073E (*SVF* II 525); τοῦ σώματος τούτον ὅρον εἶναί φασιν τὸ τριχῇ διαστατὸν μετὰ ἀντιτυπίας, Galen XIX p. 483K (*SVF* II 381). The Stoics married this view of particulars, not always happily, with pantheism and a monistic conception of οὐσία, see p. 111 n. 86.

3. Plutarch, loc. cit. Clement *Strom.* II p. 436 (*SVF* II 359).

4. See J. M. Rist, Chapter III, pp. 52–5.

5. Simplicus *In De an.* (*CAG* XI) p. 217, 36 (*SVF* II 395), ἰδίως ... ποιόν, ὃ καὶ ἀθρόως ἐπιγίνεται καὶ αὖ ἀπογίνεται καὶ τὸ αὐτὸ ἐν παντὶ τῷ τοῦ συνθέτου βίῳ διαμένει, καίτοι τῶν μορίων ἄλλων ἄλλοτε γινομένων τε καὶ φθειρομένων. Similarly Posidonius ap.

Arium Didymum (Diels *Dox. graec.* 462, 13ff.). See also Plotinus *Enn.* ΙΙ 4, 1 (*SVF* ΙΙ 320).

6. No single text supports this claim explicitly, but it is a reasonable inference from Simplicius (loc. cit.) taken with such passages as Plotinus *Enn.* VI 1, 27 (*SVF* ΙΙ 314) where Stoic 'substrate' (unshaped matter) is taken to be 'that which can become all things when shaped' (σχηματιζόμενον); Sextus *Adv. math.* ΙΧ 75 (*SVF* ΙΙ 311), who notes that 'the substance of existents, so the Stoics say, needs to be moved and *shaped* by some causal principle'; Alex. Aphr. *Mixt.* p. 224, 32 (*SVF* ΙΙ 310) who cites the Stoics as saying that 'God pervades, shapes and forms passive matter'. Void too is that which lacks σχῆμα but can receive σῶμα, Cleomedes *Circul. doctr.* ι, ι (*SVF* ΙΙ 541).

7. Shape itself is explained in terms of 'tension', Simplicius *In cat.* (*CAG* VIII) p. 264 (*SVF* ΙΙ 456); Cleomedes op. cit. ι 8 (*SVF* ΙΙ 455). On the physical aspects of the theory see Sambursky, *Physics of the Stoics*, pp. 7–11; 21–33.

8. See F. H. Sandbach, Chapter I, pp. 13ff.

9. That 'object of reference' is a correct translation of τὸ τυγχάνον is shown by the context. 'Existing thing' is generally adopted, but this would also cover φωνή. τὸ τυγχάνον is a vague word and may mean 'whatever we happen to be talking about'. Ps.–Ammonius' claim *In An. pr.* (*CAG* ΙV 6) p. 68 lines 4ff., that 'the Stoics call πράγματα τυγχάνοντα' means that the Stoics use the term τυγχάνοντα to denote visible, tangible objects for which the Peripatetic term is πράγματα.

10. As Mates observes, *Stoic Logic*, p. 11 n. 3, 'thing' is a misleading translation of πρᾶγμα, but 'entity' which he adopts has equally misleading associations. This applies to 'fact' as well. 'State of affairs' is a familiar sense for πρᾶγμα in general and least liable to misconception here. See J. M. Rist, Chapter III, p. 58 n. 11.

11. My argument, over the next few pages, has benefited greatly from the kind and critical scrutiny of Professor J. L. Ackrill, though I am solely responsible for the views expressed. Ackrill reminds me that in Plato's *Cratylus* naming someone (correctly or wrongly) tends to be assimilated to saying 'this is his name', cf. 385, 431. Something similar is needed here to square Sextus' example, Dion, with the Stoic view that, of assertions, only those which express *axiomata* are true or false, see p. 111 n. 79. For the relation between *lekta* and grammar see A. C. Lloyd, Chapter IV. The fact that I omit discussion of grammar here should not be taken to imply disagreement with his approach or conclusions.

12. Bréhier, *La théorie des incorporels*,[2] p. 15, refers here to the semitic origins of the early Stoics.

13. Diogenes' phrase above. In this I follow Zeller, *Phil. d. Gr.*[4] ΙΙΙ 1, p. 86, who translates *lekton* by 'das Ausgesprochene'. Mates and Kneale adopt 'what is meant'. In sense *lekton* can hardly be distinguished from τὸ λεγόμενον, an expression very common in the Aristotelian commentators (see n. 23). It is not the sense of the word *lekton* which makes Stoic theory distinctive, but the status they accord to 'what is said'; cf. the division of διαλεκτική into 'verba et significationes, id est in res quae dicuntur et vocabula quibus dicuntur' (Seneca *Ep. mor.* 89, 17). On the 'unstable' nature of this division and the 'natural' connexion between utterances and what they signify see A. C. Lloyd, Chapter IV, pp. 60ff.

14. *Axiomata* are defined as 'that which is either true or false' Diog. Laert. VII 65, cf. Sextus *Adv. math.* VIII 79. Diogenes (ad. loc.) gives 'Dion is walking' as an example. See Mates, pp. 27–33; W. and M. Kneale, *The Development of Logic*, pp. 144–9; Watson, *The Stoic Theory of Knowledge*, pp. 47f.

15. Sextus, *Pyrrh. hyp.* ΙΙ 104; Diog. Laert. loc. cit.

16. Diog. Laert. VII 64. See Mates, p. 17.

17. The evidence discussed suggests that 'things' means only 'particular material

objects'. But the theory of *lekton* ought to cover higher order statements, whether talk about *lekta* and other incorporeals or talk about concepts such as non-existent universals, see n. 59. The problems of reference which such discourse creates for the Stoic theory of meaning were perhaps softened by their category of τί covering incorporeals as well as material objects, see p. 88 and n. 79.

18. See J. L. Ackrill, *Aristotle's Categories and De Interpretatione* (Oxford 1963) pp. 113–15.

19. *Stoic Logic*, pp. 19–26. I. Düring, *Aristoteles* (Heidelberg 1966) p. 69 n. 97, compares Aristotle's distinction between ἔξω λόγος and ὁ ἐν τῇ ψυχῇ (*An. post.* A 76b 24) with Frege's *Sinn-Bedeutung*. But Aristotle is mainly concerned (loc. cit.) to associate ἀπόδειξις with internal discourse, not external (dialectic). For a different treatment of Aristotelian semantics and *lekta* see A. C. Lloyd, Chapter IV, pp. 64ff.

20. *In Cat.* (*CAG* VIII) p. 10, 3f.

21. Ibid. p. 397, 8ff. Mates p. 12 cites onlythe first passage.

22. *In De int.* (*CAG* IV 5) p. 17, 20ff. I am able to understand the relevance of Galen *Inst. log.* III 2 cited by Mates loc. cit. as incompatible with both Ammonius and the first quotation from Simplicius. Of some relevance is a later passage, *Inst. log.* IV 5–6 in which Galen criticises the Stoics for concentrating on λέξις rather than πράγματα (objects of reference). The point at issue is the need for a σκοπός in all discourse so that the auditor may clearly understand what is being talked about.

23. Some observations by Dexippus *In Cat.* (*CAG* IV 2) pp. 6–9 are worth mentioning here. Dexippus asks τί ἐστι τὸ λεγόμενον? Is it φωνή, πρᾶγμα or νόημα? His own answer is in line with Ammonius: 'properly νοήματα are signified but accidentally πράγματα'. πράγματα here means external objects of reference. Dexippus proceeds to refute the view that such objects are 'what is said', since this rules out the possibility of referring to (λέγειν with direct object) non-existents such as hippocentaurs. Being true or false is an accident of λόγος; the *essence* of λόγος is τὸ σημαίνειν τόδε τι προηγουμένως. Throughout σημαίνειν seems to have the sense 'refer to'. No mention is made of the *lekton*; indeed the question τί ἐστι τὸ λεγόμενον strictly rules out the Stoic answer: to them 'what is said' is 'what is said'. Dexippus goes on to say that true and false are ἐν διανοίᾳ καὶ ἐν τοῖς διεξόδοις τοῦ νοῦ, for which he appeals to the *De anima*. This suggests that Sextus may have the Peripatetics in mind when he mentions (see p. 76) those who locate true and false in the movement of thought.

24. *Adv. math.* VIII 70; Diog. Laert. VII 63.

25. The term ὑφιστάμενον is generally translated 'subsists', but without explanation this is misleading. The sense is clearly similar to that of Sextus' παρυφισταμένου (*Adv. math.* VIII 12) which I translated 'coexists with'. For a detailed discussion of the terms, which have a necessary bearing on the ontological status of *lekta*, see p. 89. I have followed Mates and the Kneales in translating λογική by 'rational' and λόγῳ by 'speech'. Originally I preferred 'expressible' or 'expressed' for λογική, and I hope to show that the term covers these senses too. But in the present context the definition of λογικὴ φαντασία becomes a tautology with the translation 'expressible'. Aristotle uses φαντασία λογιστική, *De an.* III 433b 29.

26. *Th.* 190a (206d); *Soph.* 263e.

27. Aetius (Diels, *Dox. graec.* p. 401, 14) reading αὐτό τε for ἐν αὐτῷ with ps-Galen XIX p. 305K.

28. Diog. Laert. VII 51 (*SVF* II 61). See further F. H. Sandbach, Chapter I, pp. 11f.

29. Cicero *Ac. post.* I 41–2 (*SVF* I 60); Stob. II 349, 23 (*SVF* II 74); Sextus *Adv. math.* VIII 56 (*SVF* II 88).

30. Cf. Watson, *The Stoic Theory of Knowledge*, pp. 35f. Chrysippus calls *logos* an ἐννοιῶν τέ τινων καὶ προλήψεων ἄθροισμα, *De placitis* v p. 421M (*SVF* II 841), see further p. 102.

31. Diog. Laert. VII 51. For a late Stoic catalogue of types of *phantasia* see Sextus *Adv. math.* VII 241–52.

32. So Sextus *Adv. math.* VIII 70. λόγος should be translated here by 'speech' not 'reason' (Bury, Loeb library ad loc.). In λόγος both φωνή and λεκτόν are involved, hence the definition 'significant sound dispatched by thought' (Diog. Laert. VII 56).

33. I do not think Mates is right to equate *lekton* and τὸ φαντασθέν, *Stoic Logic*, p. 22. 'The presented object' is what a *phantasia* reveals, a 'thing' not a *lekton*. If I see Cato walking I am presented with an object which can be denoted in a complete *lekton*.

34. It is impossible to distinguish clearly, if at all, between 'things' and *phantasiai* of things. But this does not mean in Stoicism an identification of thought with its object. *Phantasiai* as such are not thoughts, but the mind's awareness of things which it can express.

35. See Mates, p. 22.

36. *Adv. math.* VIII 75–8.

37. Ibid. 257–64.

38. *Stoic Logic*, pp. 13–15.

39. Diog. Laert. VII 55, 58.

40. φωνή embraces written words as well as utterances, cf. Diog. Laert. VII 56; Aristotle *De int.* 16a 3–6.

41. Sextus *Adv. math.* VIII 245. This usage of σημεῖον is a modification of Aristotle's definition, *An. pr.* II 27, 70a 7. For a general discussion see P. H. and E. A. De Lacy, *Philodemus: on Methods of Inference*, pp. 159ff.

42. *The Development of Logic*, pp. 141f.

43. *Adv. math.* VIII 276. See further p. 87.

44. Ibid. 151–3.

45. See J. B. Gould, 'Chrysippus: on the criteria for the truth of a conditional proposition', *Phronesis* xii (1967) 156–61.

46. Sextus *Adv. math.* VIII 154–5.

47. *Stoic Logic*, p. 14.

48. Sextus ibid. 264.

49. Hence we may dispense with the other 'possible explanations' offered by Mates, p. 13 n. 16. He overlooks Sextus' critical intentions.

50. *The Development of Logic*, p. 142.

51. *Adv. math.* VIII 262–74.

52. Ibid. 275ff.

53. Galen defines λόγος ἐνδιάθετος as 'that by which we recognise consequences and contradictions', XVIII p. 649K (*SVF* II 135).

54. Bury's translation (Loeb library ad loc.) is meaningless: 'the transitive and constructive impression' and his explanatory note is little better. The phrase is glossed by Diog. Laert. VII 52–3: rational presentations are thoughts (see p. 83) and among them are those produced κατὰ μετάβασιν, and κατὰ σύνθεσιν. The idea of space and *lekta* are Diogenes' examples of the former, and he illustrates the latter by the example of Centaur. In Sextus' context μεταβατικός must mean 'inferential' for which cf. *Adv. math.* III 25 εἰ καὶ τὸ νοητὸν μεταβατικὸν ἀπὸ τοῦ αἰσθητοῦ νοοῦμεν, and ibid. VIII 194 τῇ ἀπὸ τοῦ πυρὸς μεταβάσει.

55. Diog. Laert. VII 110 and *SVF* II 823–33. According to Iamblichus ap. Stob. *Ecl.* I p. 367 (*SVF* II 826) the soul's δυνάμεις are ἐν τῷ ὑποκειμένῳ ποιότητες. For their corporeal nature see Alex. Aphr. *De an.* p. 115, 37ff (*SVF* II 797).

56. Plutarch *Comm. not.* 1084c, e.g. walking is the walking animal. Origen's assertion II p. 368K (*SVF* II 318) that ἐνέργειαι are 'qualities' means that activity is a differentiation of unshaped οὐσία.

57. See Bréhier, *Théorie des incorporels*, p. 19. But there seems to be no evidence for his claim that the Stoics want to say 'a body hots' not 'a body is hot', p. 20.

58. Stobaeus *Ecl.* II p. 98 (*SVF* III 91 ad fin.); cf. Simplicius *In cat.* (*CAG* VIII p. 388 =*SVF* II 173). For the corporeality of virtue(s) see Plutarch *Comm. not.* 1084A (*SVF* II 848), Seneca *Ep. mor.* 106, 7.

59. ἔννοιαι are imprinted on the mind, Aetius *Plac.* IV 11 (*SVF* II 83); they are a species of *phantasia* (*SVF* II 847) and *noeseis*. Bréhier, op. cit. p. 18, fails to distinguish νόησις and ἔννοια from ἐννόημα. ἐννόημα is not a φαντασία but a φάντασμα, a mental picture produced from nothing real, cf. Aetius *Plac.* IV 12 (*SVF* II 54). The Stoics seem to have confined ἐννοήματα to 'general ideas' whose content is unreal since there is no body corresponding to the ideas of men, dogs etc. The description of them as neither corporeal nor incorporeal (Alex. Aphr. *In Top.*, *CAG* II 2 p. 301, *SVF* II 329) may be due to their being conceived as vacuous in content but corporeal in respect of their power to affect the mind.

60. See pp. 77, 82.

61. Sextus *Adv. math.* VIII 32–4; *Hyp. pyrrh.* II 86–7, and the texts cited at *SVF* II p. 117. See also J. M. Rist, Chapter III, p. 39.

62. Such a use of εἶναί τι is perfectly possible, sv *LSJ* τις 5. No change of accent would be necessary, cf. τι ὄν Diog. Laert. VII 61.

63. It is quite in Sextus' manner to show awareness of a Stoic distinction such as that between σημεῖον and σημαῖνον in one place and ignore it in another. For his awareness of τό τι cf. the passages cited in n. 61.

64. Sextus himself asserts that the Stoics made 'time' both ἀσώματον and a καθ' αὐτό τι νοούμενον πρᾶγμα *Adv. math.* X 218.

65. The ambiguity of ὑπάρχειν in the first two senses noted here is mentioned by W. and M. Kneale, p. 151.

66. Stobaeus *Ecl.* I p. 106 (*SVF* II 509).

67. Plutarch *Comm. not.* 1081F (*SVF* II 518).

68. X p. 155K (*SVF* II 322). This might not be the same distinction since Galen cites τὸ ὄν not τὸ ὑπάρχον! But I think we may assume that in each case ὑφίστασθαι denotes a state subordinate to that denoted by the other term.

69. Plutarch *Comm. not.* 1074D (*SVF* II 335); Sextus *Adv. math.* X 218 (*SVF* II 331); Diog. Laert. VII 140; Proclus *In Tim.* p. 271D (*SVF* II 521).

70. The Stoics argued for the infinite divisibility of time, concluding from this that 'no time is strictly present since the present consists of past and future', *SVF* II 509, 517. Chrysippus' discussion ap. Stobaeum seems to be an attempt to explain the reality of the present in terms of an event expressed in the present tense. See in general Pohlenz, *Die Stoa* i pp. 45–7; Goldschmidt, *Le système stoicien* pp. 36f.

71. It is significant that similar language is used of two other ἀσώματα: place is that which παρυφίσταται material objects (Simplicius *In. cat.*, *CAG* VIII p. 361 = *SVF* II 507); time is the interval παρακολουθοῦν (accompanying) the movement of the cosmos (Stobaeus *Ecl.* I p. 106, 5 =*SVF* II 509) and movements are bodies (Galen XIX p. 480K =*SVF* II 385).

72. Cicero *Ac. pr.* II 77 (*SVF* I 59); Sextus *Adv. math.* VII 248. I am unable to accept the view of Adorno, 'Sul significato del termine ὑπάρχον in Zenone Stoico', *Parola del Passato* XII (1957) 369, that τὸ ὑπάρχον does not denote 'the real object existing by itself' but 'what exists only in the act of sensation'. Unless τὸ ὑπάρχον is independent of the act of sensation it will not serve, as it must, to distinguish καταληπτικαί from other φαντασίαι.

73. This is the summary meaning of κατ' αὐτὸ τὸ ὑπάρχον, a phrase also used by Sextus in his Epicurean epistemology, *Adv. math.* VII 205.

74. See Mates, *Stoic Logic*, pp. 33–6; W. and M. Kneale, *The Development of Logic*, pp. 150f.

75. *Adv. math.* VIII 10.

76. op. cit. p. 151.

77. Sextus *Adv. math.* VIII 100.

78. Seneca, *Ep. mor.* 113, 23 (*SVF* II 836).

79. Certain presentations and *lekta* necessarily fall outside this scheme. The Stoics recognised that some presentations might be both true and false, e.g. those prompted by existing things which are incorrectly identified (Sextus *Adv. math.* VII 245); and others might be neither true nor false, exemplified by 'generic presentations' such as man (ibid. 246). The reason given by Sextus for the latter assertion is obscure; he seems to be saying that predicates which are true of particular members of a class could not in all cases be asserted of the class itself: man is neither Greek nor barbarian. But the Stoics would allow *lekta* describing such presentations, though these could not be propositions since neither true nor false. Universals are ἀνύπαρκτα (see n. 59) but they can obviously occur in *lekta* and form part of the content of a mental image. The theory of *lekta* permits significant discourse about non-existents. What the Stoics would have said about mathematical truths is not clear, if they discussed them at all. They regarded whole, part and limits as constructs of the mind (see p. 94) and may have argued similarly about numbers. The truth of mathematical statements could not have been explained by reference to external objects. But the Stoics did admit the existence of mathematical knowledge (ps. Galen XIX p. 529K = *SVF* II 98) and may have claimed that this knowledge, itself a material entity (see Sextus *Adv. math.* VII 38f.), was the reality corresponding to true mathematical statements.

80. *The Stoic Theory of Knowledge*, pp. 27, 28.

81. *The Development of Logic*, p. 153.

82. Sextus *Adv. math.* IX 352, Watson p. 38.

83. Proclus *In Euc.* p. 89F (*SVF* II 488), Watson p. 39.

84. Diog. Laert. VII 65.

85. Chrysippus regarded day and night, the seasons, and other extended periods of time as σώματα, Plutarch *Comm. not.* 1084C (*SVF* II 665).

86. See p. 71. Watson's interpretation seems partly based on the view that 'bodies in Stoicism are "determined" by their activity which cannot be confined within the conventional limits imposed by language', p. 39. So far as I know no text supports this view. Activities are said to be bodies, see p. 87, but bodies are not said to be activities. There is activity within bodies for they are held together by τονικὴ κίνησις, but their defining characteristics are extension in space and endurance in time, see Sextus *Adv. math.* X 7ff., Stob. *Ecl.* I p. 104 (*SVF* I 93). If the Stoics were insistent that there is but one οὐσία (body) they were equally insistent that this οὐσία is shared by a plurality of individual things (Chalcidius, *In Tim.* 292 = *SVF* I 88). The qualitative differentiation of οὐσία expressed in particular bodies is basic (Plutarch *Comm. not.* 1085E–1086A = *SVF* II 380; Simplicius *In cat.* (*CAG* VIII) p. 222 = *SVF* II 378). The cosmos is a unity, but it contains a plurality of ὄντα (Alex. Aphr. *Fat.* p. 191 = *SVF* II 945; Cleomedes *Circul. doctr.* I, 1 = *SVF* II 529; Eusebius *PE* XV 15 = *SVF* II 528). For general remarks on the tension caused by this double perspective see Chapter VIII, p. 176.

87. Alex. Aphr. *In An. pr.* (*CAG* II 1 p. 373 = *SVF* II 253; cf. Sextus *Adv. math.* VIII 111.

88. Diog. Laert. VII 81.

89. Alex. Aphr. *De an.* p. 185 (*SVF* ɪɪ 920); id. *Quaest.* p. 10 (*SVF* ɪɪ 960).

90. See my article 'Carneades and the Stoic Telos', *Phronesis* xii (1967) 61–5.

91. Diog. Laert. vɪɪ 89; Stobaeus *Ecl.* ɪɪ p. 96; 102 (*SVF* ɪɪɪ 613, 615).

92. Diog. Laert. vɪɪ 107; Stobaeus *Ecl.* ɪɪ p. 85 (*SVF* ɪɪɪ 494).

93. Stobaeus loc. cit.

94. See my article 'The Stoic Concept of Evil', *Philosophical Quarterly* xviii (1968) 334–9.

95. So Bréhier, *Théorie des incorporels*, pp. 22ff.; Pohlenz, *Die Stoa* ɪ p. 63; Sextus *Hyp. pyrrh.* ɪɪ 109.

96. *The Development of Logic*, p. 156.

97. See p. 85.

98. op. cit. p. 154.

99. Alex Aphr. *In An. pr.* (*CAG* ɪɪ 1 pp. 177ff. =*SVF* ɪɪ 202a).

100. See Mates *Stoic Logic*, p. 30, and A. C. Lloyd, Chapter IV, p. 69.

101. The distinction is mentioned briefly in standard discussions, but I know no detailed treatment of it.

102. *Adv. math.* vɪɪ 38ff. (*SVF* ɪɪ 132). More briefly *Hyp. pyrrh.* ɪɪ 8off.

103. For 'knowledge of' ἀλήθεια cf. Plato *Parm.* 134a; at *Phileb.* 64d Socrates says that νοῦς is either the same as ἀλήθεια or more like it than anything else. Aristotle (*Met. Γ* 1008b 3) observes that inquiries into ἀλήθεια should follow rules for establishing the truth of statements.

104. *Adv. math.* vɪɪɪ 10 and 85.

105. Cf. Proclus *In Tim.* p. 138E (*SVF* ɪɪ 533), and n. 86.

106. Galen *De placitis* v p. 421M (*SVF* ɪɪ 841).

107. Like σύστασις the term σύστημα is used in Stoic writing for any 'ordered structure', see Diog. Laert. vɪɪ 45; Clement *Paed.* ɪ 102 p. 160P (*SVF* ɪɪɪ 293).

108. *Ecl.* ɪɪ pp. 73f. (*SVF* ɪɪɪ 112).

109. I cannot be certain that this translation is quite accurate; my 'items' is a translation of the MSS. ἐπιστημῶν for which Wachsmuth offers the likely emendation καταλήψεων. My translation of λογικὴ 'rational apprehension' is based on the assumption that a word like κατάληψις must be supplied.

110. Cf. Aristotle *EN* 1124b 30, the good man is ἀληθευτικὸς πλὴν ὅσα μὴ δι' εἰρωνείαν. A distinction between the truth value of an uttered statement and the speaker's intention may be the point made in a battered papyrus of Chrysippus, *SVF* ɪɪ 298a col. 10 p. 107.

111. Stobaeus *Ecl.* ɪɪ p. 111 (*SVF* ɪɪɪ 554); cf. ibid. p. 99 (*SVF* ɪ 216).

112. *De Stoic. rep.* 1057A (*SVF* ɪɪɪ 177).

113. *Ecl.* ɪɪɪ p. 621 (*SVF* ɪɪ 197).

114. For the connexion between truth and destiny or causal nexus see Stobaeus *Ecl.* ɪ p. 79 (*SVF* ɪɪ 913), Bréhier *Chrysippe*, pp. 178f. My interpretation is based largely on Diog. Laert. vɪɪ 87–8.

115. Stobaeus *Ecl.* ɪɪ p. 111 (*SVF* ɪɪɪ 548).

116. *Adv. math.* vɪɪ 38.

117. See Chapter I, pp. 12f.

118. Stobaeus *Ecl.* ɪɪ p. 88 (*SVF* ɪɪɪ 378). Acts of assent by bad men are weak or false, cf. Galen v p. 58K (*SVF* ɪɪɪ 172); Plutarch *Stoic. rep.* 1057B (*SVF* ɪɪɪ 177).

119. *Ac. post.* ɪ 42 (*SVF* ɪ 60).

120. For the distinction between ἔννοια and πρόληψις see F. H. Sandbach, Chapter II. According to Diog. Laert. vɪɪ 42 the Stoics regarded 'the part of logic dealing with definitions as contributing to the discovery of truth; since by means of general ideas (ἔννοιαι) actual things are grasped'. ἔννοιαι are not universals, see n. 59. An ἔννοια is a mental image formed by reference to or inference from

one or more percepts (Diog. Laert. VII 52; Sextus *Adv. math.* VIII 60). To have the ἔννοια of man is to be able to complete a statement of the following form correctly: ('if something is a man, then it is . . .' (Sextus ibid. XI 8). In this way apparently the Stoics tried to avoid universals in their method of definition.

121. See Watson, *The Stoic Theory of Knowledge*, pp. 37, 59.

122. Cf. Cicero *De fin.* III 21; 33, and see F. H. Sandbach, Chapter II, pp. 28f, for discussion of the grasp of moral concepts.

123. Marcus Aurelius *Med.* X 5, and see p. 192.

124. See p. 87, and cf. Cicero *De off.* I 11.

125. See 'The Stoic Concept of Evil', *Phil. Quart.* xviii, 337–9.

126. Ibid. 336–7.

127. Diog. Laert. VII 83; so too *SVF* II 124; III 654.

128. cf. Bréhier, *Chrysippe*, p. 69 n. 2 (from p. 68), 'Le λεκτόν désigne non pas ce qui est exprimé par un mot quelconque, mais ce qui peut être exprimé par le mot essential de la phrase, c'est-à-dire par le verbe'.

VI

Oikeiōsis

S. G. PEMBROKE

A philosophical term with a persistent reputation for being impossible to translate might reasonably be expected to rest on assumptions for which it is no longer easy to make allowance, even in imagination, or to combine these assumptions in a way which would to-day appear forcible or contradictory. With the subject of this chapter, however, the problem is exactly the opposite. *Oikeiōsis* does not need bringing up to date. The most casual reading of the texts is likely to cause surprise at the seeming modernity of the ideas involved, and the surprise is a recurrent one in that the concepts which suggest themselves as most nearly equivalent belong to a number of different disciplines which have arisen only during the last two centuries and whose progress has often made the creation of a special terminology necessary. To combine these separate terminologies would be a task in itself, but any translation of the Stoic concept must also attempt to convey the forcefulness and consistency which it had in antiquity. The classic achievements of Greek attempts to make sense of the world are traditionally associated with their isolation of the impersonal factors which they saw as operative in it, but the contribution made by Stoics with the idea of *oikeiosis* lies in their re-introducing the personal in such a way that their view of the world has less and not more room for the exercise of arbitrary and inconsistent factors than have the systems of their predecessors. The precise date at which this step was taken, and its immediate intellectual background, have been the subject of controversy during the present century. In this chapter it will be maintained that *oikeiosis* was a central idea in Stoic thinking from the start and that the ancient tag about Chrysippus could fairly be transferred from the School's history to its doctrine: if there had been no

oikeiosis, there would have been no Stoa. But though the Stoics
made a quite distinctive use of the term, they did not actually
invent it, and consequently their originality can only be assessed
in terms of their antecedents.

Oikeiosis is a verbal noun, and the verb's immediate neighbour
is the adjective *oikeios*, itself derived from the Greek word for
house and applied both to persons who were members of the
household or had a blood-relationship to its members, and to
those connected with it either by ties of marriage or less formally
by virtually any kind of favourable association. In the household sphere, *oikeios* also denoted property and so came by a
simple extension to cover anything belonging to a person in
other senses than the strictly economic one. The word was also
used to denote a variety of relationships between things, extending from the actual classification of one thing in terms of
another to more or less any sort of appropriateness or general
relevance which did not imply conflict between the two. The
verb *oikeioun*, which is transitive, turns up in various forms in
the fifth and fourth centuries B.C. meaning to appropriate goods
or, when applied to people, to win them over—the object of
official diplomacy as well as of private intrigue.[1] This appropriation—the noun *oikeiosis* is used in this sense by Thucydides[2]—
characteristically becomes more subjective when the active form
of the verb is replaced by the Greek middle (*oikeiousthai*), and
indicates a claim to ownership rather than actual possession, for
example when the Lydians of Herodotus claim as their own the
invention of all known games except draughts.[3] But the sense of
the word most relevant to the Stoics is not directly attested in
an active form before their time: *oikeioun* could also denote the
creation of relationships between two persons or groups distinct
from the verb's subject, A 'introducing' B to C or establishing
good terms between them. Thus Epicurus uses the verb in the
passive to convey the idea of being acquainted or familiar with
something,[4] though it is less neutral than either of these words,
because strictly—and in some cases quite explicitly—its opposite is not just being unfamiliar but being on bad terms: *oikeios*,
to go back to the adjective, is regularly contrasted with *allotrios*,
what belongs to someone else or is in a wider sense alien to oneself, and in Greek as in English, to alienate people (*allotrioun*)

meant to leave them not unfamiliar with one's existence, but painfully aware of it.[5]

In the Stoa, *oikeiosis* is never used in the active sense of appropriation. What it denotes is a relationship, but this is not bilateral, and it is the subjective factor, the consciousness of such a relationship—which does not have to be reciprocated—on which most emphasis is placed. This emphasis is brought out formally by the use of a preposition after the verb, a combination which the Stoics appear to have inaugurated.[6] When *oikeiosis* has to be translated, the word most often chosen is endearment, which has the advantage of a close grammatical correspondence, with 'dear' to stand for *oikeion*, but undoubtedly sentimentalises the idea in a way which the Greek word did not. The expedient which will be adopted here is the slightly artificial one of using 'well-disposed' as a translation for the verb and where necessary representing *oikeion* with the noun 'concern'. For all its drawbacks, this can be maintained fairly consistently, since the verb is almost always used passively, and in the chief exception to this rule, which is at the same time the classic text on the subject (Diogenes Laertius), it turns out to be universal Nature that does the disposing.[7]

The prime impulse of an animal is towards self-preservation, because Nature makes it well-disposed to itself from the outset, as Chrysippus says in the first book of his work *On Ends*. He says the prime concern (*oikeion*) of every animal is its constitution and the consciousness of this; for Nature would not have been likely either to make it ill-disposed to itself or to create it and then leave it neither well- nor ill-disposed to itself. We have therefore to say that in constituting the animal, Nature made it well-disposed to itself, and it is in this way that it repels what is harmful and takes in everything which is right for it (*oikeion*).[8]

One function served by this theory is stated immediately in what follows. The view of those who represent pleasure as the prime object of animal impulses is written off on the grounds that pleasure, if there is such a thing, is purely secondary, a by-product or aftermath (*epigennēma*) and arises only when Nature has sought and found whatever is requisite for the creature's constitution. Similarly, a plant is said to 'bloom' when its needs are supplied. All that distinguishes plants from animals,

Diogenes continues, is the absence of what other texts call *psychē*, here represented by the fact that animals have impulse (*hormē*) and sensation to regulate the maintenance of their constitution, a process which in plants is simply carried out by Nature. But the process itself is natural in both cases, and it is equally natural that for human beings, on whom *logos* has been bestowed, living in accordance with *logos* should be the specifically human form for the same process to take. The *logos* supervenes not as the opponent of natural impulse but 'as the technician to take charge of it.'[9]

In mediaeval Latin, the word for impulse was consistently replaced by *instinctus naturalis*;[10] but the relation of instinct to reason is traditionally a much more direct opposition than can be detected between impulse and *logos* in Stoicism, and in antiquity *instinctus* was applied not to recurrent behaviour but to the exact opposite of this, exceptional manifestations like sudden inspiration.[11] *Logos* is or can be essentially continuous with impulse; it is not brought in from outside the biological realm but at a certain level of organisation arises spontaneously within it, and the form taken by impulse below this level is not so much irrational as prior to the rational. Man alone has the faculty of regulating impulse in accordance with *logos*, but it is only in Man and only when he fails to exercise this faculty that impulse is liable to become disproportionate and thus contravene the *logos* of universal Nature, which it cannot in any other creature.[12]

Other texts describe the means by which the *logos* does arise in human beings, a process for whose completion a period of time variously put at seven and fourteen years is required.[13] At the end of this period there again supervenes *oikeiosis* of a different and more decisive kind. Human beings encounter, during infancy, things naturally proper to them; they direct themselves towards these, keep everything which is 'alien' to them out of their way, and in the course of this, by means of a process which the sources refer to as comparison but which is at the same time distinguished from every other kind of mental operation as 'natural', they arrive at the notion of what is truly good.[14] As and when this notion is formed, it is seen to be something more profoundly proper and natural to the subject than anything he has encountered previously, so much so that the

whole range of natural things which led up to it is not merely
downgraded to a position of secondary importance but ceases
to matter at all. They turn out to be wholly indifferent by comparison with the good and its now overriding claims on his disposition.[15] The sources insist on the autonomy of moral awareness once it has been achieved;[16] ultimately, however, the
business of achieving it differs only in degree from processes at
work more obscurely at lower levels of the animal kingdom.
Moral awareness is, to use the Stoic term, the most highly
articulated form of perception possible, but what is proper
(*oikeion*) and what is alien (*allotrion*) are at all levels of consciousness not only the terms in which perception operates but
the conditions without which it could not arise.[17]

     The later, specifically moral stages of this process will be
returned to later. Before this, the account given by Chrysippus
of the preceding phases can be supplemented by two later texts,
a letter of Seneca's in which the business of self-preservation is
illustrated from the animal kingdom, and a papyrus of the
second century A.D. which contains a formal exposition of the
doctrine of *oikeiosis*, in animals and mankind alike, by the Stoic
Hierocles. Seneca admits that he is following Posidonius as well
as Archedemus, but the account given by Hierocles is undoubtedly scrupulous in its orthodoxy, to which his personal contribution is little more than the verbal mannerisms and stock
examples of the professional lecturer.[18] Both are emphatic in
basing *oikeiosis* on perception, and both of them insist that perception of external objects would be impossible without
perception of oneself.[19] Hierocles, who argues this in more
detail, does so by turning a sceptical argument upside down.
Centuries earlier, philosophers of the Cyrenaic school had
maintained that although one could be certain that one was
having particular sensations, such as that of whiteness or a
sweet taste, it was quite impossible to achieve certainty as to the
real existence of an external object corresponding to these
sensations.[20] Hierocles takes for granted the commonsense view
that external objects do exist and argues that it is impossible to
notice them without the subject's being at every stage conscious of himself as the locus of the corresponding sensations.[21]
He also gives the fullest surviving account of self-consciousness

independent of externals, in terms of the 'tensional movement'
(*tonikē kinēsis*) of the animal *psyche* which is extended through
every part of the body. Throughout this movement, the *psyche*
encounters constant resistance (*antereistikon*) from its contact
with the body and conveys a message as to this resistance back
to its headquarters, the *hēgemonikon*.[22] How the *psyche* is conscious
of itself, rather than of the body, is not made so clear, but it has
been suggested that what happens with external objects must
also take place internally, that is to say that in experiencing
resistance from the body the *psyche* must also experience itself
as the point at which this resistance is encountered.[23] Consciousness, on this view, would necessarily involve the operation of a
minimum of two factors. This is certainly consistent with what
another source cryptically describes as 'the internal contact, by
means of which we become aware of ourselves';[24] at the same
time, it gives a specific sense to the preposition with which the
word for consciousness (*synaisthēsis*)—which may well have been
used by Zeno—was constructed.[25] This would admittedly still
fail to account for the privileged position of the *hegemonikon*, or
even for its existence; but Hierocles himself no longer seems to
find the doctrine problematical. He is concerned with it only as
a preliminary to establishing the fact of *oikeiosis* attendant on
consciousness.[26]

Both Seneca and Hierocles back up their main contentions
with a number of highly perceptive, although almost certainly
inherited, observations: for Seneca, the efforts of a tortoise to
right itself when it has been turned upside down are due not to
discomfort, since no actual pain is involved, but simply to the
desire to resume its natural state, while Hierocles maintains that
the fear of the dark shown by children is due to the removal of
external stimuli, without which they are inclined to imagine
that their extinction is taking place—a hypothesis which does
much to reinforce the general theory of consciousness outlined
earlier[27]. Both writers make a good deal out of the spontaneity
with which animals put their limbs to the proper use without
having to try them out;[28] a fair amount of space is also devoted
to animal awareness of the danger constituted by other species,
the 'alienation' which is here loosely attached to *oikeiosis* as its
pendant.[29] Finally, the concept of *constitutio* is elaborated in

Seneca with the assertion, probably orthodox, that there is a
different one for each age-group and that human beings instantly accept as their own the new constitution which succeeds
each transition from one age to the next, together with the
physical changes attendant on it.[30]

This concept is for Seneca primarily a physiological one. At
the psychological level, the process by which *oikeiosis* is subsequently extended further is most fully described in Book III
of Cicero's *De Finibus*, which is generally agreed to derive from
an orthodox Stoic handbook of the time of Chrysippus' successor Diogenes or his pupil Antipater.[31] Cicero translates
oikeiosis with two alternative terms, *commendatio* and *conciliatio*;
the Latin language is unable to support either of these with a
directly related adjective corresponding to *oikeion*, but they are
both no less explicitly personal than the Greek original.[32] In this
text, acts of understanding (*comprehensiones*, formally identified by
Cicero as the Greek *katalēpseis*) are placed among those things
which are desirable for their own sake and spontaneously felt to
be so: you can see how children, without any ulterior motive, are
delighted when they manage to work out anything on their own
by the exercise of their powers of reason.[33] It would be fully
legitimate to paraphrase this by saying that human beings have
a natural impulse towards the exercise of these powers; and the
interest shown by Cicero's source in the behaviour of children
is characteristic of the Stoa from the time of Antipater onwards,
although it is not so well directly attested in the works of his
predecessors. Before the Stoics, the predominant role in which
children receive the attention of thinkers is that of a material
evaluated in terms of its susceptibility to *paideia*, the condition-
ing process of education which is already represented by Plato's
Protagoras as the accepted means of imposing *nomos* on a *physis*
distinguished from the adult as much by recalcitrance as by
immaturity.[34] In the *Nicomachaean Ethics*, child psychology is
aligned with that of animals and excluded from consideration
along with it;[35] and despite some signs of a later relaxation of
this position in the Peripatos, there is little to anticipate the kind
of interest shown in the *De Finibus*, where childhood is accorded
the status of a fully natural phenomenon and the child himself
is treated as the chief agent in his own education. There is a

definite emphasis on the continuity of childhood with maturity, just as there is elsewhere on that of animal behaviour with human life and even on that of the man who makes moral progress with the man who has actually attained to wisdom. In each case the continuity is offset by a violently sharp break. To be very close to moral perfection is to be wholly inadequate, because you drown, as Chrysippus put it, when you are just beneath the surface no less certainly than when you are at the bottom; [36] similarly, animals have no *logos* and there is no such thing as a justice which can obtain between them and humans. [37] In the present case, the violence of the break between childhood and the rationality which succeeds it is expressed by another text which declares that children do not just become bad or morally inadequate with the full development of the *logos* but that this change brings with it instant badness. [38] In each case, however, the line drawn is evaluative rather than descriptive, and ultimately, the continuity is more important than the point of demarcation, because it was the Stoics themselves who described the world in terms of this continuity, and this factor came to receive even more emphasis after Chrysippus when the insistence on moral perfection was more or less tacitly dropped.

A later section in the same book of the *De Finibus* is devoted to *oikeiosis* of a different kind, the means by which we become well-disposed not just to ourselves but to other people. [39] The validity of this doctrine was challenged in antiquity, and in modern times both its orthodoxy and the date at which it was first formulated have been disputed. [40] The arguments involved, therefore, need to be stated with some care: specifically, not so much because of their complexity but to make it clear what they leave out, a gap which in surviving texts is closed not by the Stoics but by the Peripatetics. The first point made in Cicero is that it is natural for children to be loved by their parents and that this is the starting-point from which human association is to be traced. The starting-point itself is established with a number of characteristically Stoic proofs: the human body is clearly designed by Nature for reproduction, and the conjunction of Nature both causing reproduction and failing to ensure that the resultant offspring receive affection would be

I

impossible. Furthermore, even animals can be seen to expend effort on bringing forth their young and on rearing them. So it comes about that there is a general, and natural, *oikeiosis* (*commendatio*) between people, and this is of such a kind that no man can present himself to another as something alien: that possibility is ruled out simply by his being human.[41] At this point the argument reverts to animals, which are divided into two classes and aligned with parts of the human body: eyes and ears, it is stated, are things we can use only for ourselves, but hands and legs can be put to the service of other people as well. Similarly while the wilder beasts live only for themselves, there is one case of two distinct animal species associating for their mutual advantage, while a number of other creatures—ants, bees, and the stork[42]—all perform actions of which the beneficiaries are distinct from the individual agent. The behaviour of Man is vastly more associative than any of this, and he is therefore naturally adapted to forming groups and living in society. From this point onwards the argument can be summarised more rapidly. There is, Cicero admits, a proverb to the effect *après moi le déluge*,[43] but in reality no amount of pleasures would compensate anyone for a life of total solitude; and the spontaneous nature of a life in society is again brought out by comparing it to the way we use our limbs before learning what they are for. Finally, it is stated that since Man is born for the preservation of others (and not just that of himself), the wise man will want to play a part in politics, to marry and to have children.

A fair number of the arguments in this section can be traced back with certainty to Chrysippus, and its main gist may perhaps be taken a stage earlier: the 'followers of Zeno', according to Porphyry, make *oikeiosis* the beginning of justice, and although the phrase does not necessarily include Zeno himself, there is no sign that it excludes any of his successors, even those who preceded Chrysippus, while the present tense of the verb is more likely to denote a sustained orthodoxy than a comparatively recent addition to the school's doctrine.[44] But it is not certain from the immediate context that it is other people, as distinct from oneself or from what is natural and *oikeion* in general, that are the object of the *oikeiosis* in question. Mankind at large is not in fact directly attested in the writings of Chrysippus as an object of *oikeiosis*, but it is certain that he did extend this to at least one class of persons distinct from its subject. Plutarch complains that every single book by Chrysippus, those dealing with natural phenomena no less than his ethical works, contains the proposition that 'from the moment of birth, we are well-disposed to ourselves, and to our limbs, and to our children'.[45] Elsewhere, Plutarch says that the Stoics make affection for one's children the starting-point of association (*koinōnia*) and justice;[46] and that they had the authority of Chrysippus for doing so is made certain by his statement 'The beasts are well-disposed to their offspring in direct proportion to the latter's needs'. Most if not all these words are verbatim quotation, and more important, they were taken from the first book of his work *On Justice*.[47] Finally, the example given in Cicero of co-operation between species, the bivalve *pinna* and a small crab known as its guardian and found in its vicinity, was a recurrent theme in Chrysippus' writings, again complained of by Plutarch, who points to a better example he could have given.[48]

The problem remains how, if at all, Chrysippus made the connexion between parental affection and universal *oikeiosis*. In the other passage of which Plutarch grew tired, the words 'from the moment of birth' might suggest a developmental treatment: Chrysippus, on this view, would have described the *oikeiosis* of children to other people, and its subsequent extension. A brief synopsis of this extension is in fact given by Antiochus of Ascalon, the eclectic Academic of Cicero's time who drew heavily on Stoic material in the formulation of his own doctrine. Antiochus' view was that what he called the dearness of the human race began not just at home but from the moment of conception, because, in Cicero's words, 'children are loved by their parents and the whole household is connected by the marriage-tie and by its progeny: this dearness gradually extends outdoors, first with blood-relatives, then with relations by marriage, then with friends, then neighbours, then citizens and then any kind of public association, finally embracing the entire human race'.[49]

The effortlessness suggested by this high-speed summary is hardly reassuring. It is little more convincing to be told that one is fond of all mankind than it is to discover that one has been

talking prose all one's life; and the absence of any specific
resistances to be met with and overcome in the course of this
process, for example on crossing the borderline from personal
acquaintance, however slight, to anonymous encounters, is not
offset by any formal demonstration that the total affection of
which any one person is capable can increase so as to meet the
universal demands to be made on it. Much the same goes for the
more elaborate but still defective treatment of the problem
given by Arius Didymus in the compendium of so-called
'Peripatetic' doctrine known to us from Stobaeus, which is
likely to derive, at not more than one remove, from Antiochus,
and which for reasons which will be dealt with later presents
the entire theory of *oikeiosis* as the property of Aristotle and his
successors. The second half of this work, discussing friendship
(*philia*), says that its first object is oneself, its second one's
parents; these are succeeded by other relatives and persons
outside the family.[50] If *oikeiosis* were to be substituted for friendship in this passage, it would point to an even closer anticipation of psycho-analytic doctrine than any of the texts so far considered: the process by which *libido* is directed away from the
child's own body onto its parents before its eventual transference to other goals. There is an obvious difference, in that
the final emphasis of the Greek text is on all mankind, not a
particular individual, as the object of *philia*, but the initial
convergence remains striking.[51] More precisely, however, Arius
claims to have set out the sequence of *philia* earlier in his treatise:
yet the only previous passage to which this claim could be referred is unequivocal, once the fact of *oikeiosis* to oneself has been
established, in taking as its starting-point the affection felt for
one's children and not the affection which they feel. 'Thus since
children are loved as something desirable in itself, it is bound
to happen (*anankaion*) that parents, brothers and sisters,
husbands and wives, blood-relations, other relatives and fellow-
citizens all receive affection on their own account;' and the
series is again extended so as to comprise the whole of mankind.[52]

Just why this is bound to happen is not clear, nor is the
identity of the person from whom this affection proceeds. The
analogy of Antiochus' gradual (*sensim*) extension of *caritas* might
suggest that its subject is the child and that the process starts

not of its own accord but as a response to parental affection. If this view were correct, and if the doctrine were genuinely Stoic, it would not be hard to marshal Stoic ideas whose pedigree is unquestioned and in terms of which the process could have been elaborated: the initial response could be aligned with the Stoic interest in the conferring of benefits, and in their restitution, and the transfer of affection to persons other than the child's parents might have been worked out in terms of the operations like analogy and metathesis by means of which concepts were supposed to be formed. Furthermore the lacuna in the surviving text's argument could be due not to Arius himself but to an omission by Stobaeus or any other excerptor who preceded him. But there is not the slightest trace of any such conceptual backing in any other source, and this deficiency must make it highly questionable whether the extension of *philia* set out by Arius really does represent a process of individual development beginning in infancy. The extension seems rather to be a purely logical one, flatly superimposed on an inherited doctrine of parental affection.[53] Panaetius, whose doctrine is given in Book I of the *De Officiis*, refers at once to Nature making man well-disposed to man and also to the special love it has implanted in parents towards their children, but he has nothing to say about this love being reciprocated; and though a later passage sets out different degrees of *societas*, starting with the small family, which is called the starting-point of civil society, the more distant degrees of kinship which follow this—brothers, cousins, and relations by marriage—are simply catalogued, not organised into a scheme of temporal development either individual or historical.[54]

There remains the evidence of Hierocles. A passage excerpted by Stobaeus from *How to behave to one's relatives*, one of a series of themes which also included behaviour towards the gods, to one's country, parents and brothers respectively, describes man as standing at the centre of a series of concentric circles.[55] The first is occupied by himself, his body and anything admitted to the circle to satisfy his physical needs. The second circle takes in parents, brothers, wife and children; the third one contains aunts and uncles, grandparents, nephews, nieces and cousins; other relatives are placed in the fourth circle, and outside this, circles are occupied successively by members of his deme, his fellow-tribesmen, fellow-citizens, those from neighbouring towns and then his fellow-countrymen. The largest and outermost circle is that constituted by the entire human race. What Hierocles proposes is that every effort should be made to made to draw the circumference of each circle towards the centre—a task which quite explicitly, and unlike what is suggested by Antiochus and Arius, he does not expect to be effortless.[56] It is something if persons in one circle can be treated as though they belonged to its immediate neighbour on the inside. One means suggested to effect this is the upgrading of one's more distant relatives by addressing them in terms which denote a closer relationship than that which really obtains. Cousins, aunts, and uncles are to be addressed respectively as 'brother', 'mother' and 'father', while still more remote kindred are dignified with the names uncle, nephew and cousin—a kind of 'classificatory' system of appellations, in the anthropological sense, which can be found no ancient parallel in that it is not merely Utopian but is meant for immediate adoption within the bourgeois family[57]. But the succession of circles is again a purely logical one, and the list of relatives placed in the second circle presupposes that the person at its centre is already an adult. The succession does not begin to correspond to a succession of encounters during the life of an individual, since past and future, parents and their grandchildren, are alike placed in a single circle.[58] And though the papyrus containing Hierocles' treatment of *oikeiosis* does certainly suggest a stage-by-stage approach, its evidence on this point is not decisive.

In this treatise, a section whose heading ended with the words 'what the *telos* is' sets out three distinct kinds of *oikeiosis*. That which is directed towards oneself is called 'benevolent' (*eunoētikē*), while the familial kind (*syngenikē*) receives the title 'affectionate' (*sterktikē*), and *oikeiosis* towards external goods is called 'due to choice' (*hairetikē*). But the only instance given of familial *oikeiosis* is that towards one's children, and no other members of the family are mentioned.[59] It has been suggested that this deficiency is due simply to the state of the papyrus, since more than a hundred lines of what followed are impossible to recover. Where the text resumes after this hiatus, Hierocles is found describing Man as an animal which is not solitary but gregarious (*synagelastikon*)—which is why we live in cities, since every man is part of a city. There followed a number of observations instancing the ease with which we form friendships, simply from sitting next to someone at a meal or in a theatre and 'the most surprising thing of all' which was probably the fraternisation of troops with the enemy.[60]

At this point, the text again becomes unuseable; but whatever it was that the previous gap contained, it is not likely to have established universal, or potentially universal, *oikeiosis*, since if it had done so, the proposition that Man is gregarious could hardly have been introduced as something new. Furthermore, there is no sign that Man's gregarious tendencies are essentially derived, in Hierocles' view, from his life or upbringing in the family. The word *synagelastikon* denotes a permanent and instinctive tendency, and no earlier writer applies it in this way to human beings, although Aristotle may have used it in describing certain other animals.[61] Other Stoic sources describe men as naturally 'fond of one another' (*philallēloi*),[62] a word regularly applied to herd animals and which when it is used of human beings, as it may have been by the Cynics, does not suggest any kind of association more complex or highly differentiated than that of these animals.[63] If this tendency were a permanent and innate one, there would be little need for its existence to be established via the family, and none whatsoever for relatives more distant than parents and children as a link between Hierocles' second circle and the rest of mankind. Humanity would simply consist, as Epictetus says it does, of people 'naturally well-disposed to one another'.[64]

The chief objection to this rather simplistic view, and to the corollary that justice can be derived from *oikeiosis*, is brilliantly stated in a papyrus dating from the second century A.D. which contains part of a commentary on Plato's *Theaetetus* and was found at the beginning of the present century.[65] The author is unnamed, but from internal evidence he has generally been associated fairly closely with Gaius and Albinus, the leading Platonists of the time. Whatever his identity, he is scrupulous in putting his criticisms in the Stoics' own terms. His first point is that *oikeiosis* must be subject to variations in intensity, *epitasis*

128OIKEIŌSIS

and *anesis*, the heightening and relaxation of tension to which in
Stoic theory all human dispositions other than moral perfection
were necessarily liable, although they did not themselves
formally include *oikeiosis* with these.[66] In the commentary, once
the possibility of variation is established, it is stated that *oikeiosis*
to other people will never match *oikeiosis* to oneself, and that it
is contrary to all experience to maintain that it can do so.[67]
Oikeiosis to oneself is natural and irrational, whereas that
directed towards other people, though also natural, necessarily
involves *logos*.[68] Furthermore if we disapprove of other people,
we experience actual 'alienation' towards them, whereas we do
not hate ourselves when our own behaviour falls below par. At
this point *epitasis* and *anesis* are shown to obtain even in *oikeiosis*
to oneself and to the various parts of one's body—and the sense
of alienation provoked by their loss: nail-parings and hair-
trimmings do not belong in the same way that more vital organs
do.[69] If, therefore, the fact of variation in *oikeiosis* is admitted,
benevolence (*philanthropia*) will remain a possibility, but *oikeiosis*
to oneself will inevitably have the ascendancy over it—particularly in a situation involving two people one of whom has to
die.

The papyrus has a small gap at the point where this situation
comes up, but as Diels showed when first publishing it, this can
be filled in such a way as to identify the two as survivors from a
shipwreck.[70] As he pointed out, a situation of this kind had
already been considered by the Stoic Hecaton, a pupil of
Panaetius.[71] Even before this, however, shipwreck was also the
classic instance in Carneades' demonstration that there was no
such thing as natural justice or that, if there was, it was flatly
opposed to wisdom. For each of the two survivors, there was a
straight choice: either to kill the other man—which would be
wise, especially as no third party would witness it, but unjust—
or to choose death for himself rather than lay hands on someone
else. And though anyone taking this latter option might have to
be called just, he would be a fool.[72]

This argument of Carneades' might well appear to suggest a
still closer connexion with the *Theaetetus* commentary. It might
be thought, in fact, although this possibility does not seem to
have been made explicit in discussions of the text, that the

whole case against *oikeiosis* is simply too well argued to have originated with the anonymous Platonist: that is to say, that the derivation of justice from *oikeiosis* was already in existence (and under attack from the Academy) in the time of Carneades. This is suggested very strongly by the text itself, which goes on immediately to summarise an argument used by the Academy —the attribution here is explicit—as a stick with which to beat the Stoic theory of justice and that of the Epicureans, with whom the Stoics are with characteristic sophistry made to stand or fall. Even if this were the case, however, and if Carneades did at some stage combine his onslaughts on justice with an attack on *oikeiosis* to other people, this does not mean that the case made against it here is a fair one. The validity of an argument extrapolated from a society of two people to which no values are admitted but physical survival is highly questionable, and Hecaton, both of whose survivors are wise men, may well have intended his own solution as a response to the Academy: it was that the raft should be taken by the one whose prolonged existence was more important either for his own sake or for that of his compatriots. Alternatively, if there was nothing to choose between them, their fate could be decided by lot.

This additional criterion is perfectly consistent with earlier Stoic doctrine. If Chrysippus or his predecessors did make a connexion between justice and *oikeiosis*, it is highly unlikely that in doing so they formally excluded that state of being well-disposed to moral values which is the final stage in the development of *oikeiosis* to oneself. No philosophical system before the Stoa lays so much emphasis on the importance of the total moral condition of the agent, and there is no evidence whatsoever that Chrysippus believed *oikeiosis* to other people could constitute a sort of escape route enabling a man to behave justly irrespective of his moral condition, any more than he believed in a 'free will' independent of this condition.[73] *Dikaiosynē*, like *alētheia*, must necessarily be located in a human being; and it is *dikaiosyne*, not merely 'the just' (*to dikaion*) which has been translated as justice in all the texts so far considered. Of the latter, Chrysippus has extremely little to say beyond that it exists and that its existence is natural;[74] in talking of *dikaiosyne*, he consistently treats it as an aspect of *aretē*.[75]

His successors have less to say about the perfectly wise man and from Antipater to Hierocles place increasing emphasis on the institutions of existing society;[76] they may therefore have found themselves making greater demands on *oikeiosis* also. But there is no sign that this was at any stage formally equated with impulse.[77] *Oikeiosis* is the precondition of impulse, a sort of standing equivalent to the more intermittent *epibolē*, defined by the Stoics as 'impulse prior to impulse' and instanced by sexual love, 'an *epibole* of striking up a friendship, caused by the presentation of beauty'.[78] It is, however, considerably less specific than this. To find oneself well-disposed to one's fellow-humans —in a way which one is not towards animals—indicates them as belonging within the area where justice should obtain;[79] but it is not an instant guarantee of perfect behaviour in this area, nor does it in itself define what is appropriate (*kathēkon*) in one's dealings with them. A thing found to be *oikeion* was not thereby certain to constitute a good in itself, any more than a thing seen to accord with nature would necessarily merit a higher status than the indifferent;[80] and other people, contrary to what might be suggested by assimilating *oikeiosis* to the Freudian libido, did not in themselves constitute an absolute value or one which could register in any terms independent of *arete*.

This being so, it is unthinkable that Chrysippus should have represented the real business of living as a banal process of tracing one's more distant relatives and following up increasingly casual acquaintances. What conclusions he did draw from the co-operation and parental affection shown by animals cannot be reconstructed in detail, but their general tendency is clear enough. Animals existed for Man's benefit, and there is every sign that this comprised not merely the satisfaction of his economic needs, but his edification: in this case, the spectacle of parental devotion as a natural force. In human beings, the potential of such a force would not, in Chrysippus' terms, be reduced by the accession of *logos*, as though it had to make room for it. *Logos* could so 'articulate' devotion as actually to reinforce it, and the resultant force would be capable of still higher things.[81]

It is however not likely that from this starting-point Chrysippus went on to a systematic elaboration of the various forms of human association that could be derived from it. In the hierarchy of the three degrees of organisation in the physical world, first what was called the discrete, then the composite, and finally the unified, nothing at the discrete level could for the Stoics represent a good; and of the stock examples cited for each of these categories, the only social or political institutions—a chorus, an assembly or an army—are all explicitly assigned to the discrete, because what happens to one member of such a group does not affect the remainder.[82] What these examples appear deliberately to exclude is the kind of group whose members have different roles and might therefore be linked not merely by a common task but by different kinds of *oikeiosis* towards one another. Something of this sort could reasonably be expected to figure at the composite level, but there is no sign of such groups in surviving accounts of the hierarchy;[83] and while some scattered texts refer to the 'unification of the discrete,' this is regularly presented as a paradoxical ideal or one that can be realised only by an exercise of *logos* or *arete* so total as to overrule all possible difficulties.[84] More generally, all institutions, social or political, were for orthodox Stoics purely external and could not affect people's inner morality. Both in the ideal *Politeia* of Zeno and in the pronouncements of Chrysippus on existing institutions—the latter simply divided into good and bad and aligned with wise men and the unwise respectively—these institutions are consistently treated as though they were internalised and amounted to no more than aspects of the moral state of the individual. Their external manifestations, it is implied, can even in the existing state of things be written off as totally unimportant and could, given less imperfect human beings, be dispensed with altogether.[85] It was, in any case, possible to express the community of the whole world in terms of a household no less well than in those of *politeia*;[86] and when the relationship of a benefactor such as Hercules to the rest of mankind is aligned with that of animals to their offspring, as it is in the *De finibus*,[87] it becomes clear that for the Stoics no more elaborate institutions than the family were needed to establish the two decisive categories of good and bad.

In one context, moreover, the role given to parental affection is a negative one. A text whose orthodoxy cannot be challenged describes this affection as natural (*physikē*) to the wise and not present at all in unwise people.[88] It may therefore have served not only to indicate the possibility of altruism but to account for that general perversion (*diastrophē*) of the natural which had to account for the standing world shortage of wise men and whose onset is in other texts traced back to infancy.[89] There is, however, no evidence that the effects of this deficiency on the child were elaborated in terms of emotional deprivation, and apart from Arius no extant text so much as mentions parents in the catalogue of what children encounter during infancy. *Philostorgia*, therefore, is just one of the counts on which almost all human beings are found wanting, and not the most decisive. And finally, whatever criticisms the derivation of justice from this affection may be open to, the one made by the Academy cannot be placed at all high on the list. The attempt to reduce justice to the one question of physical survival, if it was directed at the Stoa, was singularly inappropriate. The morality which the Stoics derived from self-preservation was capable not merely of condoning, but actually prescribing, suicide committed for the right reasons and by persons who had attained the full measure of this morality.[90] The prolongation of life, as such, was no more demanded by the Stoic's concern for others than it was by his concern for himself.

The originality of the doctrine of *oikeiosis* has been much disputed in the present century. Specifically, it has more than once been argued that its real home was the Peripatos: not that the materials from which the doctrine was put together were available here, nor even that their synthesis was partially anticipated by Theophrastus and his contemporaries, but that he was himself responsible for its elaboration and that the Stoics simply appropriated it wholesale and without acknowledgment. In 1926 von Arnim maintained that *oikeiosis*, while originally the property of Theophrastus, had reached Zeno via the Academy of Polemon, with which a number of passages in Cicero represent Zeno as closely associated and to which in particular Cicero says Zeno was indebted for the doctrine of *principia naturae*.[91] The chief fact, however, on which this argu-

ment was based is that Arius Didymus gives a quite elaborate
account of *oikeiosis* in his compendium of Peripatetic ethics—
most of which was, in von Arnim's view, an authentic exposition
of the moral philosophy of Theophrastus, who is at one point
quoted verbatim—whereas he has almost nothing to say about
it in his treatment of the Stoics.[92]

A similar conclusion was reached eleven years later by Dirlmeier, who not only reinforced his case by mapping out the
area occupied by the concept *oikeion* in the Peripatos but
established its connexion with κατὰ φύσιν in Aristotle and with
the τὰ κατὰ φύσιν of his successor.[93] He also pointed to evidence
of the same kind of biological approach to ethical problems as
that involved in the doctrine of *oikeiosis*: in the first place, the
words 'from the moment of birth', in the repeated declaration
of Chrysippus, which Plutarch found so tiresome, were no less
frequent in Aristotle himself,[94] while the first chapter of Book
VIII of the *Historia Animalium*—which Dirlmeier attributed to
Theophrastus rather than to his teacher—not only maintained
a much closer connexion between the psychology of animals
and that of humans than could be found elsewhere in Aristotle,
but also made use of children, the observation of whose behaviour was said to reveal traces of their future dispositions as
adults.[95] This emphasis on children was more than equalled by
a unique passage in the *Magna Moralia*, which again pointed to
their behaviour as evidence that the decisive factor in morality
was emotion rather than reason, the 'irrational impulses' (*hormai*,
the standard term of the Stoa) towards goodness which they
showed prior to the development of *logos*.[96] The upgrading of
animals, on the other hand, could be explained in terms of a
fragment of Theophrastus to which attention had already been
drawn by von Arnim. Here it is stated that all men are *oikeioi*
and akin to one another and also, in a lesser degree, to the
animals. This kinship with animals is based on the kinship or
similarity (*oikeiotēs*) of animal and human physiology and even
more on that of their psychology.[97] The fragment is quoted by
Porphyry, who does not indicate where the quotation ends, but
the text goes on shortly afterwards to argue that *oikeiosis*—in the
Stoic sense—should not be restricted to mankind and that only
if it is extended to animals can true justice be guaranteed.[98]

Finally, Dirlmeier was able to produce one certain instance of this latter word in Theophrastus, who said that the bee has a kind of *oikeiosis* to the oak-tree.[99] While therefore modifying the position of von Arnim on a number of points—he recognised the presence of neo-Peripatetic elements in the summary of Arius and, more important, denied that anything could be known about the doctrine of *oikeiosis* in the Stoa before the time of Chrysippus[100]—he was no less convinced that it was being promulgated elsewhere in Athens well before this time.

Impressive as these arguments were, when taken cumulatively, they were met by an authoritative counter-analysis by Pohlenz three years later in a survey of the entire evidence which while it has been ignored, has scarcely been challenged, except on points of detail, from 1940 to the present day.[101] The effect of this analysis was to align the position adopted by von Arnim and Dirlmeier with that taken by Antiochus of Ascalon some two thousand years earlier. Antiochus himself was a pupil of the sceptic Carneades, who had taken it upon himself to survey not merely all prevailing ethical systems, but all possible ones, and had concluded that these could be divided into three classes. All philosophers engaged in the pursuit of the highest good were, in his view, agreed as to the question that should be asked: it was only their answers that were different. Practically all of them admitted, in the words of Cicero, that 'the object with which Prudence is occupied and the end which it desires to attain must be something intimately adapted to nature; it must be of such a kind as spontaneously to arouse and elicit a psychological impulse—what the Greeks call *horme*'. The only question was the identity of this object, 'what it is that from the first moment of our existence has this effect and is naturally the object of impulse,' and there could be only three answers: either pleasure, or the avoidance of pain, or what they called *prima secundum naturam*.[102] In adopting this classification, Carneades was attributing to all his predecessors (and to all possible successors) a number of related assumptions which properly belong to his chief opponents, the Stoics, as is shown by the totalising value given to nature, by the characteristically Stoic 'impulse' and by the unquestioned assumption of a total continuity in motivation from one end of a human life to the other. It is in fact assumed here that the theme of moral philosophy is *oikeiosis*. Carneades' purpose in taking over this schema was largely polemical, but there is no sign that it was consciously dishonest, and the same is true of his successor Antiochus, who had more positive ends in adopting it and was anxious in the construction of his own philosophical system to incorporate the most worthwhile features from all those of his predecessors. He was, however, still unable to gain access to the esoteric writings of Aristotle; but Carneades had already indicated how the deficiency could be supplied by saying that the only difference between the Peripatos and the Stoa was one of terminology, not of doctrine: *non rerum, sed nominum*. Consequently Antiochus, in reconstructing the philosophy of Aristotle, the *institutum veterum* 'also used by the Stoics,' had nothing with which to fill the gap but *oikeiosis*, and this he also attributed to Plato's successors in the Academy, Xenocrates and Polemon.[103] It must therefore be Antiochus from whom *oikeiosis* has found its way into Arius' account of Peripatetic ethics—though not directly, since an intermediary is indicated by the close relation of other parts of this compendium to the then recently rediscovered *Nicomachaean Ethics*; and Cicero's Antiochus is explicit in rejecting Theophrastus owing to the undue importance which his writings attached to luck as a factor in happiness.[104] Finally, no sound argument can be drawn from the relatively little that Arius' Stoic compendium has to say about *oikeiosis*, since it is so uncertain, in Pohlenz's view, who was responsible for the omission. And while Theophrastus' doctrine of *oikeiotes* does to some extent pre-figure the Stoic theory of *oikeiosis*, there is nothing that anticipates *oikeiosis* towards oneself.[105]

In 1956 what might appear to be broadly similar conclusions were reached in a further survey of the evidence by C. O. Brink.[106] While questioning the sharpness of the line drawn by Pohlenz between *oikeiotes* as the objective fact of kinship and the subjective element in Stoic *oikeiosis*,[107] he agreed that what Theophrastus said about the bee and the oak-tree simply denoted affinity and had nothing to do with the Stoic doctrine.[108] Against this, however, he was inclined to accept the historicity of Zeno's connexion with Polemon and in particular the positive contribution made by the latter to the Stoic concept of Nature

and living in accordance with Nature, Zeno's own version of
this being primarily a response to a problem formulated in the
Academy.[109] There are, however, two larger issues, on both of
which the position adopted is a long way removed from that of
Pohlenz: in the first place, it is left an open question whether
the argument from *oikeiosis* was formulated at all before Chrysippus, and secondly, this argument is presented as essentially
subordinate to the problem of the natural. The really fundamental principles of Stoicism, it is maintained, can be stated
without recourse to *oikeiosis*, and the argument from *oikeiosis* 'is
not identical with the fundamental Zenonian axiom; it is no
more than a mode of arguing this axiom.'[110]

An unfavourable verdict as to the value of property whose
ownership is disputed, suggesting as it does that there are more
interesting cases to be conducted elsewhere, is unlikely to
satisfy either claimant even when an award is made. In this
instance, however, the verdict provides an opportunity both to
reassess the general importance of *oikeiosis* in Stoic thinking and
to abandon the strictly lexicographical approach to the question
of its antecedents. There is no evidence that Theophrastus
elevated *oikeiotes* into a general principle of conduct or applied
it to any question but the strictly limited one of animal sacrifice
in religious offerings, and the principle itself was already traditional among the Pythagoreans, who acted on it a good deal
more decisively.[111] More generally, not all instances of a word
so versatile as *oikeion* are likely to have much relevance to the
problem, and Aristotle's description of a certain kind of pleasure
as *oikeion* to a certain activity has less light to throw on *oikeiosis*
than does his discussion of the question whether a man can be
described as his own friend—which is conducted in different
terms.[112] However, it is not by any means certain that Zeno or
Chrysippus knew this discussion, and there is something to be
said for a transfer of attention from the Peripatos to the line
which goes back through the Cynics to the ideas topical in
Socratic circles earlier in the century.[113] The formula τὸ τὰ
αὑτοῦ πράττειν, which can have a more positive sense than
merely minding one's own business and not interfering in other
people's, appears to have occupied an important place in the
thinking of Antisthenes, who not only said that all wickedness

(or perhaps vulgarity) was to be regarded as 'foreign'—in a
sense closely parallel to that of the word *allotrion* in the Stoa—
but is credited with a statement repeated almost verbatim by
Chrysippus: to the wise man, nothing is foreign or impossible to
deal with.[114] In itself, the assimilation of *oikeion* to *agathon*, and
of *allotrion* to *kakon*, is nothing surprising and can be paralleled
among the Atomists: Epicurus uses the first two as synonyms,
both directly subsumed under Nature.[115] More significant is the
process of discovery implied, at least potentially, in τὸ τὰ αὑτοῦ
πράττειν, the identification and execution of one's real business in life, which points unmistakeably back to what Socrates
himself had urged upon everyone, *epimeleia*, concern for oneself,
for *arete* and for the perfecting of the *psyche*.[116] The question of
actual influence is no longer accessible, but the prestige of
Socrates among the Cynics amounted to more than mere
affectation, and it is hard to believe that the Stoic paradox about
the man who actually attains to wisdom without noticing it has
no connexion with the answer brought back by Chaerephon
from Delphi.[117] As it happens, the word *epimeleia* is used by
Zeno—and referred to a classic province of *oikeiosis*, the parts of
one's body—in one of the few texts whose authenticity is
reasonably certain;[118] and whatever value is placed on evidence
of this kind, the logical connexion is clear. It takes little more
than a heightened emphasis on the spontaneity of human
behaviour to convert *epimeleia* from something which could be
misdirected or even virtually inoperative into a universal disposition with a constant object.

The idea plays little part in the thinking of Plato, who also
effectively rejected the use of *oikeion* and *allotrion* as concepts, but
a brief consideration of his motives in doing so, while not
directly relevant to the question of influence, does have some
light to throw on their function in the Stoic system. In the *Lysis*,
a number of possible candidates for the real identity of that
which is *philon*, the object of friendship, are investigated. Both
to homoion, 'the like', and its opposite the unlike fail, as it turns
out, to meet the necessary requirements. At this stage, a third
possibility, that which is *oikeion*, comes up for scrutiny, and is
within a few lines given two senses so sharply distinct—without
the dialogue's making the distinction in any way explicit—that

K   L.P.S.

it is hard to believe Plato was unaware of the contradiction. One moment it is suggested that the object with which friendship is formed implies a deficiency in the subject and can therefore be defined as 'that in which one is deficient'—which Socrates identifies as 'that which is *oikeion*'; almost immediately after this, the adjective is used in a sense hardly distinguishable from that of similarity, a role already occupied earlier in the dialogue by *homoion*.[119] At the end the conclusion is reached that the problem as to the object of friendship is insoluble unless what is *homoion* can be shown to differ from what is *oikeion*, and finally this possibility is in turn thrown out by means of an exceptionally rapid display of logic-chopping with no apparent purpose beyond establishing the regulation uncertainty on all counts which in this case nothing but the requirements of literary form can be said to demand.[120]

It seems clear that Plato is anxious to discredit the idea, as he is in two further dialogues where it is brought in only to be dismissed as perhaps fashionable but contributing nothing new to the content of the discussion.[121] Why it should need discrediting is not altogether clear; it has been suggested that Plato has Aristippus in view,[122] but two further aspects of the word are worth further consideration. In the first place, *oikeion* is not a universalist term and would afford a dangerously large area to subjectivism of the kind associated with Protagoras: there is no formal reason why what is *oikeion* for one man should be so to his neighbour, and the idea could thus point to a thoroughgoing moral relativism. Secondly, it can be brought into relation with Plato's theory of knowledge. A fragment of Plutarch lists a number of solutions adopted by subsequent philosophers to the problem stated in Plato's *Meno*: how can one seek to find either what one knows or what one does not know? In the case of the Stoics, according to Plutarch, the answer was provided by the *ennoiai*.[123] It could, however, equally be claimed that at least the preliminary stages of this task are carried out by the concept *oikeion*, what is familiar, and that one of the main functions of this concept is to base perception and hence also human knowledge on recognition—the factor which Herder's essay on the origin of language represents as virtually co-extensive with that of speech:

Man demonstrates reflection when, emerging from the nebulous
dream of images flitting past his senses, he can concentrate on a
point of wakefulness, dwell voluntarily on one image, observe it
calmly and lucidly, and distinguish characteristics proving that this
and no other is the object. He demonstrates reflection when he not
only knows all attributes vividly and clearly, but can *recognize* one
or more distinguishing attributes: the first act of this recognition
yields a clear concept. . . . With it human speech was invented.[124]

The importance of this factor has perhaps not received
sufficient emphasis in accounts of the Stoa. At a different level,
and in sources which are admittedly not likely to go back
further than Panaetius or Posidonius, it becomes one of the
criteria in establishing the animal hierarchy, starting with such
creatures as are unable to tell members of their own species
apart and moving on firstly to the kind of animals that can
distinguish one another, even when they are not individually
distinguishable to a human observer, and lastly to Man himself,
whose institutions and whole existence depend for their maintenance on his ability to identify his fellow-men at sight.[125]
Even before these texts, however, recognition is clearly implied
when Stoic authors point to the way in which the newly born,
infants and animals, make for and accept their sources of
nourishment,[126] and more clearly still in the natural 'alienation'
shown by animals towards potential dangers such as more fero-
cious species which they have never previously encountered.[127]
At the human level, even Zeno's criterion for a satisfactory
phantasia, 'what it would not look like if it came from something
non-existent,' despite its apparent appeal to familiarity with the
appearance of non-existent objects, has recognition as its real
theme.[128] No other philosophical system in antiquity, while
consistently describing human perfection in terms of *savoir*, the
epistēmē of the wise man, at the same time derived it so consistently from *connaissance*, the direct acquaintance whose ground
is recognition.

The word *oikeiosis* cannot be directly attested with chapter
and verse of the doubtful remains of Zeno's writings. There is,
however, some evidence that the terminology was used by his
pupil Ariston, who despite heresy in other fields declared himself content with this part of his teacher's doctrine.[129] And the

foundations of the idea are so deeply laid in Stoic thinking that it is hardly possible to discern what the inheritance of Chrysippus would have amounted to without it. For while Hierocles can be justified, in his own terms, in presenting *oikeiosis* as attendant on consciousness, rather than prior to it, for Chrysippus the road to consciousness is prepared at lower levels of creation by a kind of rudimentary *oikeiosis* whose business is in plants carried out by Nature itself, while in animals even consciousness is stated to be a direct concern of the conscious subject.[130] *Oikeiosis* and *allotriōsis* are, as this statement confirms, the conditions without which consciousness could not arise. How far it would be legitimate to regard the *logos* of Stoic man as itself an extension of *oikeiosis* may be suggested by Konrad Lorenz's formulation of what Man has gained with the loss of those instinctual structures which remain fixed and unbroken in other species, and what in Man has entered in to take their place. It is, in his words, 'that conversational, questioning relationship with the environment, that "getting on good terms" (*Sich-ins-Einvernehmen-Setzen*) with external reality which is even contained in the etymology of the word *Vernunft*'.[131]

It is no accident that this language should co-incide so closely with that used by the Stoics. The relationship of *logos* to *horme* in their thinking points to the same kind of conclusions as those reached by the study of animal behaviour in the present century, and *oikeiosis* itself represents more than a casual anticipation of what has been a crucial factor in the rise of this discipline, the notion of the *Umwelt* or subjective environment of animals.[132] The Stoics' observations in this area also concentrated on behaviour which makes sense only in terms of a complex of perceptions, and if *oikeiosis* failed to provide an actual apparatus for the further investigation of these problems it did clearly demarcate the problems and not just sentimentalise the workings of nature.[133] The principle itself, moreover, was closely coherent with the Stoic view of less complex phenomena, and in conclusion, *oikeiosis* can be seen as corresponding to a more elementary force at work in inorganic matter. Recent controversy on this subject has tended to isolate Stoic ethics from other aspects of their thinking, but Nature is not a specifically ethical term, and at the lowest level of organisation to be found in the physical world, the identity of inanimate objects was not, as it had been for Plato, guaranteed once and for all by their participation in a changeless form, but actively maintained by the continual process of 'tensional movement' that took place in the *pneuma*, 'constantly going forth and returning' or, as another writer puts it, 'turning back on itself'.[134] *Oikeiosis* to oneself is the same process raised to the level of consciousness and alone capable of raising consciousness to the higher level of moral wisdom.

NOTES

1. Hdt. IV, 148, 1; Thuc. I, 36, 1, III, 65, 3; Aen. Tact. XXIV, 5; Plato *Legg.* 843e 1, cf. id. *Soph.* 223b 1.

2. τῶν δὲ οἰκείωσιν ἐποιοῦντο Thuc. IV, 128, 4.

3. Hdt. I, 94, 3, cf. I, 4, 4; III, 2, 1.

4. τοῖς ᾠκειωμένοις φυσιολογίᾳ Epicur. *Ep. Hdt.* 37; cf. also Plato *Parm.* 128a 5, *Prot.* 326b 2, *Ep.* III 317e 3 (οἰκειωσάμενον), *Ep.* VII 330a 7, *Legg.* 738d 7; [Dem.] LXI, 4. On the use of συνοικειοῦσθαι in Aristotle cf. below, n. 112.

5. Thuc. VIII, 73, 4.

6. The Stoic construction οἰκειοῦσθαι πρός τι is not attested earlier, unless the Cyrenaic proof that ἡδονή is the *telos* (Diog. Laert. II 88 = fr. 178 Mannh. τὸ ἀπροαιρέτως ἡμᾶς ἐκ παίδων ᾠκειῶσθαι πρὸς αὐτήν) is to be taken as direct quotation (so R. Philippson, 'Das "Erste Naturgemässe",' *Philologus* lxxxvii (1932) 454–5). But the language here is unlikely to be first-generation and may well be that of Panaetius, cf. ibid. 86–7 (=fr. 49 van Str.). Epicurus' use of the adjective οἰκεῖον (Philippson, p. 455) does not presuppose οἰκειοῦσθαι, and it is hard to see what purpose would have been served by adopting the verb unless the Stoics were already using it. Cf. below, n. 89.

7. So also Plut. *Comm. not.* 1060c (*SVF* III 146), cf. Alex. Aphr. *De an.* (*CAG* suppl. II 1) p. 163, 24–31.

8. Diog. Laert. VII, 85 (*SVF* III 178), cf. below, nn. 77, 130. The authenticity of the term πρῶτον οἰκεῖον (Alex. Aphr. *De an.* p. 150, 20ff., cf. Stob. II. 47, 12W.; Hierocles, 'Ἠθ. στοιχ. (below, n. 18) I, 2ff.) has been disputed, Philippson, loc. cit., pp. 463–4, cf. Pohlenz, *Grundfragen* p. 14, n. 1; the text of H. S. Long, ii, p. 333, separates the words with a comma, but this is deleted in the second impression (1966). It is not certain, however, that a strictly temporal, rather than logical, priority is denoted, cf. Plato *Lys.* 219c7 ἐκεῖνο ὅ ἐστι πρῶτον φίλον, Epicur. *Ep. Menoec.* 129 πρῶτον ἀγαθόν. The Stoics themselves contrast πρῶτα with κατὰ μετοχήν, Stob. II 82, 12W. (*SVF* III 141), and πρῶται with ὑποτεταγμέναι ἀρεταί, Diog. Laert. VII 92–3 (*SVF* III 265).

9. Ibid. 86 τεχνίτης γὰρ οὗτος ἐπιγίνεται τῆς ὁρμῆς.

10. E.g. Aquinas, *Comm. in Mag. Petr. Lomb.* lib. II, dist. 20, art. 2 ad 5: dicendum quod alia animalia non prosequuntur conveniens et fugiunt nocivum per rationis deliberationem, sed per naturalem instinctum aestimativae virtutis: et talis

naturalis instinctus est etiam in pueris; unde etiam mamillas accipiunt, et alia eis convenientia, etiam sine hoc quod ab aliis doceantur, cf. sent. II dist. 25, qu. 1, art. 1 ad 7 and for mankind *Summa c. gent.* III, 117. For the persistence of Stoic language cf. e.g. Condillac, *Traité des animaux* (Amsterdam 1755) p. 10 (arguing, like the Stoics' opponents in the Academy, for the rationality of animals): 'les bêtes veillent elles-mêmes à leur conservation; elles se meuvent à leur gré; elles saisissent ce qui leur est propre, rejettent, évitent, ce qui est contraire; les mêmes sens qui reglent nos actions paroissent regler les leurs.'

11. Cic. *Div.* I, 34; *Tusc.* I, 26.

12. For the πλεονάζουσα ὁρμή cf. Galen *De Plac.* IV 2, pp. 338–41 M. (V, 368–370K.) =*SVF* III 462; I. G. Kidd, Chapter IX p. 204.

13. Aetius, *Plac.* IV 11 (Diels, *Dox. graec.* p. 400) =*SVF* II 83; Diog. Laert. VII 52 (*SVF* II 87); Aetius, *Plac.* v 23, 1 (Diels, *Dox. graec.* p. 434) =*SVF* II 764; schol. Plato *Alc. I* p. 121E (*SVF* I 149); Iambl. ap. Stob. I 317, 21W. =*SVF* II 835.

14. *Collatione rationis* Cic. *Fin.* III 33 (*SVF* III 72), cf. Sen. *Ep. mor.* 120, 4: nobis videtur observatio collegisse et rerum saepe factarum inter se conlatio; per analogian nostri intellectum et honestum et bonum iudicant. In Diog. Laert. VII 53 (*SVF* II 87) the 'natural' contribution to this process (φυσικῶς δὲ νοεῖται δίκαιόν τι καὶ ἀγαθόν) is left indefinite but probably corresponds to the naturally evaluative quality of human consciousness, cf. Plut. *Comm. not.* 1070C and Pohlenz, *Grundfragen*, pp. 92–3. [cf. F. H. Sandbach, Chapter II, pp. 33–4, Ed.].

15. Cic. *Fin.* III 21 (*SVF* III 188), cf. Galen *De Plac.* v 5 p. 439, 2 M (V, 460 K.) = *SVF* III 229a ὁ δὲ Χρύσιππος . . . φάμενος ἡμᾶς ᾠκειῶσθαι πρὸς μόνον τὸ καλόν.

16. Cic. *Fin.* III 34 (*SVF* III 72), cf. Gell. XII 5, 7 (*SVF* III 181).

17. Cf. Plut. *Stoic. rep.* 1038C (*SVF* II 724) ἡ γὰρ οἰκείωσις αἴσθησις ἔοικε τοῦ οἰκείου καὶ ἀντίληψις εἶναι.

18. Sen. *Ep. mor.* 121, 1; von Arnim *Hierokles, Ethische Elementarlehre*, pp. vii–xi.

19. Sen. *Ep. mor.* 121, 12 necesse est enim id sentiant per quod alia quoque sentiunt, Hierocl. VI 1ff. καθόλου γ(ὰρ) ο[ὐ σ]υντε|λε[ῖται] τ(ῶν) ἐκτός τινος [ἀντ]ίληψις δίχα τ(ῆς) ἑ|αυ[τ(ῶν) αἰ]σθήσεως. Cf. Cic. *Fin.* III 16 (*SVF* III 182); Tertull. *De carne Christi* 12 (*SVF* II 845).

20. Sext. *Adv. math.* VII 191.

21. VI 3ff. μ(ετὰ) γ(ὰρ) [τ(ῆς)] τοῦ λευκοῦ φέρε εἰπεῖν | [αἰσθ]ήσεως κ(αὶ) ἑαυτ(ῶν) αἰσθανόμεθα λευκ(αι)νομ(έν)ω(ν) κ(αὶ) μ(ετὰ) <τῆς> | τοῦ γλυκέως γλυκαζομ(έν)ω(ν) κ(αὶ) μ(ετὰ) τ(ῆς) τοῦ θερμοῦ | θερμαινομ(έν)ω(ν) κἀπὶ τ(ῶν) ἄλλ(ων) τἀνάλογον.

22. IV, 44–52 τ(ε)ινομ(έν)η γ(ὰρ) ἔ|ξω ἡ ψυχ[ὴ μ(ετ')] ἀφέσεως [πρ(οσ)βάλ]λει πᾶσι τ(οῦ) σώματος τ(οῖς) | μέρεσιν, ἐ[πε]ιδὴ κ(αὶ) κέκραται πᾶσι, πρ(οσ)βάλλου|σα δ(ὲ) ἀν[τι]πρ(οσ)[βάλλ]εται· ἀντιβατικὸν γ(ὰρ) κ(αὶ) τὸ σῶμα, | [κ]αθάπ[ερ] κ(αὶ) [ἡ] ψυχή· κ(αὶ) τὸ πάθος συνερειστικ[ὸν] | ὁμοῦ κ(αὶ) ἀντερειστικὸν ἀ(πο)τελεῖται. κ[(αὶ) ἀπὸ τ(ῶν) ἀκροτά]|τ(ων) μερῶ(ν) εἴσω νε[ῦο]ν ἐ(πὶ) τ(ὴν) ἡγεμονίαν τ[ὸ τοῦ πά]|θους σ[ημ(εῖον)] ἀναφέρ[ετ]αι, ὡς ἀντίληψιν γίνεσθαι | μερῶ(ν) [ἀ]πά[ν]τ(ων) τ(ὸν) τ[ε τ]οῦ σώματος κ(αὶ) τ(ῶν) τ(ῆς) ψυχῆς. The reading σημεῖον is that of Pohlenz, *Gött. Gel. Anz.* 168. Jahrg. (1906) p. 918. For the terminology cf. ἀντερείδει Plut. *De fac.* 924D (*SVF* II 646); ἐπέρεισις Alex. Aphr. *De an.* p. 132, 32 (*SVF* II 432), Procl. *In Parm.* v p. 74 Cousin (*SVF* II 343).

23. Von Arnim, *Hierokles*, pp. xxvi–xxviii.

24. Aetius *Plac.* IV 8, 7 (Diels *Dox. graec.* p. 395, 16 =Stob. I 473, 17W., *SVF* II 852), cf. the (Cyrenaic) *tactus interior* or *intumus* of Cic. *Acad. prior.* xx 76.

25. Plut. *De prof. in virt.* 82F (*SVF* I 234), cf. tit. 75A. For the reading συναίσθησιν in Diog. Laert. VII 85 (below, n. 77) cf. Hierocl. II 3, Stob. III 56, Stob. II 47, 13W. (Pohlenz, *Die Stoa* ii, p. 63, so already Dyroff, *Die Ethik der alten Stoa,* p. 37, n. 3); συνείδησιν MSS and *SVF* III 178, ed. H. S. Long, ii p. 333.

26. Cf. below, n. 130.

27. Sen. *Ep. mor.* 121, 8; Hierocl. VII, 5–10 ταυτῆι ἄ[ρ]α δοκεῖ μοι κ(αὶ) τὰ νεαρὰ | παι[δά]ρια μὴ ῥα[ι]δίως φέρειν κ(ατα)[κ]λ(ε)ιόμ(εν)α ζοφεροῖς οἴ|κοις κ(αὶ) πάσ(ης) φων(ῆς) ἀμετόχοις. ἐντ(ε)ίνοντα γ(ὰρ) τὰ αἰσθητή|ρια κ(αὶ) μηδὲν μήτ' ἀκοῦσαι μήτ' ἰδ[ε]ῖν δυνάμ(εν)α φαντασί|αν ἀναιρέσεως αὐτ(ῶν) λαμβά[νει κ(αὶ)] δ(ιὰ) τοῦτο δυσανα[σ]χε|τεῖ.

28. Sen. *Ep. mor.* 121, 6, 13; Hierocl. I, 51–III, 19.

29. Hierocl. III, 19–52; Sen. Ep. mor. 121, 19.

30. Sen. *Ep. mor.* 121, 14–16.

31. Cic. *Fin.* III 16ff., cf. Madvig, *De finibus*, ed. 3, pp. 830–1; Hirzel, *Untersuchungen* ii (Leipzig 1882) pp. 567–80; von Arnim, *SVF* vol. I, p. xxix; Philippson, *Berl. philol. Wochenschr.* Jahrg. 33 (1913) col. 609; Pohlenz, *Grundfragen*, p. 2. Schäfer, *Frühmittelstoisches System*, pp. 276–93, argues for Antipater as the source.

32. Cf. esp. III 23 (*SVF* III 186) sed quemadmodum saepe fit, ut is qui commendatus sit alicui, pluris eum faciat, cui commendatus sit, quam illum, a quo sit; sic minime mirum est, primo nos sapientiae commendari ab initiis naturae, post autem ipsam sapientiam nobis cariorem fieri, quam illa sunt, a quibus ad hanc venerimus.

33. Ibid. III 17 (*SVF* III 189).

34. Plato *Prot.* 325c 4ff.

35. Arist. *EN* 1111a 25, cf. 1144b 8, 1152b 19, 1153a 27ff.; below, p. 133.

36. Plut. *Comm. not.* 1063A (*SVF* III 539).

37. Diog. Laert. VII 129 (*SVF* III 367), so already Arist. *EN* 1161b 1.

38. Alex. Aphr. *Quaest.* IV 3 (*CAG* suppl. II 2) p. 121, 32 (*SVF* III 537).

39. Cic. *Fin.* III 62–8, partly in *SVF* III 340–2.

40. Cf. esp. Praechter, 'Zum Platoniker Gaios,' *Hermes* li (1916) 517–29; Baldry, *The Unity of Mankind in Greek Thought*, pp. 177–94; Cole, *Democritus and the Sources of Greek Anthropology*, pp. 136–40.

41. *Fin.* III 63, cf. Terence *Heauton timor.* 77 homo sum: humani nil a me alienum puto.

42. The stork was proverbial for looking after its parents in their old age, cf. Ar. *Av.* 1355ff., Soph. *El.* 1058 and schol.; Philo, *De animalibus* (Opera omnia [ed. C. E. Richter], viii (Leipzig 1830) pp. 101–44), § 61 (p. 156 Aucher), Plut. *Soll. an.* 962E.

43. Cf. Stob. II 121, 3ff. W.; Pohlenz, *Grundfragen*, p. 34.

44. Porph. *Abst.* III 19 (p. 209, 4 Nauck) =*SVF* I 197 καὶ γὰρ οἰκειώσεως πάσης καὶ ἀλλοτριώσεως ἀρχὴ τὸ αἰσθάνεσθαι. τὴν δὲ οἰκείωσιν ἀρχὴν τίθενται δικαιοσύνης οἱ ἀπὸ Ζήνωνος.

45. Chrysippus ap. Plut. *Stoic. rep.* 1038B (*SVF* III 179) οἰκειούμεθα πρὸς αὐτοὺς εὐθὺς γενόμενοι καὶ τὰ μέρη καὶ τὰ ἔκγονα τὰ ἑαυτῶν.

46. Plut. *Soll. an.* 962A τὴν γοῦν πρὸς τὰ ἔγγονα φιλοστοργίαν ἀρχὴν μὲν ἡμῖν κοινωνίας καὶ δικαιοσύνης, cf. id. *De amore prolis* 495B, where the parental affection given by Nature to animals is described as ἀτελὲς καὶ οὐ διαρκὲς πρὸς δικαιοσύνην. The word quoted from Erasistratus at 495C virtually proves that he is not the source.

47. *Stoic. rep.* 1038B (*SVF* II 724) ἐν δὲ τῷ πρώτῳ περὶ Δικαιοσύνης καὶ τὰ θηρία φησὶ συμμέτρως τῇ χρείᾳ τῶν ἐκγόνων ᾠκειῶσθαι πρὸς αὐτά.

48. Plut. *Soll. an.* 980AB, cf. Chrysippus ap. Athen. III 89D; Cic. *ND* II 123–4; Philo *De animal.* §§ 60, 93 (pp. 155, 169 Aucher) =*SVF* II 728–30.

49. Cic. *Fin.* V 65.

50. Stob. II 143, 11–14W.

`51. More generally, *oikeiosis* towards oneself must suggest an analogy with the concept of primary narcissism, 'the libidinal complement to the egoism of the instinct of self-preservation', first made public by Freud in 1914, cf. 'On Narcissism', Standard Edition, xiv (London 1957) pp. 73–102; *Introductory Lectures*, No. xxvi (ibid., xvi (1963) pp. 412–30), and the section added in 1915 to *Three Essays* vii (1953) p. 218; further discussion in Herbert Marcuse, *Eros and Civilization*,[2] (Boston 1966) pp. 22ff., 168–70. Antecedents apart, however, the hypothesis that narcissism might be a universal phase in the regular course of human development was first arrived at via the observation of extreme manifestations (and the variety of disorders in which these occurred); on the Stoic side, there is no sign that exaggerated φιλαυτία provided a similar starting-point, but Hierocles (vII 16ff.) observes that *oikeiosis* persists even in pathological conditions (κ[ἀν τ(οῖς)|π(αρὰ)φ[ύ]σ-ι[ν]) enabling a man to put up with himself despite the most unsightly or foul-smelling diseases, even when these are more than other people can bear to confront, vII 19 τ(ὴν) κ(ατ)αρχήν | γε [ἡ] πρ(ὸς) [ἑα]υτοὖ[s οἰκεί]ωσ[ις παρέ]χει, δι᾽ ἣν οἰστὸς (ἐστιν) ἕ|κα[σ]τος ἑ[αυτ]ῷ[ι, κἂ]ν ἄλ[λοις ἀ]φόρητος ἦι. ἕλκη γο(ῦν) | τὰ δυ[σο]σμότα[τ]α κ(αὶ) πρ(ὸς) τ(ὴν) [ὄψιν] ἀπηνέστατα φέρο|μ(εν) ἑα[υ]τ(ῶν) [κ(αὶ)] τ(ὴν) ἄ[λ]λην ἀηδ[ία]ν ὑπὸ τ(ῆς) φιλαυτίας ἐ(πι)|[σ]κοτουμ(έν)ην.

52. Stob. II 120, 8–20W.

53. Among other inconsistencies in this account, it may be noted that *oikeiosis* to oneself, the fact of which is postulated at 118, 11–14, is at 122, 16–18 inferred back from *oikeiosis* towards other people.

54. Cic. *Off.* I 12; 53–4. Cf. also Alex. Aphr. *De an.* p. 162, 18ff.; Apul. *De Platone* II 2 p. 105, 6–11 Thomas, with the corrections of Praechter, *Hermes* li (1916) 517–18, 522–3, who shows that *intimatum* represents the Greek ᾠκειωμένον. [For a different approach to the natural development of social feeling, see Gerard Watson, Chapter X, pp. 228ff. Ed.]

55. Stob. IV 671ff. Hense; for the other capita cf. ibid. I p. 63, II 181W.; III 730ff., IV 502, 603, 640, 660ff. and V 696H.; Praechter, *Hierokles der Stoiker* pp. 7ff.; Philippson, *Rh. Mus.* lxxxii (1937) 97–114, esp. 108–9.

56. IV 672, 16–18 ἀφαιρήσεται μὲν γάρ τι τῆς εὐνοίας τὸ καθ᾽ αἷμα διάστημα πλέον ὄν· ἡμῖν δ᾽ ὅμως σπουδαστέα περὶ τὴν ἐξομοίωσιν, cf. ibid. 664, 9-10 μέγας δὲ βοηθὸς ὁ λόγος, καὶ τοὺς ὀθνείους καὶ μηδὲν καθ᾽ αἷμα προσήκοντας ἐξιδιούμενος.

57. IV 673, 2–11.

58. γονεῖς ἀδελφοὶ γυνὴ παῖδες 671, 18.

59. Hierocl. IX, 3ff. ἡ μ(ὲν) πρ(ὸς) ἑαυτὸ εὐνοητ[ική, στερ]|κτ[ι]κ[ὴ δὲ ἡ συγ]γεν[ι]κ[ή]· καλεῖται γ(ὰρ) [......] | πολλ[ο]ῖς [ὀνόμασ]ιν, ἡ δ(ὲ) πρ(ὸς) τὰ ἐκτὸς χ[ρήματα αἱ]|ρετι[κ]ή. καθάπερ [ο(ὖν)] στε[ρ]κτικῶς μ(ὲν) κ[....οἱ]κε[ι]ούμεθα τοῖς τέκνοις, αἱρετικ[ῶς] δ(ὲ) [τοῖς ἐκ]τὸ]ς χρήμασιν, οὖ[τ]ω κτλ. Praechter, *Gött. Gel. Anz.* 171 Jahrg. (1909) p. 545, suggests κ(αὶ) γ(ὰρ) ἡ μ(ὲν) (ἐστι) κ[ηδεμονική] at IX, 12, cf. *Anon. comm. Plato Tht.* (below, n. 65) where *oikeiosis* to oneself and to other people is said to be κηδεμονική, not αἱρετική, vII 28–vIII 6.

60. Hierocl. XI 14–21.

61. Arist. fr. 321 R.=Athen. vII 309A, cf. *HA* 610b 1. συναγελάζεσθαι in Polybius' history of culture (vI 5, 7) is the response to a specific situation, rather than a permanent tendency.

62. Stob. II 109, 16 (*SVF* III 686), cf. ibid. 120, 14 (Peripatetics); Epictet. *Diss.* III 13, 5; IV 5, 10, cf. also Iambl. *Protr.* p. 123, 12 Pist.

63. Plut. *Soll. an.* 977C, 979F; Babrias 124, 9; Eust. 1126, 29 ad *Il.* xvii, 755 (συναγελαστικά), cf. Basil. *Homil. in Ps. XIV* i, 6 (*PG* xxix 261C Migne) ἐπὶ τὸ κοινωνικόν, καὶ φιλάλληλον, καὶ τῇ φύσει οἰκεῖον, ὁ λόγος ἡμᾶς προκαλεῖται. πολιτικὸν γὰρ ζῷον καὶ συναγελαστικὸν ὁ ἄνθρωπος, Nemes. *Nat. hom.* c. 1 p. 52 Matth. (*PG*

xl 521A Migne). φιλαλληλία is one bright spot in the otherwise black picture given by Tzetzes of the herd-like existence of primitive mankind, schol. Hes. *OD* 42 (pp. 68–70 Gaisford (Demokr. 68 [55]B5 § 3 p. 137, 39; 138, 7 D–K), cf. ibid. schol. *OD* 115, 116, 118), to which Moschopulos adds δικαιοσύνη (schol. 111, 118 p. 114, 1; 117, 27 Gsf.). On the source cf. W. Spoerri, *Mus. Helv.* xiv (1957) 184 and Cole, *Democritus* p. 22 n. 16 and p. 152.

64. Epictet. *Diss.* III 24, 11 ἀνθρώπων φύσει πρὸς ἀλλήλους ᾠκειωμένων.

65. *Anonymer Kommentar zu Platons Theatet* (*Papyrus* 9782), hrsg. Diels und Schubart (Berlin 1905 (Berliner Klassikertexte, Heft II)).

66. Col. v, 22ff. cf. VI, 17ff.; for the Stoic doctrine of ἕξεις and διαθέσεις cf. Simplic. *In Cat.* p. 237, 25ff. (*SVF* II 393); Porph. *In Cat.* 137, 29ff. (*SVF* III 525); Diog. Laert. VII 101 (*SVF* III 92).

67. v, 34 παρὰ γὰ[ρ τὴν] | ἐνάργειάν ἐστιν [κ]α[ὶ] > | τὴν συναίσθησιν, cf. Plut. *Virt. mor.* 447A παρὰ τὴν ἐνάργειαν καὶ τὴν αἴσθησιν.

68. v, 36ff. ἡ > | μὲν γὰρ πρὸς ἑαυτὸν | οἰκείωσις, φυσική ἐστιν | καὶ ἄλογος, ἡ δὲ πρὸς | τοὺς πλησίον φυσικὴ | μὲν καὶ αὐτή, οὐ μέν|τοι ἄνευ λόγου.

69. VI, 3ff. οὐκ ἔστιν τοίνυν ἴση | ἡ ο[ἰ]κε[ί]ωσις πρὸς ἐ|αυτὸν [καὶ π]ρὸς ὀντιν-|οῦν, ὅπου μηδὲ πρὸς | τὰ [ἑ]αυτῶν μέρη ἐπ' ἴ|σης ᾠκε[ι]ώμεθα. οὐ γὰρ | ὁμοίως ἔχομεν πρὸς | ὀφ[θα]λμ[ὸ]ν κα[ὶ] δάκτυ|λον, ἵνα μὴ λέγω πρὸς | ὄνυχας [κ]αὶ τρίχας, ἐπεὶ | οὐδὲ πρὸς τὴν ἀποβο|λὴν αὐτῶν ὁμοίως > | ἠλλοτριώμ[εθ]α, ἀλλὰ | μᾶλλον κ[αὶ ἧτ]τον. The argument here put to a destructive use had in fact been employed by Zeno in advocating the concentration of ἐπιμέλεια on those persons most likely to be ὠφέλιμοι, A. Mai, *Scriptorum veterum nova collectio* ii (Rome 1827) p. xxvii n. 1 (*SVF* I 236) καὶ γὰρ καὶ τῶν μερῶν τοῦ σώματος ἐκείνων ἐπιμελούμεθα μᾶλλον, ἅπερ ὠφελιμώτερα ἑαυτοῖς πρὸς τὴν ὑπηρεσίαν νομίζομεν εἶναι. Cf. below, n. 118.

70. VI, 20ff. ἐλέγξου|σι δὲ τ[ούτους α]ἱ πε|ριστάσεις [ναυαγῶ]ν, ὅ > | που ἀνάγ[κη μό]νον > | σώζεσθαι τὸν ἕτε|ρον αὐτῶν.

71. Cic. *Off.* III 90.

72. Cic. *Rep.* III 20, 30 (Lactant. *Div. inst.* v 16, 9–10).

73. Cf. A.A. Long, Chapter VIII pp. 189ff.

74. Diog. Laert. VII 128 (*SVF* III 308).

75. Plut. *Stoic.rep.* 1041AB (*SVF* III 297); Procl. Diad. *In Plato Alc. I* 115A (p. 148, 20ff. Westerink) = *SVF* III 310; Stob. II 63, 22 W. (*SVF* III 280); Diog. Laert. VII 92 (*SVF* III 265).

76. Cf. esp. Antipater Περὶ γάμου Stob. IV 507, 6 H. (fr. 63 *SVF* III p. 254).

77. An equation of this kind is perhaps implied by Philippson, *Philologus* LXXXVII 455, and almost explicit in Pohlenz, *Grundfragen*, p. 9: both maintain that the distinction in Alex. Aphr. *De an.* p. 150, 28–33 (*SVF* III 183) between those Stoics who regarded 'the animal itself' as its πρῶτον οἰκεῖον and the subtler formulation of those who made σύστασις and τήρησις the object of οἰκείωσις (150, 30 οἱ δὲ χαριέστερον δοκοῦντες λέγειν αὐτῶν καὶ μᾶλλον διαρθροῦν περὶ τοῦδέ φασιν πρὸς τὴν σύστασιν καὶ τήρησιν ᾠκειῶσθαι εὐθὺς γενομένους ἡμᾶς τὴν ἡμῶν αὐτῶν) represents the refinement of Zeno's formula by Chrysippus. But this view is not consistent with Diog. Laert. VII 85 (*SVF* III 178; above, p. 116). Here the οἰκειοῦσθαι πρός construction undoubtedly has ἑαυτό as its object; σύστασις (and συναίσθησις) serve to identify the almost substantival πρῶτον οἰκεῖον, but the two propositions reinforce one another and no such contrast is implied. Only the 'prime impulse' (which is not synonymous with οἰκείωσις) is expressed in the strictly verbal form of a κατηγόρημα: τὴν δὲ πρώτην ὁρμήν φασι τὸ ζῷον ἴσχειν ἐπὶ τὸ τηρεῖν ἑαυτό, οἰκειούσης αὐτὸ τῆς φύσεως ἀπ' ἀρχῆς, καθά φησιν ὁ Χρύσιππος ἐν τῷ πρώτῳ Περὶ τελῶν, πρῶτον οἰκεῖον λέγων εἶναι παντὶ

ζώῳ τὴν αὐτοῦ σύστασιν καὶ τὴν ταύτης συναίσθησιν . . . . ἀπολείπεται τοίνυν λέγειν (τὴν φύσιν) συστησαμένη αὐτὸ οἰκειῶσαι πρὸς ἑαυτό. This is wholly compatible with Stob. II 88, 2ff. (*SVF* III 171) ἤδη δὲ ἄλλων μὲν εἶναι συγκαταθέσεις, ἐπ᾽ ἄλλο δὲ ὁρμάς· καὶ συγκαταθέσεις μὲν ἀξιώμασί τισιν, ὁρμὰς δὲ ἐπὶ κατηγορήματα, τὰ περιεχόμενά πως ἐν τοῖς ἀξιώμασιν, οἷς συγκαταθέσεις, but there is no evidence that for Chrysippus the object of *oikeiosis* (οἰκειοῦσθαι πρός τι) had to be a κατηγόρημα, cf. above nn. 15, 45, 47, and the real contrast is not that of the animal with its preservation but of the latter with mere gratification.

78. ἐπιβολὴν δὲ ὁρμὴν πρὸ ὁρμῆς Stob. II 88, 18 (*SVF* III 173), ἐπιβολὴ φιλοποιίας διὰ κάλλος ἐμφαινόμενον Diog. Laert. VII 113, 129 (*SVF* III 396, 716), cf. Stob. II 66, 13 (*SVF* III 717); 91, 15 (*SVF* III 395); 115, 1 (*SVF* III 650); Cic. *Tusc.* IV 72. Strictly, however, the common factor is φαντασία, cf. Plut. *Adv. Col.* 1122C τῇ ὁρμῇ φυσικῶς ἀγούσῃ πρὸς τὸ φαινόμενον οἰκεῖον . . . ἡ γὰρ πρᾶξις δυοῖν δεῖται, φαντασίας τοῦ οἰκείου καὶ πρὸς τὸ φανὲν οἰκεῖον ὁρμῆς. [For Posidonius' three *oikeioseis* corresponding to his three capacities in the human *psyche*, see I. G. Kidd, Chapter IX, p. 205. Ed.]

79. The Stoic use of ἐπιπλοκή to denote the involvement of men with one another and with the gods (but not animals) points to the same conclusion, Sext. *Adv. math.* IX 126, 131 (*SVF* III 370), cf. Stob. II 108, 22 (*SVF* III 630).

80. Plut. *Comm. not.* 1070A (*SVF* III 123), cf. 1060C (*SVF* III 146).

81. For similar ideas in Aristotle cf. esp. *Gen. an.* 753a 7–17, where the parental concern shown by different species (ἡ τῶν τέκνων αἴσθησις ἐπιμελητική) is measured primarily by its duration, *EN* 1162a 17–29 (τεκνοποιία) and *HA* 588b 30–589a 3.

82. τὸ μηδὲν ἐκ διεστηκότων ἀγαθὸν εἶναι κατ᾽ αὐτούς Stob. II 94, 24 (*SVF* III 98), cf. Sen. *Ep. mor.* 102, 7 (*SVF* III 160). Classification and examples of ἡνωμένα, συναπτόμενα and διεστῶτα in Sext. *Adv. math.* IX 78–81 (*SVF* II 1013), Plut. *Conjug. praec.* 142E (*SVF* II 366), Achilles *Isagog. in Arat.* 14 p. 41, 25 Maass (*SVF* II 368), cf. Philo *De aeternit. mundi* § 80, Plut. *Def. orac.* 426A (*SVF* II 367), Sen. *Nat. qu.* II 2, 1–4.

83. συνάπτεσθαι is used as synonymous with οἰκειοῦσθαι by Nemes. *Nat. hom.* c. 4 p. 153 M. (*PG* XL 616AB), but the stock examples of συναπτόμενα do not include human groups, and Sext. *Adv. math.* IX 80 makes no distinction between composite and discrete in this respect, ἐπὶ μὲν γὰρ τῶν ἐκ συναπτομένων ἢ διεστηκότων οὐ συμπάσχει τὰ μέρη ἀλλήλοις.

84. Plut. *Conjug. praec.*, loc. cit. (a marriage based on love and not just the (composite) profit motive or wanting children); M. Aur. IX 9, 2–3, cf. VII 13 οἷόν ἐστιν ἐν ἡνωμένοις τὰ μέλη τοῦ σώματος, τοῦτον ἔχει τὸν λόγον ἐν διεστῶσι τὰ λογικά. Critolaus in Philo *De aeternit. mundi* § 75 (*SVF* II 459, there attributed to Chrysippus) uses τὴν ἕνωσιν τῶν διεστηκότων to characterise the whole universe.

85. H. C. Baldry, 'Zeno's Ideal State,' *JHS* LXXIX (1959) 3–15; for Chrysippus cf. e.g. Diog. Laert. VII 121–2 (*SVF* III 355, 617) and Baldry, *Unity of Mankind*, pp. 164–6. [Gerard Watson suggests a relation between *oikeiosis* and the ideal association of Zeno's *Politeia*, Chapter X, p. 220. Ed.]

86. Chrysippus in Plut. *Stoic. rep.* 1050A (*SVF* II 937); Philo *De animal.* § 91 p. 168 Aucher (*SVF* II 733); id. *De Josepho* § 38 (*SVF* III 323).

87. Cic. *Fin.* III 66 (*SVF* III 342).

88. Diog. Laert. VII 120 (*SVF* III 731).

89. Chalcid. *Comm. in Plato Tim.* § 165 (*SVF* III 229) describes how the newly-born infant (encouraged by its nurses) is liable to be led astray by pain and pleasure right from its first emergence into the cold air. Behind this admission almost certainly lies a particularly well-aimed hedonist critique of *oikeiosis*, directed precisely at 'the moment of birth' and pointing out that at this moment the infant shows itself anything but well-disposed to its constitution, Philo *De opif. mund.* § 161 (1 56, 7ff. Cohn) τά τε γεννώμενα οὐδενὶ πρῶτον οἰκειοῦσθαι πέφυκεν ἢ ταύτῃ, χαίροντα

μὲν ἡδονῇ, τὴν δ' ἐναντίαν ἀλγηδόνα δυσχεραίνοντα· παρὸ καὶ ἀνακλαίεται τὸ βρέφος ἀποκυηθέν, ἀλγῆσαν ὡς εἰκὸς τῇ περιψύξει· ἐκ γὰρ θερμοτάτου καὶ πυρωδεστάτου χωρίου τοῦ κατὰ τὴν μήτραν, ᾧ πολὺν χρόνον ἐνδιῃτήθη, προελθὸν ἐξαπιναίως εἰς ἀέρα, ψυχρὸν καὶ ἀσυνήθη τόπον, ἐπλήχθη καὶ τῆς ὀδύνης καὶ τοῦ δυσχεραίνειν ἀλγηδόνι τὰ κλαύματα δεῖγμα παρέσχεν ἐναργέστατον. The language of Diog. Laert. II 88 (above, n. 6) is most easily explained in terms of such a critique.

90. Diog. Laert. VII 130 (*SVF* III 757–68); for Stoic indifference to length of days cf. Plut. *Comm. not.* 1061F (*SVF* III 54).

91. Von Arnim, *Arius Didymus* esp. 131ff., 157–61; Cic. *Fin.* IV 3, 14, 45 (*SVF* I 198), cf. *Acad. post.* 34, *Acad. prior.* 131.

92. Stob. II 118, 11–123, 27 (Peripatetics); 47, 12–48, 5 (Stoics).

93. Dirlmeier, *Die Oikeiosis-Lehre Theophrasts*, pp. 20ff., 67–72, cf. p. 11 (Thphr. in schol. Plato *Legg.* 631c).

94. Ibid., pp. 50–2, esp. Arist. *Pol.* 1254b 23.

95. *HA* 588a 31–b 2.

96. *MM* 1206b 17–25. Cf. Walzer, *Magna Moralia und aristotelische Ethik*, Neue philologische Untersuchungen, VII (Berlin 1929) pp. 195ff.

97. Porph. *Abst.* III 25 (p. 220, 15–221, 20 Nauck = fr. 20 Pötscher), cf. Bernays, *Theophrastos' Schrift über Frömmigkeit* (Berlin 1866) pp. 96ff.; von Arnim, op. cit., p. 142; Dirlmeier pp. 72, 90.

98. Porph. *Abst.* III 26 (p. 223, 10ff. Nauck); cf. Iambl. *VP* §§ 168–9 (p. 95, 3–16 Deubner).

99. Thphr. fr. 190 Wimmer = Phot. *Bibl.* cod. 278, p. 529b 22 Bekker ἔχει δέ πως ἡ μέλισσα οἰκείωσίν τινα πρὸς τὴν δρῦν.

100. Op. cit. pp. 77, 48–9.

101. Pohlenz, *Grundfragen* pp. 1–81.

102. Cic. *Fin.* V 17–18.

103. Cic. *Fin.* V 21ff.; IV 15.

104. Cic. *Fin.* V 12, cf. *Acad. post.* 33.

105. *Grundfragen*, p. 13, cf. Praechter, *Hermes* li (1916) 528 n. 1.

106. Brink, 'Οἰκείωσις and Οἰκειότης: Theophrastus and Zeno on Nature in moral theory,' *Phronesis* i, 2 (1956) 123–45.

107. Ibid., p. 138, n. 83.

108. Ibid., p. 140, n. 98, cf. Pohlenz, *Grundfragen*, p. 12 n. 1. For the sense cf. also Posidonius ap. Str. VI 2, 3, p. 269 καθάπερ οὖν τὸ πήγανον τῇ ξυλίνῃ σποδῷ τρέφεται, τοιοῦτον ἔχειν τι οἰκείωμα πρὸς τὴν ἄμπελον εἰκὸς τὴν Αἰτναίαν σποδόν and for the construction with πρός cf. Thphr. in Porph. *Abst.* II 22 (p. 151, 14 N. = fr. 12 Pötscher) οἰκειότητος οὔσης ἡμῖν πρὸς τοὺς ἀνθρώπους. The φυσική τις οἰκείωσις of human beings towards one another, however, mentioned in an Epicurean context by Porph. *Abst.* I 7 p. 89, 22 N. as one factor militating against the tolerance of homicide, is probably an addition by Porphyry himself and can only be taken in the Stoic sense.

109. Loc. cit., pp. 141ff. Some emphasis might also be placed on the tripartite division of philosophy which is attributed to Xenocrates (fr. 1 Heinze = Sext. *Adv. math.* VII 16) and attested for Zeno, Diog. Laert. VII 39 (*SVF* I 45).

110. Ibid., pp. 141–2.

111. Cf. the verdict of Bernays, op. cit. p. 102. The implication of *Abst.* III 25 (p. 221, 15 N.), possibly re-phrased by Porphyry, that animals are capable of λογισμοί is elsewhere explicitly rejected by Theophrastus, cf. the text of Περὶ τῶν ζῴων ὅσα λέγεται φθονεῖν (Diog. Laert. v 43) in Phot. *Bibl.* cod. 278 p. 528a 40ff., esp. 528b 13 πόθεν γὰρ τοῖς ἀλόγοις ἡ τοσαύτη σοφία, ἣν καὶ οἱ λογικοὶ μετὰ συχνῆς μελέτης μανθάνουσιν;

112. Arist. *EN* 1175a 29–b 24; 1168a 28ff. In the first of these passages, the opening phrase φανείη δ᾽ ἂν τοῦτο καὶ ἐκ τοῦ συνῳκειῶσθαι τῶν ἡδονῶν ἑκάστην τῇ ἐνεργείᾳ ἣν τελειοῖ clearly cannot imply the presence of consciousness in ἡδονή and simply means that it is connected with the activity (so also 1172a 16 μάλιστα γὰρ δοκεῖ (ἡδονὴ) συνῳκειῶσθαι τῷ γένει ἡμῶν). Consequently at 1161b 19ff. μᾶλλον δ᾽ ἴσασιν οἱ γονεῖς τὰ ἐξ αὐτῶν ἢ τὰ γεννηθέντα ὅτι ἐκ τούτων, καὶ μᾶλλον συνῳκείωται τὸ ἀφ᾽ οὗ τῷ γεννηθέντι ἢ τὸ γενόμενον τῷ ποιήσαντι the verb again denotes only a kind of connection and does not in itself imply consciousness, cf. ibid. 1162a 1 ἀνεψιοὶ δὲ καὶ οἱ λοιποὶ συγγενεῖς ἐκ τούτων συνῳκείωνται. There is therefore no real anticipation of Stoic ideas or language in this text.

113. Cf. Grumach, *Physis und Agathon*, pp. 76–7.

114. Diog. Laert. VI 12 (Antisth. frr. 73, 81 Caizzi), cf. also Epictet. *Diss.* III 24, 67 (fr. 118 C.) and for Chrysippus the quotation in Plut. *Stoic. rep.* 1038B (*SVF* III 674): ʼκατὰ ταὐτὰ δὲ τῷ μὲν ἀστείῳ ἀλλότριον οὐδὲν τῷ δὲ φαύλῳ οὐδὲν οἰκεῖόν ἐστιν, ἐπειδὴ τὸ μὲν ἀγαθὸν τὸ δὲ κακόν ἐστιν αὐτῶν.ʼ On Antisthenes cf. Zeller, *Philos. d. Gr.*,[4] ii 1 pp. 303–4 and more fully Maier, *Sokrates, sein Werk und seine geschichtliche Stellung* (Tübingen 1913) p. 392 n. 2. The same criterion was put to a less productive use in Antisthenes' atomistic doctrine of language, the οἰκεῖος λόγος, which vetoed predication, cf. Arist. *Met.* 1024b 32–4 and Alex. Aphr. *In Met.* p. 435, 2ff. (fr. 47b Caizzi).

115. τὸ τῆς φύσεως ἀγαθόν, τὸ τῆς φύσεως οἰκεῖον ΚΔ VII (Diog. Laert. X 141).

116. Plato *Ap.* 29d 7–e 3, 30a 7–b 2, 31b 1–5; Xen. *Mem.* I 2, 2–4.

117. Plato *Ap.* 21a; for the διαλεληθὼς σοφός cf. Plut. *Prof. virt.* 75D, Stob. II 113, 12ff., Philo *De agric.* § 160 (*SVF* III 539–41).

118. *SVF* I 236 (text above, n. 69). According to Mai, this comes from a letter to Cleanthes and would therefore have been accepted as genuine by Panaetius and Sosigenes, Diog. Laert. VII 163. The manuscript, still unpublished, is cod. Vatic. n. 739 (saec. XII), Wachsmuth, *Studien zu den griechischen Florilegien* (Berlin 1882) p. 103. Cf. also *Gnomol. Vatic.* ed. Sternbach no. 299 (Zeno); Stob. II 109, 1ff. (*SVF* III 656) λέγουσι δὲ καὶ ἄριστον αὐτοῦ ἰατρὸν εἶναι τὸν σπουδαῖον ἄνδρα. ἐπιμελῆ γὰρ ὄντα τῆς ἰδίας φύσεως παρατηρητὴν ὑπάρχειν, Alex. Aphr. *De an.* p. 163, 36 (*SVF* III 194), Basil. *Homil. in hexaem.* ix, 3 (*PG* XXIX 193A Migne) πόση τοῖς ἀλόγοις τούτοις ἐνυπάρχει ἀδίδακτος καὶ φυσικὴ τῆς ἑαυτῶν ζωῆς ἐπιμέλεια.

119. Plato *Lys.* 221d 7–222a 3.

120. Ibid., 222b 3ff.

121. Plato *Charm.* 163c 4—d 4 *Smp.* 205e 5ff.

122. von Arnim, *Platos Jugenddialoge* (Leipzig–Berlin 1914) pp. 58–59. The onslaught on the identification of σωφροσύνη as τὸ τὰ αὐτοῦ πράττειν (*Charm.* 161d 1ff.), however, could equally point to Antisthenes.

123. Plut. fr. 215f. Sandbach (cod. Marc. gr. 196), cf. Plato *Meno* 80d 5ff.

124. Herder, *Abhandlung über den Ursprung der Sprache* (1770) = *Werke*, ed. Suphan, v (Berlin 1891) p. 34.

125. Nemes. *Nat. hom.* c. 42 pp. 339–42 Matth. (*PG* XL 788C–792A Migne); Basil. *Homil. in hexaem.* VIII 1 (*PG* XXIX 165A), IX 4 (ibid. 197AB); cf. also Philo *De animal.* § 22 p. 134 Aucher (hirundo) in alienum nidum minime intrat, sed falli nescium ad suum venit in reditu ob desiderium curae propriae.

126. Cic. *ND* II 128, cf. Ps. Clem. *Recognit.* VIII 25, 2 (p. 231, 19 Rehm) ac statim ut natum fuerit, nullo docente scit ubi alimoniae suae horrea requirat, Hierocl. V 56ff. κ(αὶ) τὰ μ(ὲν) ἐ(πὶ) θήλας | μητρῴας ὁρμήσα[ντ]α σπᾶι τὸ γάλα, τὸ δ᾽ ὑπὸ | πτέρυξ[ι τ(ῆς)] γ(ε)ιναμ(ένης) κ(ατα)δύεται.

127. Cf. above, n. 29.

128. Sext. *Adv. math.* VII 248; Diog. Laert. VII 50(*SVF* I 59). Cf. F. H. Sandbach, Chapter I, p. 10.

129. Sext. *Adv. math.* VII 12 (*SVF* I 356) ἀρκεῖν δὲ πρὸς τὸ μακαρίως βιῶναι τὸν οἰκειοῦντα μὲν πρὸς ἀρετὴν λόγον, ἀπαλλοτριοῦντα δὲ κακίας, κατατρέχοντα δὲ τῶν μεταξὺ τούτων, περὶ ἃ οἱ πολλοὶ πτοηθέντες κακοδαιμονοῦσιν.

130. Hierocl. VI 43ff. δ(ιὰ) ταῦτ[α ο]ὐκ ἄν μοι δοκ[[ῳ]]εῖ τις, | οὐδ(ὲ) Μ[αρ]γείτης ὤν, [εἰ]πεῖν ὥς τε γεννη|θὲν τὸ ζῶιο(ν) ἑαυτ[ῶι] τε κ(αὶ) τῆι φαντασίαι τῆι | ἑαυτοῦ δυσαρεστεῖ· κ(αὶ) μὴν οὐδ' ἀρρεπῶς ἵ|σχει· οὐχ ἧττον γ(ὰρ) τ(ῆς) δυσαρεστήσεως κ(αὶ) αὐ|τὸ τὸ μὴ εὐαρ[ε]στ[εῖ]ν πρ(ός) τε ὄλεθρον τοῦ ζώ(ιου) | κ(αὶ) πρ(ὸς) κ(ατά)-γνωσιν [φέρ]ει τ(ῆς) φύσεως· ὅθεν ὁ συν|λογισμὸς οὗτο[ς ἀν]αγκάζει ὁμολογεῖν ὅτι | τὸ ζῶ(ιον) τ(ὴν) πρώτη[ν αἴ]σθησιν ἑαυτοῦ λαβὸν εὐ|θ[ὺ]ς ὠ[ικ]ειώθ[η πρ(ὸς) ἑ]αυτὸ κ(αὶ) τὴν ἑαυτοῦ σύστα|σιν. In Diog. Laert. VII 85 (*SVF* III 178) the agent is Nature: οὔτε γὰρ ἀλλοτριῶσαι εἰκὸς ἦν αὐτὸ ⟨αὐτῷ⟩ τὸ ζῷον, οὔτε ποιήσασαν αὐτό, μήτ' ἀλλοτριῶσαι μήτ' [οὐκ] οἰκειῶσαι. The word *oikeiosis* is normally used of animals and human beings only, although in the polemic of Philo *De animal.* § 94 (p. 169 Aucher = *SVF* II 730), it is said to obtain even between plants, such as the ivy and the olive tree: hae etiam etsi nullam habeant animae partem, tamen familiaritatis abalienationisque non minorem praeferunt manifestationem. For Philo's own abuse of the term cf. esp. *Quod det. potiori insid. soleant* § 129 (I 287, 14 Cohn) ἴδιον δὲ λόγου τὸ λέγειν, πρὸς ὃ οἰκειώσει φυσικῇ τινι σπεύδει.

131. K. Lorenz, 'Ganzheit und Teil in der tierischen und menschlichen Gemeinschaft,' *Studium Generale* iii (1950) 491 = *Gesammelte Abhandlungen* (München 1966) ii p. 187.

132. Jakob von Uexküll, *Umwelt und Innenwelt der Tiere*, 2. Aufl. (Berlin 1921), pp. 218–19; id. (Engl. tr.) 'A stroll through the worlds of animals and men' in Claire M. Schiller (ed. and tr.), *Instinctive Behaviour: The Development of a Modern Concept* (New York and London 1957) pp. 5–80.

133. A striking testimony to the Stoics' achievement in this field is provided by their opponents in the Academy, who in arguing for the rationality of animals were able to draw heavily on material gathered by the Stoics themselves. Cf. Philo, *De animal.* §§ 10–71 (pp. 126–61 Aucher), with Sext. *Hyp.* I 62–77; Porph. *Abst.* III 1–15 and G. Tappe, *De Philonis libro qui inscribitur Ἀλέξανδρος ἢ περὶ τοῦ λόγον ἔχειν τὰ ἄλογα ζῷα* (diss. Göttingen 1912).

134. πνεῦμα ἀναστρέφον ἐφ' ἑαυτό Philo *Quod deus sit immort.* § 35 (II p. 64, 4 Wendl.) = *SVF* II 458, cf. Simplic. *In Cat.* p. 269, 14–16 (*SVF* II 452), Nemes. *Nat. hom.* c. 2 pp. 70–1 Matth. (*PG* XL 540A) = *SVF* II 451.

VII

Stoic Intermediates and the End for Man[1]

I. G. KIDD

The Stoics maintained that virtue was the only good; every-thing else, therefore, was not good. On the other hand, regarded by itself, this huge class was not equally valueless. Vice, of course, was bad; but everything else was thought to be 'indiffer-ent': wealth, health, for example; indifferent, that is, with regard to the *summum bonum*. Of these Intermediates, men, from human nature, had a leaning to some; these were 'in accordance with nature' (κατὰ φύσιν, *kata physin*), had value, were called προηγμένα (*proēgmena*) that is, preferred, and virtue itself lay in choice exercised among them. Yet they were not good—their actual acquisition did not count against the exercise of virtue, the only good. So that although Zeno defined happiness, to live in harmony with nature, the Intermediates, although some were *kata physin*, were indifferent. This is the bare core of Stoic ethics, and naturally met with the main attack of criticism.

That this is the crux can be seen from the ancient criticism of the Stoa in the ethical sphere from Carneades on,[2] and can be briefly illustrated for my purpose by Plutarch, who, while criticising the Indifferents generally throughout the two essays, *De stoicorum repugnantiis* and *De communibus notitiis*[3], advances the following three points:

(1) *Comm. not.* XXIII 1069E. In beginning from 'the things in accordance with nature', natural advantages (*ta kata physin*), Zeno and the Stoics were merely following the Peripatetics and the Old Academy; in fact they cling to *ta kata physin* in their actions as goods, while it is in the language they use that they play them down.[4]

(2) Ibid. IV 1060C. Nature inclines us towards what is not regarded by the Stoa as good.[5]

(3) Ibid. XXVI 1071. One can offer Stoic ethics a dilemma

which it implies: (a) There are two ends. (b) There is one end, yet every action is to be referred to something else, i.e. *ta kata physin*.[6]

I bring forward these points to show that the difficulty is focused on *ta kata physin* and their relationship to the *summum bonum*. The opponents of the Stoa maintained that *ta kata physin* should have been included in the End as goods, otherwise there was a contradiction, or that the Stoics were hedging and that their thought implied this.

Modern scholars are well aware of this difficulty to the Stoa, and the tendency has been to show that the later members of the School changed their attitude on this crucial point. This may be illustrated by three recent examinations of the problem, each proceeding by a different method.

Pohlenz stresses the difficulties that arise for the Stoa from the two-sidedness of man's nature, and shows how the split widened under the blows of criticism.[7] His standpoint seems to be that Zeno insisted on the development of the intelligent nature of man (i.e. the *logos*) as the goal, yet the Stoics refused to deny some value to the animal side, and *ta kata physin*, as some kind of standard for our everyday actions. 'In this way a dichotomy threatened to develop between the doctrine of Goods and the doctrine of action in accordance with nature, the *kathē-konta*.'[8] Thus he argues that the reformulation of the *telos* up to Antipater was due to Carneades' criticism of the Stoic relation of *ta kata physin* to the End. He maintains, certainly, that Antipater held on to the self-sufficiency of virtue—'One feels clearly how he is making concessions to Carneades, but at all costs wishes to preserve the central position, the self-sufficiency of virtue';[9] but by the words 'at all costs', he implies that the Stoa was being driven into a corner, and that new and desperate methods were being taken to save the position. Diogenes and Antipater, then, held on to Zeno's main position, but their attempts at new definitions were barren in the face of Carneades' criticism, because their methods were dictated by his point of view. There is a difference, however, with Panaetius, 'who ignoring previous attempts, took new directions'.[10] He, by departing from Chrysippus' intellectual interpretation of the soul, gave natural importance to the impulses (*hormai*), and while adhering to *to kalon* as the true good for man, held that *ta kata physin* had real value. 'He did not think he was endangering the moral ideal, when he declared his adherence to the heretical proposition that virtue was not self-sufficient, but that for complete *eudaimonia* health, strength and moderately favourable circumstances were necessary.'[11]

Miss Reesor, by examining statements of the different members of the School, reaches the following conclusions: after Zeno 'the concept of the "indifferents" was modified by the later Stoics';[12] for example, 'a right choice among the "indifferents" was emphasised in the definitions of the end of life used by Diogenes of Babylon and Antipater of Tarsus'.[13] 'Panaetius was the first of the Stoic philosophers to argue that virtue was not sufficient for happiness.'[14] 'In the first book [of the *De officiis*] position, wealth, and age, which were regarded as "indifferents" by the Old Stoa, are used to determine what actions should be considered fitting or appropriate (*decorum*)';[15] and *decorum* is identical with *honestum*.[16] The statesman is urged to exercise his virtue that he may win *gloria* and *fides*;[17] 'indifferents' thus being the goal towards which the virtues are directed.[18] 'Posidonius believed that the "indifferents" had a positive effect upon the emotions, and seems to have argued that they should be regarded as good or evil but not as a matter of indifference.'[19]

Dr M. van Straaten[20] makes a detailed study of one Stoic philosopher, Panaetius, who is a crucial figure in this problem. He interprets Panaetius' definition of the *telos*[21] that human happiness is determined 'selon les aspirations et les tendances de la nature individuelle';[22] this comes from his reading of *De officiis* I. In this the stress is shifted from *la nature cosmique* of the Old Stoa to *la nature humaine*, concentrating on the impulses (*hormai*).[23] *ta kata physin* are equated with 'ces objets qui sont conformes à la nature humaine'.[24] They are the objective content of all acts, the 'what', and Panaetius stresses this rather than the mentality of the act, the 'how', underlined by the Old Stoa.[25] In this Panaetius, although his method of formulation is the same, is saying something different from the Old Stoa up to Antipater, who agreed in substance although there was variation of formulae.[26] For Panaetius thought it not only necessary for *eudaimonia* to have 'la *tendance* vers τὰ κατὰ φύσιν, mais il exigeait aussi dûment la possession réelle de ces objets'.[27] From such an interpretation van Straaten summarizes three general points where Panaetius differs in stress from previous Stoics:[28] (1) in the central doctrine of nature (*physis*), Panaetius concentrates on the *physis* of human nature instead of *physis* in the cosmic sense. (2) He shifts from the subjective to the objective element in human actions (i.e. *ta kata physin*). (3) There is a change of accent from the functions of knowing to the impulses (*hormai*) of the human nature (*physis*). In spite of this van Straaten holds that Panaetius did not differ so much from the Old Stoa as other scholars think,[29] and in fact that he also maintained the essential dogma that only that which is morally good can make a man happy.[30] But to bring this into line with the above interpretation, he is forced to give a new exposition of virtue (*arete*) in which 'the things according to nature' (*ta kata physin*) now play a decisive part.[31] Thus in the end, if Panaetius differs at all from previous Stoics in this problem, it is in the relation of *ta kata physin* to the good.

This brief account of three views on the subject is not, of course, meant to be an exhaustive survey of relevant modern scholarship; but the position can, I think, be illustrated thus by the conclusions reached through these three distinct methods. They seem to be based primarily on the following evidence: (1) the formulae of the *telos* given by members of the School. (2) the precise statement of Diogenes Laertius, VII 128. (3) Cicero, *De officiis*, I and II as a general source for Panaetius' ethical philosophy. (4) passages showing that Panaetius and Posidonius, in opposition to Chrysippus, recognised an irrational element in the human soul, leading to a changed interpretation of human impulses (*hormai*) and thus of *ta kata physin*, their objects. As for the conclusions themselves, it appears to be agreed that the attitude to *ta kata physin* changed. Diogenes and Antipater, in seeking to defend their position against Carneades' criticism of the importance of *ta kata physin* in moral action, brought *ta kata physin* more into prominence in their definitions of the End. In this they may or may not have deviated from the exposition of Zeno and Chrysippus. Panaetius certainly gave positive value to *ta kata physin* with regard to the moral act, and in consequence his whole ethical philosophy takes on a complexion different from that of his predecessors. There is a certain hesitation and reluctance to draw the conclusion that in this Panaetius was departing from the fundamental Stoic dogma of the moral ideal. But since the positive value assigned by Panaetius to *ta kata physin* was of the rank of 'goods' (*agatha*), in that their attainment in the moral act, i.e. the end (*telos*) of human action, was necessary, while in the Old Stoa they were regarded as indifferent, it can hardly be denied that Panaetius held different views on the *telos* from Zeno and Chrysippus, and that this difference lay in the position of *ta kata physin* with regard to the *telos*, where this position was decisive. Moreover, if the interpretation of the strenuous efforts of Diogenes and Antipater on this subject is correct, Panaetius' views would appear not only different in the sense of unorthodox, but contradictory in the sense of non-Stoic.

Now the Stoics did not regard their founder's views as divine sayings that held good for all time, like the Epicureans, and were philosophers enough to change ground if they thought previous dogmas were wrong; so the brilliant work which has shown these changes is an immense contribution to the disentangling of the Stoic skein. It is true, moreover, that in this particular context the form of the Stoic definitions of the End did alter. But there comes a time when one is led to ask the question, 'When is a Stoic not a Stoic?', and I for one would find difficulty over a member who contradicted the characteristic and fundamental tenet of the School, the *summum bonum*. I am further heartened in this by the backing of Cicero, who maintains that a School may diverge on other points but not on this.[32]

This chapter then wishes to question the view that the Stoa changed on this fundamental point; and since the root of the matter has been shown to be 'the things according to nature' (*ta kata physin*), to attempt to assess the position of this concept in Stoic philosophy, and its bearing on Stoic teaching.

The method suggested is (*a*) to examine the use and meaning of the various technical terms employed, and (*b*) to call in to assist another part of their philosophy, namely physics, without which their ethics cannot properly be understood.

II

Diogenes Laertius[33] gives a number of subdivisions of Stoic ethics classified by Chrysippus, but a more fruitful division for *ta kata physin* is the threefold specification of Cicero, *De fin.* IV 39: 'naturalem enim appetitionem, quam vocant ὁρμήν, itemque officium, ipsam etiam virtutem volunt [sc. Stoici] esse earum rerum quae secundum naturam sunt' (natural impulse, which they term *hormē*, and again appropriate acts, virtue itself even, Stoics hold to be in the category of those things which are according to nature); fruitful because *ta kata physin* have some place in all sections, yet, as I would stress, each of the sections is distinct because of the different part played in each by *ta kata physin*. The terms in the three divisions are familiar from the sources; the intention is to show their interrelation with respect to *ta kata physin* as briefly as possible.

(1) *ta prōta kata physin, prōton oikeion*[34]

ta prota kata physin, i.e. the initial natural impulses, are the springs of *ta kata physin*.[35] They are instanced in babies or young children,[36] and therefore can have nothing to do with the *logos*, which according to the Stoics flowered late;[37] on the contrary they seem centred on the body.

(2) *ta kata physin, adiaphora, proēgmena, kathēkonta*[38]

In this section *ta kata physin* occupy the position of prime importance, since they are the object of *kathekonta* (appropriate acts, *officia*, often misleadingly translated: duties), their base[39] and their *archē*[40], and the whole stress of *kathekonta* lies in the object of the act being achieved, as opposed to the attitude of mind of the agent.[41]

But such an act is not right action; it does not lie in the sphere of good or evil—*id officium nec in bonis ponamus nec in malis*.[42] This follows for two main reasons:

(a) *ta kata physin* are not 'goods' (*agatha*). Since they cover the triple sphere of τὰ περὶ τὴν ψυχήν, τὰ περὶ σῶμα and τὰ ἐκτός (mental, physical, external),[43] while having a certain amount of positive value and their opposites a negative value,[44] this value is relative[45] not absolute like virtue alone.[46] Hence the introduction of the term *proegmena* (preferred), a kind of second rank of value, a *proxime accessit*.[47]

(b) No account is taken of the agent's attitude of mind—only the object of the act is important.[48]

It seems that the worth (*axia*) of *ta kata physin* was formed objectively; for the stimulus for the agent is external.[49] I suggest that this external stimulus was in the form of a rule. *Kathekonta* are expressly linked with *praecepta* in Cicero, *De off.* 1 7.[50] Again Seneca[51] refers to M. Brutus' περὶ καθήκοντος in which 'he gives many rules (*praecepta*) to parents, children, brothers'; while in *Ep. mor.* 94, 32, he thinks that if the mind is 'untrained in discovering the path of appropriate acts,' (*officiorum*), *admonitio*, part of the *praeceptiva pars* of philosophy, points this out; the form of the rules is given in *Ep. mor.* 94, 50, 'Avoid this, do that' (*hoc vitabis, hoc facies*). In *kathekonta* these rules are laid down for the use of the agent for the attainment of a certain object, but do not apply to his attitude of mind in the performance of the act.[52] The agent accepts the rules, like the opinions of a legal expert,[53] but does not form them or think out the situation for himself.

It is from these two positions that the following objections in our sources are derived: (1) sometimes the general rule is wrong;[54] (2) *kathekonta* may be done by a bad man or a good man, or without knowing, or for the wrong or insufficient reason;[55] (3) owing to external circumstances it is not completely in our power to achieve or possess Intermediates;[56] (4) a man can possess any of the Intermediates and yet be unhappy;[57] conversely, a man can be happy apart from these.[58]

Hence *kathekonta*, or acts performed for the attainment of *ta kata physin* guided by external rules as to which of these are 'preferred' (*proegmena*), are 'indifferent' (*adiaphora*) with regard to happiness, good and evil.

(3) *agatha, aretē, katorthōmata, eudaimonia*

The objects of perfect morally right acts (*katorthomata*), as goods (*agatha*), are the virtues, or the right attitude of mind in any situation, as the only thing in our power: so the central Stoic dogma μόνον τὸ καλὸν ἀγαθόν (only what is morally fine is good).[59] Yet *ta kata physin* have a part to play in this section also as the material with which moral intelligence works—its *hylē* or *materia*.[60] In this *katorthomata* are like *kathekonta*, but the all-important difference is given by Plutarch;[61] *ta kata physin* are also the *arche* of appropriate action, they are merely the material (*hyle*) of virtue, not its *arche*. So the stress shifts completely in *katorthomata* to the attitude of mind;[62] the result of the action, the attainment of *ta kata physin* is incidental and does not matter. 'It is the choosing and adopting of those things wisely which is the end, whereas those things themselves and their possession are not the end' (τέλος μὲν γὰρ τὸ ἐκλέγεσθαι καὶ λαμβάνειν ἐκεῖνα φρονίμως, ἐκεῖνα δ' αὐτὰ καὶ τὸ τυγχάνειν αὐτῶν οὐ τέλος).[63]

What follows from this brief survey of *ta kata physin*? It might be said that this is merely a presentation of orthodox Stoic doctrine, and is no argument against change in the later Stoa. But the point brought out is that *kathekonta* and *katorthomata* are distinguished precisely because of the different part played by *ta kata physin* in them. Elevate *ta kata physin* in *katorthomata* and the two sections are confounded. Yet all our sources regard the distinction between *kathekonta* and *katorthomata* as continuing to be fundamental to Stoic ethics.[64] Then if the position of *ta kata physin* is altered, the whole fabric of Stoic ethics tumbles, even their very technical terms lose meaning.

III

The second inquiry is how Stoic physics bear on their ethics. I take this to be an important point, because: (1) it is the reference-point of the definition of happiness; (2) whereas the Stoics laid down that ethics should be taught before physics, in practice they always prefaced moral questions with some physical explanation; Chrysippus said there can be no other *arche* for justice than from physics, and in one place indeed that speculation of nature was learned for nothing else;[65] further in one of their similes, ethics is the fruit of the trees of physics;[66] (3) Stoicism was noted for its internal unity and consistency all through.[67]

Of the two principles in the universe, active and passive, the active was the *logos* or the governing force of the universe.[68] It was this, in terms of the four elements, as a creative fire (πῦρ τεχνικόν)[69] with cosmic supremacy which was the substance of the human soul.[70] The latter, therefore, could not be put on the same footing (like the additional Peripatetic fifth element)

as the body in the *physis* of man, being a different nature altogether as part of the guiding force of the universe. Therefore the
same holds for the goods of the soul and the body. So the *logos*
in man as in the universe is all-important, and happiness
depends on it alone.[71] But the *logos* in the universe is the rational
element, and therefore the duty of the *logos* in man is the development of his rational part in knowledge, and on knowledge are
founded all the virtues.[72] Moreover the *logos* in man being the
same *logos* which is the governing force of the universe,[73] the
knowledge of man and his duties cannot be complete until it
comprises the universe and man's place in it.[74] To put this in
another way, as right reason is identical with God (ὁ ὀρθὸς
λόγος . . . ὁ αὐτὸς ὢν τῷ Διί),[75] a man will never make sufficient progress until he has conceived a right idea of God.[76] This
is what the Stoics mean by *physis* and what they must mean by
their common definition of the End for Man, ὁμολογουμένως
τῇ φύσει ζῆν, i.e. to live in harmony with nature. It must follow
that in man the rational as displayed in the virtues is the only
good, and compared with them *ta kata physin* are indifferent. To
contradict this would be to contradict their physics or their
views on the universe, and blur the distinction between the
Stoa and the Academy and Peripatos.

IV

If the previous sections are a correct account of the structure of
Stoic philosophy, it is difficult to see how the logic of the system,
both in physics and in the use of technical terms, could lead a
Stoic to maintain anything else than that virtue and the right
attitude of mind in action was the only good. Further, this
seems the main point of the evidence. Cicero, who surely had
some familiarity with the later Stoa, maintains this consistently
throughout the *De finibus*,[77] with the strengthening view that
this is the only point where members of a school may not differ.[78]

What positive evidence is there against this? In the first
place we have different forms of the definition of the End;
Diogenes and Antipater bring *ta kata physin* more into prominence in their definitions,[79] no doubt because of Carneades'
polemic; but this is no more than a recognition in the definition

that *ta kata physin* are the material of *katorthomata*, not that they are their *arche*; that is, their formulae differ in form but not in meaning.[80] Here again we may refer to Cicero: 'the Stoic definitions (*of bonum*) do indeed differ from each other in a very minute degree, but they all point in the same direction.'[81] Even Antipater did not deny that virtue was sufficient for happiness,[82] and Zeno presumably held *ta kata physin* were the *materia* of *phronesis* and human *logos*.

When we come to Panaetius we meet the one bald statement to the contrary. Diogenes Laertius, VII 128, says in passing that Panaetius and Posidonius 'say that virtue is not self-sufficient, but maintain that there is need (*chreian*) for health, supplies and strength' (οὐκ αὐτάρκη λέγουσι τὴν ἀρετήν, ἀλλὰ χρείαν εἶναί φασι καὶ ὑγιείας καὶ χορηγίας καὶ ἰσχύος).[83] In the face of all the rest of the evidence, I find it not too difficult to disbelieve Diogenes. In the first place we do not know the context of this remark, and it seems to me more difficult to explain, if there was such a change of view, why continuous tracts of criticism, such as we find in Cicero and Plutarch, did not use this as a cudgel when dealing with this point;[84] and continuous exposition is infinitely more valuable than isolated reference out of context. For without any context, one can see only too clearly from Plutarch, *Stoic rep.* xxx, how easily such a statement could arise. Plutarch digs up a quotation of Chrysippus,[85] where the latter permits the use of customary language to the extent of calling 'preferred things' (*proegmena*), 'goods' (*agatha*), as long as one understands the meaning of what one is saying. Plutarch deduces from such evidence that sometimes to the Stoa *proegmena* are 'goods', sometimes 'indifferents'. The Stoics seem to have been untechnical in their use of language on occasion, no doubt when forced to argue with opponents in their opponents' language.[86]

It has been suggested to me by a correspondent that perhaps a closer explanation for the statement could arise from a point given by Alexander of Aphrodisias in his section ὅτι οὐκ αὐτάρκης ἡ ἀρετὴ πρὸς εὐδαιμονίαν (that virtue is not self-sufficient in relation to happiness).[87] Here Alexander preserves an unwelcome dilemma doubtless offered to the Stoa in the course of the controversy: 'if virtue in conjunction with *proegmena* and virtue on its own were separate and distinct' (δίχα κειμένων ἀρετῆς τε σὺν τούτοις [i.e. προηγμένα] καὶ ἀρετῆς μόνης), which would the wise man choose? And the Stoic answer given is 'that the sage would never choose the isolated case, if it were in his power to get the case where virtue was combined with the rest' (μηδέποτ' ἂν τὸν σοφὸν τὴν κεχωρισμένην ἐλέσθαι, εἰ εἴη αὐτῷ δυνατὸν τὴν μετὰ τῶν ἄλλων λαβεῖν). Now, either the conclusion drawn by the opponents of the Stoa and Alexander here, namely 'but if the latter, obviously the sage will have need (chreian) of these things' (εἰ δὲ τοῦτο, δῆλον ὡς χρείαν ὁ σοφὸς ἕξει τούτων), could be maliciously assigned to the Stoa itself, or through lapse of time taken to be part of the Stoic answer (the similarity of expression with chreian both here and in Diogenes is suggestive); or the Stoic phrase itself, 'the sage would never choose the isolated virtue', could be lifted out of context and come to be the father of the statement in Diogenes. The reason for choosing Panaetius and Posidonius as foster-parents should, I think, be clear from the rest of this chapter. Such a line of reasoning seems to me very possible. On the whole, since the controversy in which, according to Alexander,[88] the dilemma occurred—the reference-point of choice in action—was such a famous one,[89] I am inclined to think tendentious misrepresentation rather less likely than an unguarded statement or careless language by Panaetius taken out of context. However it is not necessary for my purpose, nor indeed is it possible, to trace exactly the family tree of Diogenes' sentence, but merely to show that such a misstatement could quite reasonably occur.

Again for the customary ὁμολογουμένως τῇ φύσει ζῆν, to live in harmony with nature,[90] Panaetius has a different formula, ζῆν κατὰ τὰς δεδομένας ἡμῖν ἐκ φύσεως ἀφορμάς, to live in accordance with the starting points granted us from nature.[91] But in meaning this does not contradict previous Stoic thought.[92]

I see no departure from the view I put forward when hunting for Panaetius in the De officiis. For I take it that the general rules for kathekonta are merely classified under the headings of the different virtues, from which they may as rules be derived.[93] Cicero seems to understand the position, and sums up well in De off. III 11ff., in a passage where Panaetius' name occurs at the beginning. Moral goodness alone is good, honestum solum *bonum est* (11), but the subject for discussion in the *De officiis* is not *perfectum honestum*, but something that bears a resemblance to moral goodness, *similitudines honesti*—

atque illud quidem honestum, quod proprie vereque dicitur, id in sapientibus est solis neque a virtute divelli umquam potest; in iis autem, in quibus sapientia perfecta non est, ipsum illud quidem perfectum honestum nullo modo, similitudines honesti esse possunt. Haec enim officia de quibus his libris disputamus, media Stoici appellant (13-14).

what is properly and truly termed moral goodness occurs in sages only and cannot ever be separated from virtue; but in men whose wisdom is not perfect, this perfect moral goodness itself cannot possibly occur, but a semblance of moral goodness can. These appropriate acts which are the object of discussion in these books are called by the Stoics intermediates.[94]

These *officia* are a kind of second rank moral goodness—'haec igitur officia, de quibus his libris disserimus, quasi secunda quaedam honesta esse dicunt', not the prerogative of the sage, but common to all mankind, 'non sapientium modo propria, sed cum omni hominum genere communia' (15). Once again[95] Cicero stresses the subject-matter as if determined to prevent a mistake. What else can follow from this than that (1) *officium* is *not honestum*;[96] (2) there is such a thing as *honestum*; (3) what is discussed in the *De officiis* (and therefore in Panaetius' περὶ καθήκοντος) is not *honestum* but *officium*? The very title of Panaetius' book should have been sufficient to show this. In that case we must remember that in the *De officiis* we have Panaetius' views on *kathekonta/officia*, but not on *katorthomata, agatha, honestum*. And indeed the statements and arguments of the *De officiis* bear the characteristic stamp of the *kathekon* group illustrated above. So the three general characteristics singled out by van Straaten,[97] (1) the concentration on human nature and not on the physical cosmos; (2) the stress on the objective rather than the subjective element in human actions, that is, the importance of attaining *ta kata physin*; (3) a moral system based on the appetites of human nature instead of based on knowledge; all these if applied purely to the doctrine of *officium* do not seem to me to be a shift of stress and emphasis; and, as I said, Cicero seems to take pains to point out that the subject is *officium* and

not *honestum*. Hence it appears to me false to relate Panaetius'
stress on individual endowments to a new interpretation of the
End. In van Straaten's argument,[98] there seems to be a confusion
as to the importance given to individual endowments and
universa natura. For one must distinguish (*a*) which of the two is
important to Panaetius for the moment in connexion with the
type of philosophical problems with which he is dealing, and
(*b*) which is of more basic importance, i.e. which in the last
resort cannot be disregarded. In the latter sense, which after all
must be the sense of the *telos*, Cicero says quite plainly *universa
natura*.[99] It is put first, and only *ea conservata* can we go on to take
account of individual endowments.[100] Then the *propria* are
important here to Panaetius as a practical guide among *officia*—
ta kata physin; that is, as part of the *materia* of the moral reason;
but they are subordinate to reason and not to be assigned more
importance in the End than *ta kata physin* with Antipater. It is
the subject-matter which puts 'la nature cosmique' in the background.[101] In the same way the stress on *appetitus* is natural in
a study of *officium*, as *ta kata physin* are the developments of the
hormai. But Cicero, *De off.* 1 141, puts it in its proper place.[102]

Posidonius may have regarded riches and wealth and such *ta
kata physin* in a different way from his predecessors because of
his admittedly new theory of the emotions dependent on his
new psychology;[103] but however one interprets Diogenes
Laertius VII 103, Ποσειδώνιος μέντοι καὶ ταῦτά [i.e. πλοῦτον
καὶ ὑγίειαν] φησι τῶν ἀγαθῶν εἶναι (Posidonius however says
that these too [wealth and health] are in the category of
goods),[104] the fact remains that they are contrasted by Posidonius with goods (*agatha*).[105] Posidonius himself discussed with
Pompey 'seriously and fully on this very point, that nothing was
good that was not morally good' (*honestum*).[106] The End as before
is to live in harmony with nature, which is precisely to live in
accordance with virtue, τὸ ὁμολογουμένως τῇ φύσει ζῆν, ὅπερ
ἐστὶ κατ' ἀρετὴν ζῆν. But it is true that Posidonius recognised
illogical virtues from the illogical faculties of the soul;[107] yet the
final point is the absolute control and importance of the rational
faculty.[108] So either D. L. VII 103 is to be regarded with suspicion in the same way as D. L. VII. 128;[109] in which case it is
interesting to trace how the misinterpretation is taken a stage

further by *Doxographi graeci*, p. 593, 9: Ποσειδώνιος 'Απαμεὺς
ἔλεγε τὸ μέγιστον ἐν ἀνθρώποις ἀγαθὸν εἶναι πλοῦτον καὶ ὑγιείαν
('Posidonius of Apameia used to say that the greatest good for
man was wealth and health'); or, with regard to Posidonius'
new psychology, it is to be interpreted in some such way as by
Edelstein,[110] but with reference to the illogical faculties of the
soul, and as such wealth, health, and *ta kata physin* in general do
not have positive value for sages (*sophoi*). We are told that
Posidonius criticised Chrysippus strongly on the doctrine of the
End;[111] but the criticism was not directed against what
Chrysippus thought the End was, but against Chrysippus'
interpretation of the End, which was faulty in Posidonius'
view because the earlier philosopher had recognised only the
rational in the soul; he could not, therefore, rightly interpret
the part played by the emotions for vice and virtue.[112] Posidonius, on the other hand, held that one could only understand
the End, if one understood the difficulty to mankind of the
emotions, and they were to be explained by positing irrational
faculties of the soul as well as a rational faculty. But the End lay
in the complete supremacy of the rational faculty.[113] Is there
room here for making wealth, health, and other similar *ta kata
physin*, goods (*agatha*) in the Stoic sense of the objects of the
sophoi, or for the conclusion that Posidonius thought virtue insufficient for happiness? Moreover Posidonius thought he was
in all this interpreting Zeno and Cleanthes.[114] I am not arguing
that Posidonius did not differ from former Stoics,[115] but only
that as a Stoic (and he seems to have been regarded as one), he
did not differ in the fundamental tenet. His whole approach to
the problem seems to have been different, and consequently his
view of *ta kata physin* may have been individual, but I suggest
they were not regarded as *agatha* in relation to the *telos*.[116]

V

If there was no change of opinion in the Stoa on this point, one
must ask how the confusion with regard to the position of *ta kata
physin* arose. I suggest a principal reason may be the failure to
appreciate the double nature of Stoic teaching exemplified by
kathekonta and *katorthomata*.[117] Perhaps a hint of how this worked

may come from the passage of Cicero referred to above,[118] when coupled with Seneca, *Epp.* 94, 95. In the *De officiis* the division between *honestum* and *similitudines honesti* (or *secunda quaedam honesta*, i.e. *officia*) is referred respectively to *sapientes* and *ii, in quibus sapientia perfecta non est*.[119] Now Seneca considers in *Epp.* 94, 95 whether *praecepta* are important in moral training and if so how, and suggests that the Stoics were divided on this point. I have tried to show that *praecepta* are closely linked with *kathekonta* and thus bound up with *ta kata physin*, their *axia* and *proegmena*. But what purpose would *praecepta* serve for the *sapiens*? So Seneca,[120]

Precepts will perhaps help you to do what should be done; but they will not help you to do it in the proper way; and if they do not help you to this end, they do not conduct you to virtue. I grant you that, if warned, a man will do what he should; but that is not enough, since the credit lies, not in the actual deed but in the way it is done.

The wise man does not need *praecepta*, since he does not act by external rules, but by his internal *logos*, therefore it is superfluous to give rules to one who knows, *praecepta dare scienti supervacuum est*.[121] Seneca does not argue against this dictum, but against the added *nescienti parum* (to one who does not know it is insufficient). But if this part of our philosophy is to be useful (*utilis*)[122] it must be so for Cicero's class of those who do not have perfect wisdom, *ii, in quibus sapientia perfecta non est*. To the Stoics these were the *prokoptontes* (those progressing, i.e. on the road to virtue), and in our sources we find them specifically connected with this.[123] Perhaps the best illustration is in Seneca, *Ep. mor.* 94, 50–1, which I should like to quote in full.

Furthermore what you mention is the mark of an already perfect man, of one who has attained the height of human happiness. But the approach to these qualities is slow and in the meantime, in practical matters, the path should be pointed out for the benefit of one who is still short of perfection, but is making progress. Wisdom by her own agency may perhaps show herself this path without the help of admonition; for she has brought the soul to a stage where it can be impelled only in the right direction. Weaker characters, however, need someone to precede them, to say: 'Avoid this', or 'Do that'. Moreover, if one awaits the time when one can know of oneself what the best line of action is, one will sometimes go astray, and by going astray will be hindered from arriving at the point where it is possible to be content with oneself. The soul should accordingly be guided at the very moment when it is becoming able to guide itself. Boys study according to direction. Their fingers are held and guided by others so that they may follow the outlines of the letters; next they are ordered to imitate a copy and base thereon a style of penmanship. Similarly the mind is helped if it is taught according to direction. Such facts as these prove that this department of philosophy is not superfluous.[124]

So in § 20 it is compared to doctors' advice in eye treatment of preparatory process, '. . . begin with darkness, and then go into half-lights, and finally be more bold, accustoming yourself gradually to the bright light of day'. Again it is a method referred to the *inexercitata mens*.[125] Now Seneca tells us[126] that Ariston denied any value to *praecepta*; but this fits in, for Ariston had no interest in *proegmena* or the *prokoptōn* but only in knowledge and the *sapiens*. But if Ariston rejected *praecepta*, Zeno must have upheld them, and again we know Zeno was interested in *kathekonta*. Not only did he write a treatise περὶ τοῦ καθήκοντος[127] but first introduced the term,[128] as he was also the first to use *axia* (value) and *apaxia* (disvalue) in their technical sense;[129] and he was also responsible for the term *proegmenon* and its classification in 'the second place'.[130] Finally Chrysippus is not the first to deal with the *prokoptontes* but Zeno.[131] Cleanthes, his pupil, thought rules useful 'utilem quidem iudicat et hanc partem [i.e. the *praeceptiva pars*] sed imbecillam nisi ab universo fluit,'[132] and once more we know he wrote three books περὶ τοῦ καθήκοντος.[133]

I suggest then that we have here a type of educative moral teaching not directed towards the *sapiens* but to the *prokoptōn*. For it must be true that the real way to educate the *sapiens* was by the *logos*-philosophy. So it seems to follow that *praecepta*, *kathekon*, *ta kata physin*, was a second-best philosophy, as the *De officiis*[134] says, intended for the guidance of the *prokoptontes* who had not the training, opportunity, or brain for the *logos*-philosophy to be true *sapientes*.[135] Then the Stoa had two philosophies, and from this one might be led to suggest, with Plutarch,[136] two ends. But this is strenuously denied by the Stoics,[137] apart from Herillus, [138] whose position, however, at least gives some colour to the arguments above. This must mean that there is only the one true *telos*, which is led up to by various stages. In that case it is perhaps more informative to think of the three divisions examined above as three stages of progress in their human philosophy: (1) the child, governed by *proton oikeion—ta prota kata physin*; (2) the adult, governed by *kathekonta —ta kata physin*; (3) the *sapiens* governed by *logos-arete-physis*. Something of the sort seems borne out by Philo,[139] where he considers to which moral types words like command (πρόσταξις), prohibition (ἀπαγόρευσις), injunction (ἐντολή), advice (παραί-νεσις) belong. He classifies: There is no need to command, forbid or advise the perfect sage; the man who is perfectly wise needs none of these; but the inadequate fool needs command and prohibition, and the child advice and teaching. Compare, too, Seneca, *Ep. mor.* 121, 14f. An objector asks, 'How then can a child, being not yet gifted with reason, adapt himself to a reasoning constitution?' The answer comes, 'Each age has its own constitution, one for the child, another for the boy, different again for the old man; all adapt themselves to the constitution they are in.' This is not quite the same, but it helps as a pointer.

If then the triple division be accepted, the different members of the Stoa could concentrate more on the second or on the third part without holding any different views on *ta kata physin*; Ariston certainly went to extremes on the third,[140] while Panaetius was more interested in the second.[141] This was sufficient to give him the reputation of being more compliant, 'softer' (*mitior*).[142] Zeno, Cleanthes, and Chrysippus, I have tried to show, were interested in both, with perhaps more stress on the *sapiens*. Now since all sections refer to nature, but since either nature in each refers to something different, or at least the technical phrases in which the word *physis* occurs have different reference, the confusion of the first and second division with the third in criticism leads to a confusion between the spheres of teaching of *kathekonta* and *katorthomata*.

It may be objected here that with this difference of reference with respect to *physis* we retain unanimity among members of the Stoa on a fundamental point of doctrine, at the cost of destroying internal unanimity within the system itself, which has already been stressed in this chapter.[143] There may be two ways of facing this.

With regard to the *sapiens*, *physis* means universal Nature in its broad sense; in *kathekonta*, *physis* in *ta kata physin* refers to human nature, *ta prota kata physin* being the first springs of this. But Seneca, *Ep. mor.* 121, 14f., shows that human beings are regarded as having a different *constitutio* (i.e. nature) at different stages in life, and they are assigned to these by universal Nature. That is, human nature goes through several stages controlled by universal Nature; but this progression is designed to culminate in a human nature which is in complete unanimity with universal Nature, through the perfection of *logos*, that is *homologoumenōs tēi physei*. So in all stages, neither of the two senses of *physis* is completely lost sight of, and certainly neither contradicts the other. Man was not born perfect; it is Nature's decree that only gradually should his nature progress to the culmination where not only is it under Nature's direction, but hand in glove with Nature itself and most like its workings. The problem is like two converging lines, the second being gradually attracted by the first until the two meet.

Secondly, it might conceivably be argued that *physis* means the same in all sections, with the meaning of universal Nature, and that the difference lay between *kata* 'in accordance with the direction of', *secundum* of Cicero, and *homologoumenos* 'complete unanimity with', *convenienter naturae*. Some sources seem to point to this,[144] and it may have been sometimes intended by Stoic writers, but the bulk of the evidence seems to point to the first explanation.

At all events, in the details of exposition there is one common thread which runs through the three sections, namely *ta kata physin*. They are developed from *ta prota kata physin* of the first section, form both the material (*hyle*) and the principle (*arche*) of the second, and are the material of the third. Cicero noted the thread in *De fin.* III 23:

Since all appropriate acts arise from the base of the primary natural impulses, it must be that wisdom itself springs from them too . . . at first we are introduced to wisdom by the primary natural impulses, but afterwards wisdom itself becomes dearer to us than the source from which we have come to it.

cum autem omnia officia a principiis naturae proficiscantur, ab iisdem necesse est proficisci ipsam sapientiam ... primo nos sapientiae commendari ab initiis naturae, post autem ipsam sapientiam nobis cariorem fieri quam illa sint a quibus ad hanc venerimus.

But the triple division remains distinct because of the different part *ta kata physin* play in each section. I suggest then that it was the failure to recognise this division in teaching that was the root of much subsequent confusion in criticism of the Stoa.

NOTES

1. This chapter was originally printed under the title, 'The Relation of Stoic Intermediates to the *Summum Bonum*, With Reference to Change in the Stoa', in *Classical Quarterly* NS v (1955) 181–94. I have translated most quotations in the text, and transliterated some recurring technical terms, in order to make the article more accessible to a wider circle of readers, in accordance with the general policy of this book. I gladly repeat my original acknowledgement of the criticism and encouragement of Prof. C. O. Brink.

2. Cf. Cic. *De fin*. v. 16–20.

3. Plutarch, *Moralia* 1033ff. and 1058ff.; contained in the Teubner edition of Plutarch's *Moralia*, VI 2, edited by Pohlenz.

4. This line of criticism is more developed in Cicero, *De fin*. IV and v, where the Stoics are accused of not departing from the Peripatetics in fact, but only in terminology.

5. Cf. Cic. *De fin*. IV 78.

6. Cf. Cic. *De fin*. IV 40; 41; 46.

7. Pohlenz, 'Plutarchs Schriften gegen die Stoiker', *Hermes* lxxiv, 23–6. Cf. *Die Stoa* i 186ff.; 191ff.

8. *Hermes* lxxiv, 23. Cf. *Die Stoa* i 186–90.

9. *Hermes* lxxiv, 24.

10. *Die Stoa* i 189.

11. *Die Stoa* i 199; derived from Diog. Laert. VII 128.

12. Reesor, 'The Indifferents in the Old and Middle Stoa', *TAPhA* lxxxii (1951) 109.

13. Op. cit., p. 109.

14. Ibid. p. 110; based on the doctrine that the 'indifferents' were necessary, from Diog. Laert. VII 128 (ibid., p. 106).

15. Ibid., p. 110.

16. Ibid., p. 107.

17. From Cic. *De off*. II.

18. Reesor, op. cit., p. 110.

19. Ibid., p. 110; based on the arguments of Edelstein, *AJPh* lvii (1936) 308–9.

20. van Straaten, *Panétius* (Amsterdam 1946).

21. Fr. 96 of van Straaten's collection of the fragments.

22. Op. cit., pp. 140–1.

23. Ibid., pp. 143–4.

24. Ibid., p. 145.

25. Ibid., pp. 147f.

26. Ibid., pp. 152–3.

27. Ibid., p. 154. The evidence for this is our old friend Diog. Laert. VII 128.

28. Ibid., pp. 191–200.

29. Ibid., p. 191.

30. Ibid., pp. 191–2; 167.

31. Ibid., pp. 166ff.

32. Cic. *De fin.* V 14; 15.

33. Diog. Laert. VII 84.

34. In general see *SVF* III 178–89; Cic. *De fin.* III 16; *De off.* I 11; Sen. *Ep. mor.* 121, 14ff.; the evidence catalogued by Pohlenz, *Die Stoa* ii 65–6; Philippson, 'Das Erste Naturgemässe', *Philol.* lxxxvii 445ff.; Brink, 'Theophrastus and Zeno on Nature in Moral Theory', *Phronesis* i 123–45.

35. Cic. *De fin.* III 20ff. [On *prot*ɘn *oikeion* see S. G. Pembroke, Chapter VI, pp. 116ff. Ed.].

36. *SVF* III 178; 179; 181; 182.

37. *SVF* I 149.

38. For sources see *SVF* I 230–2; III 491–543.

39. *proficisci ab*, Cic. *De fin.* III 22; 60.

40. καὶ τίνα λάβω τοῦ καθήκοντος ἀρχὴν καὶ ὕλην τῆς ἀρετῆς, ἀφεὶς τὴν φύσιν καὶ τὸ κατὰ φύσιν; Plutarch *Comm. not.* 1069E (=*SVF* III 491); cf. op. cit. 1070A (=*SVF* III 123).

41. E.g. Cic. *De fin.* III 22.

42. Cic. *De fin.* III 58. Cf. ibid. III 59; *Acad. post.* I 37 (=*SVF* III 231).

43. Stob. *SVF* III 136; cf. *SVF* III 117ff.; Cic. *De fin.* III 62ff.

44. Cic *De fin.* III 50–1; *SVF* III 124–6.

45. *nisi si quid impedierit*, Seneca, *De otio* III 2 (=*SVF* I 271); Cic. *De fin.* III 23.

46. Diog. Laert. VII 107 (=*SVF* III 117); Sextus *Adv. math.* XI 59 (=*SVF* III 122); Plut. *Stoic. rep.* 1048C (=*SVF* III 123).

47. Cic. *De fin.* III 51–2; cf. Stob. *SVF* I 192; *SVF* III 126ff.

48. Cic. *De fin.* III 22.

49. Shown by the application of the term *kathekon* in its wider form to plants and animals (*SVF* I 230), and the attempt at etymology in Diog. Laert. VII 108.

50. Cicero classifies: 'omnis de officio duplex est quaestio: unum genus est quod pertinet ad finem bonorum' (this is *officium* in its wider sense as shown by the example given of this class, *omniane officia perfecta sint*. See previous note; in this sense in the human sphere *kathekon* may be applied to perfect human action, but as such is always qualified by τέλειον in contrast to μέσον καθῆκον. When unqualified it is always used in the narrower sense of a restricted technical term in human ethics—so *De fin.* IV 39), 'alterum, quod positum est in praeceptis, quibus in omnis partis usus vitae conformari possit'; and just below, 'quorum autem officiorum praecepta traduntur . . . de quibus est nobis his libris explicandum'.

51. Sen. *Ep. mor.* 95, 45.

52. So Cicero, *De fin.* III 58–9: 'ut si iuste depositum reddere in recte factis sit, in officiis ponatur depositum reddere; illo enim addito "iuste" fit recte factum, per se autem hoc ipsum reddere in officio ponitur'. Cf. Clement, *SVF* III 515; Sextus, *SVF* III 516.

53. I take the anecdote in Diog. Laert. VII 25 to apply here, where immediately after the sentence that Zeno is said πρῶτον καθῆκον ὠνομακέναι, καὶ λόγον περὶ

αὐτοῦ πεποιηκέναι, the story follows that Zeno changed Hesiod, *Op.* 293 to κεῖνος μὲν πανάριστος ὃς εὖ εἰπόντι πιθῆται.

54. Cic *De off.* I 39; 59; Philo, *SVF* III 513; Diog. Laert. VII 102 (=*SVF* III 117).

55. Cic. *De fin.* III 59; Sextus *Adv. math.* XI 199ff.; Sen. *Ep. mor.* 95, 5; 39; 40; 43; id. *De ben.* VI 11, 1–2 (=Cleanthes *SVF* I 579; Philo, *SVF* III 512: ὁ φαῦλος ἔνια δρᾷ τῶν καθηκόντων οὐκ ἀφ' ἕξεως καθηκούσης, where by ἕξις καθήκουσα is meant ἕξις λογική and ἕξις καὶ διάθεσις εὐλόγιστος.

56. Cic. *De fin.* IV 15: 'hoc non est positum in nostra actione'; cf. Fronto *SVF* III 196: 'nec quidquam quod in manu fortunae situm videat concupiscet'; cf. Epictetus *passim*.

57. Stob. *SVF* III 510: ὁ δ' ἐπ' ἄκρον, φησί, προκόπτων ἅπαντα πάντως ἀποδίδωσι τὰ καθήκοντα καὶ οὐδὲν παραλείπει. τὸν δὲ τούτου βίον οὐκ εἶναί πω φησὶν εὐδαίμονα . . .

58. Diog. Laert. VII 104: ἐνδέχεται γὰρ καὶ χωρὶς τούτων (i.e. πλοῦτος, δόξα, ἰσχύς, καὶ τὰ ὅμοια) εὐδαιμονεῖν.

59. *SVF* I 188; III 29–37, 129, 181, 498.

60. Plutarch *Comm. not.* XXIII 1069E: καὶ τίνα λάβω . . . ὕλην τῆς ἀρετῆς, ἀφεὶς τὴν φύσιν καὶ τὸ κατὰ φύσιν; id. op. cit. XXVI 1071 B: ἀλλ' ὥσπερ ὕλη τις ὑπόκειται; Cic. *De fin.* III 23; 'ab iisdem (principiis naturae) necesse est proficisci ipsam sapientiam'; ibid. 31: 'quid autem apertius quam, si selectio nulla sit ab iis rebus quae contra naturam sint earum rerum quae sint secundum naturam, tollatur omnis ea quae quaeratur laudeturque prudentia?'; cf. 58–61, especially 'prima autem illa naturae sive secunda sive contraria sub iudicium sapientis et dilectum cadunt, estque illa subiecta quasi materia sapientiae' (61).

61. Plut. *Comm. not.* XXIII 1069E.

62. See n. 52. This is the force of the added *iuste* of Cicero, the ἀπὸ φρονήσεως of Sextus. So Sen. *Ep. mor.* 95, 43, forcibly: 'amico aliquis aegro adsidet: probamus. at hoc hereditatis causa facit: vultur est, cadaver expectat. eadem aut turpia sunt aut honesta; refert quare aut quemadmodum fiant.'

63. Plut. *Comm. not.* XXVI 1071B; cf. Cic. *De fin.* III 32. They are like the ball in a ball game, Epict. *Diss.* II 5, 15.

64. So the title of Panaetius' book is περὶ καθήκοντος

65. Plut. *Stoic. rep.* IX; cf. Cic. *De fin.* III 73.

66. The authorities, Diog. Laert. VII 39f. and Sextus *Adv. math.* VII 16ff., are much confused here between order of teaching and interconnexion of the subjects.

67. *SVF* II 41; Cic. *De fin.* III 74; IV 54; V 83. This seems to me the point of Plutarch's method of criticism by contradictions.

68. E.g. *SVF* I 85; II 299ff.

69. E.g. *SVF* I 120; 171; II 423; 774.

70. *SVF* I 134.

71. Diog. Laert. VII 88: ὁ νόμος ὁ κοινός, ὅσπερ ἐστὶν ὁ ὀρθὸς λόγος . . . εἶναι δ' αὐτὸ τοῦτο τὴν εὐδαίμονος ἀρετήν. And virtue is τελειότης τῆς ἑκάστου φύσεως, *SVF* III 260.

72. Plut. *Stoic. rep.* VII 1034 C (Pohlenz's emendation, or something like it must be right); Plut. *De virt. mor.* II. So Sextus *Adv. math.* XI 200 (=*SVF* III 516); cf. Diog Laert. VII 92. Seneca shows how this works *Ep. mor.* 95, 5; 57.

73. Diog. Laert. VII 88. [For some consequences concerning human action which seem to follow from this common *logos*, see Chapter VIII, pp. 178f. Ed.]

74. Sextus *Adv. math.* XI 13 (=*SVF* II 36): τὴν δὲ σοφίαν ἐπιστήμην θείων τε καὶ ἀνθρωπίνων πραγμάτων; Epict. *Diss.* I 10, 10: παρακαλῶ σε παρὰ Χρυσίππου ἐπισκέψασθαι τίς ἐστιν ἡ τοῦ κόσμου διοίκησις καὶ ποίαν τινὰ χώραν ἐν αὐτῷ ἔχει τὸ λογικὸν ζῷον.

75. Diog. Laert. VII 88.

76. Sen. *Ep. mor.* 95, 48.

77. E.g. *De fin.* III 24; 34; 36; 40; 44; IV 45.

78. Ibid. V 14; 15.

79. *SVF* III 2, 44; III 3, 57.

80. So v. Straaten, op. cit., p. 152: 'une différence dans la façon de formuler'

81. Cic. *De fin.* III 33: 'paulum oppido inter se differunt, et tamen eodem spectant'.

82. *SVF* III 3, 56; 57.

83. Panaetius fr. 110, v. Straaten. For its importance as evidence, see v. Straaten, op. cit., pp. 154f., 159; moreover v. Straaten thinks the three objects named by Diog. Laert. are representative of the whole class of *ta kata physin*; Pohlenz *Die Stoa* i p. 199; *NGG* I (1936), 4; Reesor, *TAPhA* lxxxii (1951) 106, 109.

84. For Galen, see below.

85. Plut. 1048A =*SVF* III 137.

86. Cf. Plut. *Stoic. rep.* xv; Cic. *De fin.* III 52.

87. *De anim.* p. 163, lines 4ff. Bruns (=*SVF* III 192).

88. Ibid. lines 8–9 Bruns.

89. Cf. points (2) and (3) of Plutarch, pp. 150f.

90. Panaetius fr. 109.

91. Clem. Pan. fr. 96.

92. Cf. Cleanthes *SVF* I 566; Chrysippus, Diog. Laert. VII 89 (=*SVF* III 228). v. Straaten, who thinks Panaetius is saying something different, although his method of formulation is practically identical with that of his predecessors (op. cit., p. 152), notes, 'on ne pourra donner que difficilement une réponse à la question de savoir pourquoi Panétius a précisément choisi cette façon de formuler' (p. 152, n. 3.).

93. E.g. 'quae quattuor quamquam inter se colligata atque implicata sunt, tamen ex singulis certa officiorum genera nascuntur', I 15; 'honestum, ex quo aptum est officium', I 60; 'sed ab iis partibus, quae sunt honestatis, quem ad modum officia ducerentur, satis expositum videtur', I 152; cf. Sen. *Ep. mor.* 94, 33: 'et prudentia et iustitia officiis constat, officia praeceptis disponuntur'.

94. Cf. *De off.* I 46: 'quoniam autem vivitur non cum perfectis hominibus planeque sapientibus, sed cum iis, in quibus praeclare agitur si sunt simulacra virtutis'.

95. Cf. *De off.* I 7.

96. *Officium*, that is, in its restricted technical sense in human ethics. See above n. 50.

97. v. Straaten, op. cit., pp. 191–200.

98. Op. cit., pp. 140ff.

99. *De off.* I 110.

100. Cf. *De off.* I 107. We are invested by nature with two characters, 'quarum una communis est ex eo, quod omnes participes sumus rationis praestantiaeque eius, qua antecellimus bestiis, a qua omne honestum decorumque trahitur, et ex qua ratio inveniendi officii exquiritur, altera autem, quae proprie singulis est tributa.'

101. v. Straaten, op. cit., p. 143.

102. 'in omni autem actione suscipienda tria sunt tenenda, primum ut appetitus rationi pareat . . . horum tamen trium praestantissimum est appetitum obtemperare rationi.'

103. See Edelstein, 'The Philosophical System of Posidonius', *AJPh* lvii (1936) 305ff. For this paragraph see also my chapter , 'Posidonius on Emotions.'

104. Cf. Edelstein, op. cit., pp. 308–10.

105. E.g. Sen. *Ep. mor.* 87, 35; 31.

106. Cic. *Tusc.* II 61; cf. Gal. *De plac.* 370, 3 M: οἱ σοφοὶ μέγιστα καὶ ἀνυπέρβλητα νομίζοντες εἶναι ἀγαθὰ τὰ καλὰ πάντα.

107. Gal. *De plac.* 446 13 M.

108. Ibid. 449, 7; Clem. *Strom.* II 129.

109. See above, pp. 159.

110. Edelstein, loc. cit.

111. Gal. *De plac.* 449 8ff.; 450 3ff.; 451 2–5 M.

112. Gal. *De plac.* 450ff. M.

113. See above, n. 108; also Gal. *De plac.* 451 15–452. 10 M, which ends σοφία δὲ καὶ πᾶν ὅσον ἀγαθόν τε καὶ καλὸν ἅμα τοῦ λογικοῦ καὶ θείου; also 453 10f.

114. Gal. *De plac.* 456 M.

115. Edelstein, op. cit., has shown his heresies.

116. Cf. Rieth, 'Über das Telos der Stoiker', *Hermes* lxix (1934) 39–44.

117. Augmented, of course, by the fragmentary nature of our sources; e.g. we have quite a lot of information about Panaetius on *kathekonta* but little on *katorthomata*.

118. *De off.* III 11ff.

119. So also *De off.* I 46.

120. Sen. *Ep. mor.* 95, 40.

121. Ibid. 94, 11.

122. Cic. *De fin.* III 58; Sen. *Ep. mor.* 94, 21.

123. E.g. *progressio* in Cic. *De off.* III 17.

124. The translations of the Letters are from Gummere in the Loeb edition.

125. Sen. *Ep. mor.* 94, 29.

126. Ibid. 94.

127. Diog. Laert. VII 4; 25.

128. Diog. Laert. VII 25.

129. Stob. *SVF* I 192.

130. τὴν δευτέραν χώραν καὶ ἀξίαν ἔχον συνεγγίζειν πως τῇ τῶν ἀγαθῶν φύσει, Stob. *SVF* I 192; cf. Cic. *De fin.* III 52: '... sed eos qui in aliquo honore sunt quorum ordo proxime accedit, ut secundus sit, ad regium principatum, sic in vita non ea quae primo ordine [Madvig] sunt, sed ea, quae secundum locum obtinent, προηγμένα . . . nominentur.'

131. E.g. Plut. *Mor.* 82F.: ἠξίου (sc. ὁ Ζήνων) γὰρ ἀπὸ τῶν ὀνείρων ἕκαστον αὑτοῦ συναισθάνεσθαι προκόπτοντος; and what else is the comparison of Plato and the tyrant Dionysius in Cic. *De fin.* IV 56?

132. Sen. *Ep. mor.* 94, 4.

133. Diog. Laert. VII 175.

134. Cic. *De off.* III 15; see above, p. 161.

135. Cf. Sen. *Ep. mor.* 94, 30: 'hoc qui dicunt (i.e. that *praecepta nihil adiuvant*) non vident alium esse ingenii mobilis et erecti, alium tardi et hebetis, utique alium alio ingeniosiorem'; cf. Epict. *Diss.* I, II 33f.

136. Plut. *Comm. not.* XXVI 1071; see above, p. 151.

137. Cic. *De fin.* III 22.

138. Ibid. IV 40.

139. *SVF* III 519; twisted typically by Plut. *Stoic. rep.* XI.

140. Sen. *Ep. mor.* 94, 2.

141. Ibid. 116, 5 (=Pan. fr. 114).

142. Cic. *De fin.* IV 79 (=Pan. fr. 55). Besides, Cicero seems more concerned with language and style, cf. *De off.* II 35 (=Pan. fr. 62).

143. Prof. C. O. Brink pointed out this difficulty to me.

144. E.g. Cic. *De fin.* IV 14–15; Sen. *Ep. mor.* 121, 16.

VIII

Freedom and Determinism in the Stoic Theory of Human Action

A. A. LONG

In antiquity the Stoics gained the reputation of being strict determinists and this reputation has generally persisted up to the present day. Their attempts to give man some power of self-determination have found little support. Either the Stoics are accused of holding contradictory positions or, it is argued, their distinctions between causes are merely verbal quibbles which leave man at best in a position of semi-slavery. *Prima facie* it would be surprising if philosophers whose main concern was ethical robbed the human mind of *libera voluntas* as Carneades alleges.[1] The wise man certainly gets the credit for his goodness and other men are culpable for falling short of his moral status. But this, in the opinion of Alexander of Aphrodisias, shows the absurdity of the Stoic thesis: neither praise nor blame has any justifiable basis if men cannot act contrary to the nature given them by destiny.[2]

A detailed study of the arguments directed against the Stoic theory of determinism would not be appropriate here.[3] But even a selective reading of Alexander's lengthy treatise *De fato* will show that an Aristotelian scholar of the third century A.D. was capable both of misrepresenting and misunderstanding the Stoics. A comparable bias blinkers most of our secondary sources for the early Stoic attitude on freedom and human action. It is arguable that many of the claims against particular Stoic propositions on this question fall short of full cogency in failing to grasp the concept of freedom which the Stoics did entertain. Nor is the disagreement between Stoics and other ancient philosophers as great as the heat of ancient polemic might suggest.

In this chapter I hope to prove two related propositions: first, that Stoic determinism does not exclude a coherent theory of voluntary human action; second, that the Stoic concept of moral responsibility, though unsatisfactory, represents an advance on Aristotle in raising sharply the problems of heredity and environment.

Before turning to the Stoics proper we need to ask briefly how far freedom/determinism is a valid antithesis in Greek philosophy, and if valid, what it denotes.[4] Although a form of subjectivism won some adherents among sophists and sceptics no theory of ethics which exercised serious influence denied the possibility of designating certain types of action culpable or commendable. It is a matter of general agreement that there are circumstances in which men can be praised or blamed for what they do, or for what they are. For Aristotle the circumstances which exclude praise or blame are ones in which it can be shown that a man acted under external constraint or venial ignorance of his circumstances.[5] It is common ground to him and Plato that internal forces, desire and appetite, may 'compel' a man against his better judgement to act viciously, but 'internal constraint' is no excuse. The fact that some peoples' character (*hexis*) becomes more or less fixed by a certain age may rule out, for Aristotle, the possibility of their moral improvement.[6] But it does not rule out 'moral responsibility', since the agent acquired his character by repeatedly *and deliberately* acting in a certain way. In Plato the question of improvement or deterioration is complicated by the belief in a cycle of incarnations for the soul (the moral person). But if Plato thinks that the nature of the soul is generally determined by a dominant characteristic, as the theory of temperaments outlined in *Republic* x would suggest, it is also his belief that the soul chooses its new life deliberately in the light of its previous experience.[7]

A form of ethical determinism is common then to Plato and Aristotle. It is not, in their view, open to a man to act quite independently of the character acquired by previous acts of choice. Both are alive to the influences for good or bad of upbringing on character, Plato more than Aristotle, but neither entertains the belief that deleterious background removes moral

responsibility. Moral ignorance is culpable.[8] The determinism
exercised by character on action reappears in a similar, if more
extreme form, in Stoicism.

If freedom to act out of character is a concept generally
denied or ignored in Greek philosophy it is clear that the Stoics
were not regarded as determinists in antiquity merely for
asserting a necessary connexion between character and action.[9]
The charge was brought against them because of their theory
of causation.[10] Neither Plato nor Aristotle accepted the notion
of a totally uncaused event, but they did not take the further
step with the Stoics of asserting a strict causal nexus whereby
every event is necessarily tied to an antecedent and is itself
necessarily the cause of a consequent.[11] If all events are regarded
in Stoic theory like the 'unwinding of a rope' (Cic. *De div.* 1, 127)
and this includes human actions the Stoics were liable to answer
charges of making choice and deliberation meaningless. How
indeed could a man be regarded as an agent in the Aristotelian
sense of an ἀρχὴ κινήσεως? Was he not merely an instrument
for transmitting a predetermined effect? It was one thing to
assert that character determines action: a man might perform
at any moment one of a number of possible actions without
behaving out of character. But the Stoics were taken to be
claiming much more—the impossibility of acting otherwise.
That is to say, the action I perform is the only action which I
can perform since it and it alone is the necessary consequence
of a necessary antecedent.

How far these accusations are justified in fact remains to be
seen. But there is one point which should be mentioned at once.
Even if they are all valid an essential aspect of the Stoic concept
of freedom would not be touched. What matters to the Stoic sage
is his disposition, how he is inside. He is free because he feels
free, because he makes up his own mind about moral action in
accordance with the values prescribed by *orthos logos*.[12] At the
very least he can have the consciousness of determining his own
attitude to events and a feeling of freedom about the actions he
performs. How a man feels about himself is fundamental in
Stoicism. Whether vulnerable or not this concept of freedom
was not attacked by critics of Stoic determinism.

I

The Stoics prided themselves on the consistency and coherence of their system. The divisions of philosophy, which they made, into physics, logic and ethics were necessary for exposition, but they do not constitute independent subjects. Logic and physics are associated by the theory of knowledge, and the ethical goal is to attain self-fulfilment by living consistently with reason or, as Chrysippus phrased it, 'living in accordance with experience of natural events'.[13] Indeed, virtue and vice are 'physical' dispositions of the mind, distinguished from one another by different *pneumatic* tension. But this fact does not make ethics merely a branch of physics. Ethical and physical explanations, though inter-dependent, are different but equally valid ways of accounting for the world. To say of God that he is 'good, provident and benevolent' is as true and basic, in Stoic thought, as the statement that he is all-pervading *pneuma*. We may expect therefore that physical theories of causation and theories about human action will be necessarily related, but we should also expect differences of subject-matter to produce different, though mutually consistent, types of explanation.

The Stoics can be shown to meet these expectations with considerable skill (see Chapter V, pp. 95f.). A greater source of tension in their system is the presentation of reality through bifocal lenses. The world is one and many; it is God and his parts. There is an eternal perspective and a human viewpoint. At one moment it is necessary to view the totality and inter-connexion of all events; at another time attention must be given to a particular fragment of this totality. Then it may be proper to use terms like 'possible' and 'non-necessary', to assign priority to one causal explanation over another, to make use of distinctions which are irrelevant when we try to see things outside the time-scale, from God's viewpoint.[14] Above all, a belief in the continuum of events has to be reconciled with a belief in individual material objects, whose essential characteristics persist throughout their history. For a modern commentator this is the central problem posed by the Stoic concept of human action.

The following propositions (a representative selection from hostile witnesses and attested fragments) assert a form of determinism which could be taken to rule out any autonomy of action, whether preceding or following the formation of character:

(1) 'Prior events are causes of those following them, and in this manner all things are bound together with one another, and thus nothing happens in the world such that something else is not entirely a consequence of it and attached to it as cause. . . . From everything that happens something else follows depending on it by necessity as cause.' (Alex. Aphr., *Fat.* XXII p. 192, 1ff. [*SVF* II 945]).

(2) 'Nothing occurs which was not to be, and in the same way nothing is to be, the efficient causes of which are not contained in nature (Cic. *De div.* I, 125) . . . The passage of time is like the unwinding of a rope, bringing about nothing new.' (ibid., 127.)

(3) (The Stoics say that) 'All things have been fixed and arranged from the beginning, including those which are said to be situated in our power and those said to be fortuitious and subject to chance . . . The movements of our minds are nothing more than instruments for carrying out determined decisions (*ministeria decretorum fatalium*) since it is necessary that they be performed through us (*per nos*) by the agency of fate (*agente fato*). Thus men play the role of a necessary condition, just as place is a necessary condition for motion and rest.' (Chalcidius, *In Tim.* CLX-CLXI [*SVF* II 943].)

(4) (Chrysippus says that) 'No particular event, however small, takes place which is not in accordance with universal nature and its principle.' (Plut. *Stoic. rep.* 34, 1050A [*SVF* II 937].)

What links these passages is not only their assertion of determinism but the fact also that they assume a common perspective, the cosmic one. As we shall see, Stoic writers also approach the problem from the other vantage-point, that of the human individual. Hostile sources naturally fasten on propositions which seem favourable to denigration. But it is clearly incumbent on the Stoics to do more than merely assert 'God's ways are not our ways' or 'I feel free, even if I'm not'. The two dimensions must be brought together if the issue is to be decided without undue partiality to one side or the other.

By destiny the Stoics meant an eternal nexus of causes.[15] According to Cicero superstitious views of *fatum* are to be contrasted with the Stoic conception (*De div.* 1 125). To them, *fatum* is the answer to the questions, why has X occurred, why is X occurring and why will X occur. It is, in brief, the law of cause and effect, the law that every event is completely determined by antecedent causes and will, itself, help to determine subsequent events. But though identical, in some aspects, to necessity this law is not mechanical but divine ordinance itself.[16] Effects follow causes and become causes themselves because this is 'universal nature', the principle or *logos* by which God's plan is effected. We may be confident that the primary motive behind the Stoics' advocacy of a closed and ordered system was teleological, the desire to refer all events to divine purpose.

Logos itself is a term interchangeable in its cosmic sense with destiny.[17] When the Stoics made this identification it is probable that they had 'seminal reason' (*spermatikos logos*), the principle of growth, primarily in mind.[18] The law of cause and effect is also a law of ordered development. Nothing new is brought about by the passage of time since the seeds from which things grow are contained in the basic structure of the universe. God, it seems, not only plans the world with foreknowledge of the result, but fulfils the plan in his capacity as causal principle, immanent in all things. From this it is an easy inference to assert with Chalcidius that 'the Stoics regard even those things which are said to be in our power as decreed *ex initio*; man is merely the necessary condition for carrying out decisions under the direction of *fatum*'.[19] If this is correct, and Chalcidius claims to be reporting the Stoics directly, human decisions are completely pre-determined.

Now from one perspective Chalcidius' remarks are probably accurate; but, if taken just as they stand, they give a thoroughly false impression of the complete early Stoic position on destiny and human action. As I have remarked, the world can be viewed as nothing but the activity of all-pervasive *pneuma*. Yet *logos*, the causal principle, is inside the individual man as well as being an external force constraining him. God is expressed in the whole, the sum of all substances, which includes particular *logoi*; to describe man as nothing more than a necessary condition for the fulfilment of God's plan is misleading. For man is a particular *logikos*, a subordinate partner of the gods, a rational being in his own right, and how plan the planner?[20]

Some progress towards resolving the problem may perhaps be achieved if we follow through the implications of Stoic pantheism. Not all of God has planned the individual man's life in isolation (whether temporal or spatial) from him since there is a portion of God which is not external but inherent in every human being, namely his own *logos*. This is but a fragment of the whole, and its powers are naturally weak, so weak that 'following' rather than 'initiating' events is stressed as its proper function.[21] But man has some autonomy, and the nature of Stoicism is grossly mistaken by late sources which isolate the individual's *logos* from the determining process in the universe. The relationship between the individual *logos* and that of the world at large is expressed in the *telos* formula τὸ ἀκολούθως τῇ φύσει ζῆν, explained as 'life in harmony with one's own nature, and that of the universe'.[22] The implications of this for determinism are not expressed as clearly as we should like in any extant fragment, but they can, I think, be shown to refute the idea that man is nothing but a mechanical link in the causal chain. Indeed, Cleanthes comes most of our way in his *Hymn to Zeus*.[23] There it is denied that the decisions of evil men are planned by God, a flat contradiction of part of Chalcidius' claim. But Cleanthes does not rule out the interpretation suggested above. He is thinking of God as an absolute power, embracing all things and uniting good and evil. Yet evil actions are not planned by God in his identity as one omnipotent ruler.[24] What he does is to unite all things in a harmonious whole. Can we say that evil actions are ones purposed by certain fragments of his *logos*? They would bear no more resemblance to God as such than does a brick to the house it helps to form. It is hard to avoid this conclusion, and it does explain how God can reconcile individual good and evil while expressing only good in the whole.

Of the four deterministic passages cited above only Chalcidius' refers specifically to human action. The rest, though not necessarily inconsistent with his statement, allow the possibility of a more significant place for human decisions than the mechanical service of destiny. For instance, Alexander does not say that *one and only one* effect is compatible with each antecedent cause. He does say that every event is necessarily linked to *some* antecedent cause and necessarily becomes itself a cause of *something* else. We have, of course, to preserve God's omniscience, but to know that something will take place need not entail causing it (in any or every sense) to happen.[25] Nor do the references to everything happening in accordance with universal nature exclude human autonomy completely since man, like everything else (though unlike in his possession of *logos*), is a part of that nature.[26] The cosmic and individual perspectives are brought together in an illuminating passage from Alexander.[27]

II

The Stoics, though removing the possibility of choosing and performing either of two contrary actions, assert that what occurs through our instrumentality (δι'ἡμῶν) is attributable to (in the power of, ἐφ'ἡμῖν) us. For, they argue, since things and events have different natures . . . the result of any individual's action accords with its specific nature. The action of a stone accords with the nature of a stone, that of fire with the nature of fire and that of a living thing with the nature of a living thing. No event performed by anything in accordance with its nature can happen otherwise than it does, but they all happen so from necessity though not perforce, since it is impossible that something which has a nature to act in one way, given certain necessary circumstances, should act differently in that situation. If a stone is released from a height, it cannot fail to fall unless something prevents it. This is because it possesses weight within itself, the weight serving as cause of its natural movement. When external causes are available to assist the stone's natural movement, the stone necessarily moves in its natural way . . . not only is the stone unable not to move given such external causes, but necessarily at such time it does move. Such a movement occurs by the agency of fate through the stone's instrumentality. It is the same with other things. . . . Living creatures possess a natural movement, that is, movement prompted by impulse. For every living creature, so far as its own self is concerned, moves by impulsive movement, which comes about by the agency of fate (ὑπὸ τῆς εἱμαρμένης) through the creature's instrumentality (διὰ ζῴου). . . . Movements which occur in this way are regarded by the Stoics as attributable to (in the

power of) animals, and they are related to necessity in the same way
as all other events by the fact that external causes must be available
at the particular time, which results in the animals' realising of
necessity their internal capacity for impulsive movement.[28]

Here it is argued that all events are necessary in the sense (1)
that something must act when it is prompted by external
causes, and (2) how a thing acts in consequence of external
causes is necessarily accordant with its nature. But this second
point (at least as Alexander has expressed it) is quite innocuous
to defendants of free will. A man cannot fail to act humanly (in
the biological sense of that word) any more than a stone can
fail to fall if dropped from a height. But this only shows that all
human actions are necessarily human, a bare tautology. What
the Stoics mean is that man does not choose his nature in the
sense of his basic capacities. Human action is controlled from
within by assent and impulse,[29] and the fact that man has no
choice but to act by these powers tells us nothing against his
freedom to act *as a man*. To say that man's nature is fated only
means here that the basic capacities with which a man is born
are determined by external causes.[30] It would mean much more
if the powers of assent and impulse in particular actions were
entirely determined externally, but the first argument for the
necessity of all events does not assert this. It merely asserts that
assent and impulse are necessarily activated by external circumstances, and cannot be activated otherwise. This does not entail
that the necessary response of the mind takes one and only one
form, like the falling of a stone. True, Alexander opens the
passage with a denial from the Stoics of the possibility of choosing either of two contraries. But his discussion does not prove
this claim. It *is* proved in a Stoic argument which he cites elsewhere (see p. 183), but there it makes a point about the difference between good and bad men, not an assertion of the extrinsic
determination of every human volition.

The distinction between external and internal causes, pre-
supposed by Alexander, is familiar from Cicero's *De fato*.[31]
There Chrysippus is quoted as follows: 'When we say that all
events are determined by antecedent causes we do not mean
they are determined in virtue of principal and perfect causes
but in virtue of their auxiliary and proximate ones' (cum

dicimus omnia fato fieri causis antecedentibus, non hoc intellegi volumus: causis perfectis et principalibus, sed: causis adiuvantibus et proximis, 41). In this way Chrysippus claimed to make human actions fated but not necessary. He continues:

If auxiliary and proximate causes are not in our power it does not follow that even impulse (*adpetitus*) is not in our power . . . this conclusion will hold against those who so introduce destiny that they (also) annex necessity; but it will not hold against those who distinguish antecedent causes from perfect and principal ones. . . . For although assent (*adsensio*) cannot take place unless it has been prompted by a presentation, yet . . . assent has this as its proximate not principal cause. . . . Just as someone who pushes a drum forward gives it a beginning of movement, but not its capacity to roll, so the visual object which presents itself . . . will mark its image on the mind; but assent will be in our power and . . . once it has been given an external stimulus it will move itself for the rest by its own force and nature (*suapte vi et natura*, 41–3).

Necessity is apparently avoided by making the internal cause 'principal and perfect', and this is something which is referable to the agent and to him alone.[32] In explaining a deliberate act as the combination of a presentation and an internal response Chrysippus is in line with the general position of Aristotle (*De an.* III 10–11).

Cicero does not attribute to Chrysippus the view, evidenced by Alexander (and Nemesius, *SVF* III 991), that the internal powers are themselves the gift of fate or destiny. But Chrysippus' argument is perfectly consistent with this. He is concerned with explaining how action takes place at any moment; assent is a power given to man by fate which enables him to accept or reject the impressions presented to the mind. His judgement will not be free, in the sense 'totally uncaused', since it is an axiom of Stoic psychology, as we shall see (p. 187), that environment *and* character determine acts of choice. But that is common to much of Greek and more recent thought.

Before passing to consider what the Stoics meant by denying the possibility of 'acting otherwise' let us try to sum up this section of discussion. Any internal power of action requires an external cause for its actualisation. These 'proximate' or 'antecedent' causes are outside the individual's control. But the consequence which they promote, or can promote, requires the cooperation of the thing acted upon, just as this requires the external stimulus. A man cannot act without taking up an attitude towards his environment. Hence the times at which he acts and the range of actions available to him are determined by circumstance. But we have no evidence yet, outside Chalcidius', to hold that within these limits no alternative actions are available. It is not determined independently of a man's own volition that he will become a father.[33] The will of the agent, according to Chrysippus, is a necessary cause of many events. To say of a particular child's birth 'it was fated' means that the causal sequence leading to it entailed an act of volition by the parents as well as external circumstances. From the cosmic perspective the agent's will forms part of the causal nexus, but the event in which it issues is 'co-determined' by his external situation and a conscious act of choice. A man will not fight for his country unless certain conditions outside his control are satisfied. But given these we do not yet know that how he fights is determined by anything but himself.

III

The Stoic concept of $ἐφ'ἡμῖν$ ('attributable to us'/'in the power of us'), on which much of the debate about free will rests, is recorded by Alexander as follows:[34]

If, they argue, those things are $ἐφ'ἡμῖν$ of which we can perform the opposites as well, and it is under such conditions that praise and blame, encouragement and dissuasion, rewards and punishments are given, then wisdom and virtue will not be attributable to those ($ἐπὶ$ $τοῖς$) who have them since they are not now ($μηκέτι$) capable of receiving the vices contrary to virtues; similarly, vices are not attributable to those ($ἐπὶ$ $τοῖς$) who are vicious, since it is not open to them ($ἐπὶ$ $τούτοις$) now not to be vicious. But it is quite absurd to deny that virtue and vice are attributable to us ($ἐφ'ἡμῖν$) or that praise and blame are awarded for these; therefore $ἐφ'ἡμῖν$ does not mean 'being able to perform either of two contrary actions'.

It is most important to see what this passage asserts and what it does not assert. Alexander, whose intentions are polemical, seems to take Chrysippus (the presumed Stoic author) to be claiming that virtue and vice are dispositions which cannot be lost (ἀναπόβλητοι); that men are born with a particular moral quality, so that their present condition and future development is *necessary*.[35] Nothing however in Chrysippus' own quoted remarks justifies these assertions, and there is ample evidence elsewhere to refute some of them. The Stoics did claim that virtue is a permanent disposition in principle (whether or not it can be lost gave rise to some casuistical discussion); but neither virtue nor vice is innate.[36] Man is born morally neutral, with a natural inclination towards virtue.[37] Good or bad dispositions are acquired in maturity as a result of training or neglect.[38] Clement, who authorises this last assertion, seems to introduce Christian thought when he adds that those of a bad temperament by nature can become virtuous by proper education; and those whose nature is amenable to goodness can become bad through inattention.[39] But the entire Stoic claim that virtue is teachable was based by Chrysippus and other Stoics on the fact than bad men *can become* good.[40]

What then is Chrysippus arguing here? He appears to be asserting, what Alexander himself states with approval, that it is not open to a man who has become x (say a painter) not to be x. Yet the actions which follow from this characteristic are attributable to the man himself and nothing else. The passage tells us that good men cannot fail to act well, and bad men have no option but to act badly. That is, men cannot act contrary to their present character. The passage does not say that every action performed by good or bad men is logically the one and only action open to them at the time. It is the moral character of the action, not its spatio-temporal aspect, which cannot be otherwise. And it cannot be otherwise for a reason which is not expressed in Alexander's quotations from Chrysippus. In Stoic ethics a man is either virtuous or vicious. Hence the change from vice to virtue was regarded as instantaneous in order to avoid breaking the law of contradiction.[41] The moment of conversion, or 'surfacing' as the Stoics put it, would not give time to say 'here we have a bad man acting well'. A man cannot act well *and* badly since he is either good or bad. But the fact that it is not open to him to perform both types of action with his present character does not mean he neither was nor ever will be in a position to acquire a different character. Bad men can become good, hence μηκέτι in Alexander's text means not 'no longer capable of change', but 'not now capable'. It states a fact, not a prediction. What the Stoics reject is the possibility of acting inconsistently with present character. From bad character bad actions follow necessarily.[42] The man must instantly become a saint if he is to change at all; he must acquire a totally new character, become a new man.

ἐφ'ἡμῖν then in Stoic theory does not entail 'free at any time to act virtuously or viciously' but 'liable for praise or blame regarding the actions now attributable to oneself.' A drum rolls in virtue of its roundness and a man acts in consequence of his disposition. In order for either to act an external stimulus is required. But it would be absurd to say, when confronted by a barrel rolling down a hill, that its shape did not contribute to its movement; and it would be even more absurd to say of a man who rescued a child from a burning house that the sole reason for his action was the visual image he received. It is the immediate efficient cause which matters in Stoic theory, and to which responsibility is pinned.[43] Medea is the cause of her children's murder, not Jason's perfidy, because she and she alone planned and performed the action. And no one but she was in a position to plan and perpetrate *that* particular murder.

IV

By distinguishing an external and an internal cause for every human action the Stoics made purposeful bodily movements follow directly from an act of will and only secondarily from the environment. The environment necessarily evokes some response from the will but the particular nature of the response is apparently 'up to us'. Now this might seem to open the door wider than the Stoics can consistently permit. In theory, at least, they accepted the validity of divination and therefore the predictability of events, including those issuing from human actions. Somehow the autonomy of the agent, the aspect of action which is 'up to us', has to be reconciled with the interdependence of all events. The crucial text here is an argument of Chrysippus recorded by Aulus Gellius: it is an answer to the

charge that 'if all things are caused and controlled by unavoid-
able *fatum* human actions constituting crimes and offences
should not be an object of blame'.[44]

Quamquam ita sit . . . ut ratione quadam necessaria et principali
coacta atque conexa sint fato omnia, ingenia tamen ipsa mentium
nostrarum proinde sunt fato obnoxia, ut proprietas eorum est ipsa
et qualitas. nam si sunt per naturam primitus salubriter utiliterque
ficta, omnem illam vim quae de fato extrinsecus ingruit, inoffensius
tractabiliusque transmittunt. sin vero sunt aspera et inscita et rudia
nullisque artium bonarum adminiculis fulta, etiamsi parvo sive nullo
fatalis incommodi conflictu urgeantur, sua tamen scaevitate et
voluntario impetu in assidua delicta et in errores se ruunt. idque
ipsum ut ea ratione fiat, naturalis illa et necessaria rerum con-
sequentia efficit, quae 'fatum' vocatur. est enim genere ipso quasi
fatale et consequens, ut mala ingenia peccatis et erroribus non
vacent. . . . sic ordo et ratio et necessitas fati genera ipsa et principia
causarum movet, impetus vero consiliorum mentiumque nostrarum
actionesque ipsas voluntas cuiusque propria et animorum ingenia
moderantur.

Although it is the case that all things are held together by a certain
necessary and fundamental principle and that they are linked to fate,
yet the actual dispositions of our minds are only subject to fate
according to their particular quality.[45] For if their form from the
beginning is naturally healthy and they are suitably fashioned, they
pass on without opposition or hindrance all the pressure which
comes externally from fate.[46] If on the other hand they are intract-
able, uneducated and crude without the support of any civilised
culture then they plunge into continuous vices and errors of their
own will and vicious nature, even when they are harassed by little or
no opposition from fated misfortune. The very fact that men behave
in these different ways is the result of the natural and necessary
sequence of events called fate. For it is as it were the fate of their
actual human type and a consequence of this that bad dispositions
are not free from wrong-doing and error.

This argument is now illustrated by the simile of a drum placed
upon a slope: the first cause of a drum's movement is external:
something has to set it in the situation. But the continuing
movement is referable to its peculiar shape.

So the various categories of things in the world and the beginnings of
causes are set in motion by the order, the law and the necessity of

fate. But the prompting of our decisions and thoughts, and our actions, are controlled by each man's particular will and disposition.[47]

This text, which often passes without comment in modern discussions, is fundamental. It confirms and supplements the point made earlier, that character determines action. Not only are the basic human instruments of activity fated, in the sense that man cannot fail to act via impulse and assent. But the individual's character, which prompts his behaviour, is also determined since it follows from his particular nature *and* upbringing. Hence the causal sequence which finally issues in an act of will can be traced back both to the environment and to the nature given at birth. This does not mean that men do not genuinely will their actions. But it does mean that an act of will is not independent of character *and* the causes which go to form that.

Chrysippus gives little guidance here on the phenomenon of choice itself since he is apparently concerned with explaining the different moral categories of men and their causes. There are two moral types and every individual is true to one or the other. Though morally neutral in infancy every man possesses potentialities which make him more or less receptive to good or bad influences in the environment. The fully developed disposition is thus a necessary consequence of heredity (the individual quality which is given at birth) and environment. What results from these, and from the exercise of will or assent, is good or bad men; that is to say, men who deliberately in consequence of their characters choose actions meriting praise or blame.

So much for interpretation of the argument. Merely as it stands the text of Aulus Gellius is typically Stoic in reducing all human types to their basic moral category. But it does not deny, any more than the passage from Alexander, that before a bad man chooses *p* it is compatible with his moral character that he will choose some other bad act *q* or *r* instead. Nor does it rule out the possibility of moral improvement. The characteristics with which Chrysippus defines the bad dispositions are a product of bad upbringing as well as initial nature; and a change of environment would not, on this view, rule out the possibility

of good capacities in the innate character being developed.[49]
Unlike Aristotle the Stoics recognise that 'causes beyond those
in us' (*EN* III 1113b 17ff.) must be accorded a place in establishing the moral character. But Aristotle's account can only
appear less determinist by failing to consider adequately the
facts of heredity and environment.

There remains one Stoic theory which might seem to count
against any significance for choice. I have argued that the
majority of statements concerning the actions of a person do
not logically preclude the possibility of his choosing alternatives
within the same moral category. But Nemesius and Alexander
call attention to the theory that, 'given the same causes the same
effects must follow and the impulse of a living creature must
take an identical form in such a causal situation'.[50] Clearly
what the critics want is a statement of indeterminacy in a man's
response to the identical situation. But such a statement would
certainly be unverifiable and also irrelevant to our present
problem. The Stoics could not mean by 'the same causes' only
external circumstances. In any human action an internal cause
is also required. That is to say, a human impulse will be the
same in two situations where both the external causes and the
nature of the individual are identical. For impulse follows from
assent, and the nature of a man's assents is determined internally by his character. The passages from Aulus Gellius and
Cicero (*De fato* 41-4) emphatically refute the notion that
external causes alone determine the quality of an individual's
response. The assertion that from the 'same causes, the same
effects must follow' means that a man cannot fail to act in the
same way if external circumstances *and* his own nature, including his acts of assent, are identical; which is both true and
trivial. What the Stoics have in mind here, I suggest, is not the
phenomenon of choice, as it arises at any moment, but the
cyclical nature of events.[51] History, according to them, repeats
itself identically over infinite time. The nature of this queer
belief need not concern us here. But if the values of all the
variables which contain human action are fixed for each cycle
the theory says that 'given the same external situation and an
absolutely identical human character then at time t in cycle
p action x is the same as the action performed in cycle p^1 at time

t^1.[52] The theory does not say anything which is relevant to action now. It denies the possibility of acting differently at the identical point in the next cycle, because from an eternal perspective that is the same time as now.[53] But before the particular event x has been reached in this cycle the Stoics would allow that alternatives y and z are possible in any cycle. After x they would deny that y and z are possible in any cycle.

This does not mean that the Stoics admitted any objective uncertainty in the world. Here we return to the dual perspective mentioned earlier. Possibility exists to the extent that, but only to the extent that, men are ignorant of the future.[54] To God only what will take place is possible. But man recognises as possible anything which he has no reason for knowing to be impossible. Hence the definition of the possible recorded by Diogenes Laertius: 'the possible is that which admits of being true if externals do not prevent it from being true' (VII 75). Thus if it is the case that a gem is of a nature to be breakable then 'this gem is broken' is a possible event, even though it will not take place.[55] *Pari passu* it is possible that a man will realise any of those capacities which are compatible with his external situation and character. No contradiction before the event is involved in saying both 'it is possible that Cato will go to the forum at noon' and 'it is possible that Cato will stay at home at noon'. But this does not entail a break in the causal nexus, a 'free' volition by Cato. For he has the power only to do what he wills, and what he will will to do is co-determined by his character and external situation.

V

The major lines along which the Stoics moved to answer libertarian criticism have now been indicated. But there is to Stoicism a positive conception of freedom which needs at least some mention. It is most easily described as the state of mind enjoyed by good men. They, and they alone, are able to 'act as they will'[56]; for freedom is 'the possibility of determining one's own actions', or the 'knowledge of what is permitted and what is not'.[57] The legal language of this second definition is complemented in Philo's remark that 'all who live according to the law are free', that is the law embodied in natural events.[58] No adequate context for these statements is provided by the evidence for early Stoicism. But page after page of Epictetus gives clarification and substance to them. His discussion is all the more valuable since it shows what freedom meant in the experience of a committed Stoic. Without his subjective statements the concept would be unintelligible, and these also help to relate it to the ethical determinism already discussed.

The first discourse in Arrian's collection is devoted to the topic: 'the things which are and are not under our control'. Man is answerable for and free in his use of one thing, according to Epictetus: his *logos*, the faculty of impulse and desire which has the impressions presented externally to the mind as its field of activity.[59] (These, as we have seen, are the proximate cause of action.) Over the existence of external presentations he has no control, but he does possess the power to make good or bad use of them. In Stoic terms that means the power to adapt or fail to adapt one's actions and goals to the natural course of events.[60] This power, Epictetus claims, is a gift of God, which is subject to constraint neither by God nor anything else.[61] The words 'free from all restriction, compulsion and hindrance' compel the reader's attention by repetition.[62] For Epictetus the human reason is a fragment of God identified as individual man.[63] The relation between man and God which Cleanthes' *Hymn to Zeus* implies is spelled out precisely here. God oversees all human actions since he is co-substantial with men and all things.[64] But the individual has identity in his own right: 'in the region of assent he is free and unhindered'.[65] And assent embraces choice, purpose and decision, that is to say, the planning of one's life and the actions which follow from this.

The plight of the majority, in Epictetus' view, is their failure to exercise assent correctly. Assent enables men to be free, but it also allows them to inflict slavery on themselves.[66] The reasoning behind this thinking belongs to the core of Stoic ethics. In brief, to be prompted by passions or false judgements of value about things wrongly supposed to be good is the source of unhappiness, moral corruption and slavery since it involves an abrogation of self-sufficiency and a pursuit of what is un-

certain. 'If you will, you are free.'[67] Freedom entails taking up
that attitude to events which is proof against every check and
uncertainty since it is based upon a knowledge of what must
happen as a natural consequence.[68] The attitude is both positive
and negative. By self-knowledge a man can know what he is
able to initiate successfully;[69] and by experience of nature he
knows what he must accept as external necessity. In either event
he wills what happens.

How, we must now ask, does this tie up with the causal nexus
and ethical determinism of the old Stoa? Epictetus is as convinced as any Stoic of the divine ordination of the world.[70] He
has little to say about fate or causes,[71] but his pantheism is
orthodox and he continuously stresses that human freedom is
confined to the exercise of *logos*. That however is a confinement
which the most ardent libertarian could accept with certain
provisos. In fact, though he is not explicit on the point, Epictetus' freedom of the *logos* seems to be subject to the same
qualifications as Chrysippus', and for the same reasons.

A subject on which Epictetus dwells constantly is one already
mentioned, the need for suitable education. Reason, he argues,
in the case of the uneducated, leads to errors of judgement and
moral choice.[72] Their vices are a consequence of ignorance, and
freedom is incompatible with error.[73] The relation between lack
of proper training and moral corruption, though it is not set in
any context which mentions fate, is as necessary for Epictetus as
it is for Chrysippus. It is also Epictetus' view that a change of
moral attitude can be achieved by education, and this finds
justification in the early Stoic concept of 'progress'.[74] The
ethical determinism of Chrysippus is implicit in the freedom of
Epictetus. To be free is to possess knowledge, but this requires
training lacked by the majority of men. Epictetus differs from
early Stoics in the more charitable attitude he adopts towards
moral weakness. Teaching and exhortation take the place of
outright condemnation. But nothing in his theory of the influences which determine human action is fundamentally
different from the Stoicism of Zeno and Chrysippus. The personal experience of Epictetus, for much of his life a slave, must
account for part of his preoccupation with freedom. In spite of
this bias and his philosophical naïvité, Epictetus is the Stoic

who most ably demonstrates how autonomy of the personality
can find a place within the causal nexus.

VI

To will or not to will. On this disjunction the Stoic concepts of
freedom and enslavement are based. But, as Pohlenz remarks,
'to will' in Greek thought is not to exercise some independent
mental faculty called 'the will' but to adopt a pro-attitude
to some specific object, and for the Stoics this object is given
and necessary.[75] 'Guide me, o Zeus, and thou, Fate, whither I
have been appointed by you. For I will follow freely; and if,
grown evil, I prove unwilling I shall follow no less.'[76] The sense
of these well known verses by Cleanthes is graphically illustrated
by the simile attributed to Chrysippus and Zeno: 'just as a dog
tied to a cart follows while being pulled, if it is willing to follow,
making its own self-determination comply with necessity; yet it
will be in all respects subject to compulsion if it is unwilling to
follow. So it is too with men'.[77] As these two passages show the
object of the Stoic's will is external and determinate. He can
accept what will happen, or he can reject this. But in neither
case can he alter it. This looks like an assertion of the strictest
determinism, but is it? All turns upon what is embraced under
the term 'will happen'. If 'what will happen' means 'all of the
future which is undetermined by me' then the assertion is both
true and necessarily true. There is however a part of the future
which cannot happen independently of me.[78] A dog which is
dragged is a different event from a dog which runs with a loose
rope. This simile seems to have been misinterpreted from a
failure to distinguish the *tertium comparationis*. What it illustrates
is the nature of human action, not the determined course of
one's life (the particular cart to which a man is tied). It is open
to a man to fit his life to the circumstances in which he finds
himself or not to do so. And 'fitting one's life' includes adopting
policies and attempting to initiate them. If a man fails to take
full account of his circumstances his plans will necessarily
encounter resistance. For he is pitting himself against causes
outside his control. Such a man's inner life, and his external
actions, will differ fundamentally from the Stoic who has

achieved εὔροια βίου (a smooth-flowing life). In neither case does the theory entail that his actions, that is, 'what follows from his own disposition', have been planned in advance without reference to his agency. Otherwise there would be no meaning in the distinction between willing or not willing.

The Stoics are at one with Aristotle in relating the concept of human action to moral character. Actions meriting praise or blame are the results of conscious choice, and what men choose depends upon their character. But the Stoics also argue that character itself cannot be isolated from the law of cause and effect. The moral history of a man includes not only, with Aristotle, all his deliberate acts but also the inherited nature and external causes which help to form his character. This insight enables the Stoics to reject the impossibility of becoming a sage from 'incorrigible badness' since what a man is may be changed by external causes.[79] Heredity, which gives the faculty of choice along with certain necessary reactions, determines the character to some extent.[80] But what is given initially remains adaptable to the environment, and within these limits men decide their own future by following out the consequences of their particular adaptation. Without adequate education they remain prisoners of emotion and environment, but the fact that their actions issue directly from the will and character is taken to be proof of moral responsibility. Through the right training men can learn to plan their lives on rational criteria: these are based upon a grasp of what is necessary both in the inner and outer life thus assuring complete autonomy within the area of the possible. To be sure, this theory far from solving the problem of moral responsibility raises it in a most acute form. The Stoic account of character development requires them, in consistency, to lay down educational minima before making moral judgements, and this they failed to do. But it would be scarcely fair to twit the Stoics for failing to see all the implications of questions which are still far from settlement. They were humane as well as precocious when they denied any innate moral determination and traced the causes of wrong-doing to infantile experiences and corrupting environment.[81]

There remains the problem of the causal nexus, and doubtless the Stoics were too ready to keep their cake and eat it. The demands of teleology and providence, combined with pan-theism, impose an undeniable strain on the credibility of their ethics. Yet the universal causal principle is present to man, however little, in his own *logos*: he 'makes history as well as being history's product'.[82] His *logos* is equal in quality to all the divine which is outside. And it constitutes a unique sub-stance whose identity is unaffected by external events. A man can be free, can act as a man, if and only if the external move-ments of his body follow from a decision which reconciles his own will and moral choice to what is necessarily the case.[83]

NOTES

1. Cf. Cicero *De fato* IX 29. Later (ibid. 39) Cicero, perhaps under Antiochus' influence (see Albert Yon, *Cicéron. Traité du destin* (Paris 1950) p. xlv), calls Chry-sippus *tamquam arbiter honorarius* between the determinists and libertarians. Cf. Augustine, *Civ. Dei (PL* 41) v 10, p. 152 (*necessitatem*) formidando Stoici laboraver-unt causas rerum ita distinguere ut quasdam subtraherent necessitati, quasdam sub-derent, atque in his, quas esse sub necessitate noluerunt, posuerunt etiam nostras voluntates.

2. Alex. Aphr. *De fato (CAG* suppl. II 2) XXVII, pp. 197f., cf. pp. 187, 189. For a discussion of Stoic and Aristotelian elements in this work see G. Verbeke, *Archiv. f. Gesch. d. Phil.* 1 (1968) 73–100. Undoubtedly the Stoics are Alexander's main object of attack; but he never refers to them by name in this work, and it should not be assumed (as Verbeke seems to assume) that his reports and critiques of determinist theses are all fair to Stoic doctrine. Alexander makes a generalised attack on determinism; as a polemic purely against the Stoics it often misfires, as I hope to show in an article forthcoming in the same journal.

3. Much of the evidence is assembled by A. Gercke, 'Chrysippea', *Jahrb. f. Klass. Phil.* suppl. 14. In addition to Alex. Aphr. the main sources are Nemesius, *De nat. hom.*, Chalcidius, *Comm. in Plat. Tim.*, and Diogenianus ap. Eusebium, *Praep. ev.* J. H. Waszink, in his brilliant edition of Chalcidius (*Plato Latinus* iv), argues that Nemesius and Chalcidius derive their views from Porphyry, who based himself on Numenius, and to a lesser extent, Alexander, pp. LXIIf. A most learned study of theories of determinism, with particular reference to the first and second centuries A.D., is provided by Willy Theiler, 'Tacitus und die antike Schicksalslehre', *Phyllobolia für Peter von der Mühll*, pp. 35–90.

4. Pohlenz, *Griechische Freiheit*, gives a useful survey of ancient attitudes to free-dom. His book sets political and philosophical conceptions together with admirable clarity. Its chief shortcoming, in my view, is a tendency to regard the '*innere Freiheit*' of Stoicism as typical of Greek thinking before the Hellenistic period. Bréhier, *Chrysippe*, pp. 170–6, has important remarks on the historical background to Stoic determinism. It is sometimes forgotten that determinism was a philosophical issue before the Stoics, cf. Aristotle *De int.* IX; *EN* III 1114a 31–b 12; X 1179b 20–3; Epicur. *Ep. Men.* 134.

5. *EN* III 1.

6. Ibid. 5, especially 1114a 13–15. See Furley, *Two Studies in the Greek Atomists*, pp. 190f.; W. F. R. Hardie, *Aristotle's Ethical Theory* (Oxford 1968) pp. 173–9.

7. *Rep.* x 617e; cf. *Tim.* 41e–42c; *Laws* x 904b–c.

8. Aristotle, perhaps, unlike Plato accepts that a man may knowingly, in the strong sense of 'know', do what he ought not to do. It is weakness of will which distinguishes the *akratēs* from the morally insensitive *akolastos*, *EN* VII 2–7.

9. Epicurus has often been regarded as an advocate of *acte gratuit* owing to his swerve of atoms. For a new interpretation of this theory which brings Epicurus much closer to Greek thinking in general, especially Aristotle, see Furley op. cit. pp. 161–237.

10. So Pohlenz, *Die Stoa* i p. 103. Cf. Alex. Aphr. *Fat.* XI; Cicero *De fato* XIV. Destiny (εἱμαρμένη) is described as συμπλοκὴ αἰτίων (Diels, *Dox. graec.* 322), cf. εἱρμὸς αἰτίων, τουτέστι τάξιν καὶ ἐπισύνδεσιν ἀπαράβατον (ibid. 324); ἀμεταθέτους εἶναι τὰς ἐξ αἰῶνος προκατειλημένας . . . αἰτίας (Chrys. ap. Euseb. *Praep. ev.* VI 8, 11 Dindorf). For Stoic causal theory see Rieth, *Grundbegriffe*, pp. 134–68; Pohlenz, *Grundfragen*, pp. 104–12.

11. In spite of their causal nexus the Stoics did recognise a place for the 'possible'. Its definition, as given by Diog. Laert., is 'that which admits of being true if externals do not prevent it from being true' VII 75, cf. Cic. *De fato* 13. In this the Stoics went further than the Megarians who allowed nothing to be possible which was not actual, cf. Arist. *Met.* Θ 1046b 29ff., with discussion by Schuhl, *Le dominateur et les possibles*, p. 48. For a study of the relation in Stoicism of fate to possibility see Reesor, *Phoenix* XIX (1965) 285–97, and below p. 189.

12. See Epictetus, *Ench.* I; *Diss.* IV 7.

13. Diog. Laert. VII 87f. For further comments on the coherence of Stoicism see p. 104.

14. Cf. Cic. *De div.* I 128, non est . . . ut mirandum sit ea praesentiri a divinantibus, quae nusquam sint; sunt enim omnia, sed tempore absunt; Nemesius, *Nat. hom. PG* xl 801B Migne, τῷ θεῷ καὶ τὰ μέλλοντα ὡς παρόντα. See Theiler, op. cit., pp. 49f., and below p. 189.

15. See n. 10. As we shall see, Chrysippus drew an important distinction between fate or destiny, and necessity. This is not the place to expound that distinction in detail, but it seems to be parallel or identical to a distinction he drew between external antecedent causes (fate) and the internal nature of a thing (necessity), see p. 181. If so, it helps to explain the inconsistencies fastened upon by Diogenianus (ap. Eus. *Praep. ev.* VI 8, 1–2D): 'Chrysippus in his first book on destiny wishes to show that all things are embraced ὑπὸ τῆς ἀνάγκης καὶ τῆς εἱμαρμένης . . . [but in his second book] he wishes to arrange that many things occur παρ'ἡμᾶς.' From the cosmic perspective we have an inviolable causal nexus, but in any individual event a distinction may be drawn between the 'fated' external antecedents (*necessitas fati*, cf. Aulus Gellius, p. 186) and the internal necessity, a response which is referable to and only referable to the body in question.

16. For 'divine ordinance' and the causal nexus, cf. Augustine, *Civ. Dei.* v 8; Seneca, *Benef.* IV 7, 2; Chalcidius, *In Tim.* CXLIV.

17. Stobaeus, *Ecl.* I p. 132 (*SVF* I 87); ibid. p. 79 (*SVF* II 913); Lactantius, *De vera sap.* 9 (*SVF* I 160); Plutarch, *Stoic. rep.* 1050C, 1056C (*SVF* II 937).

18. Stobaeus (first citation above) compares the relation of fate-*logos* to the world with ἐν τῇ γονῇ τὸ σπέρμα. For *spermatikos logos* cf. Diog. Laert. VII 136. Aetius, *Plac.* I 7, 33 (*SVF* II 1027) says 'God contains the "seminal principles" in accordance with which each thing comes about by fate'.

19. Elsewhere fate is defined as 'eternal motion', Theodoretus VI 14 (*SVF* II 916).

20. Arius Didymus fr. 29 (Diels *Dox. graec.* p. 464, 9 = *SVF* II 528); Cicero *ND* II 78f. (*SVF* II 1127), 133, 154 (*SVF* II 1131).

21. Most famously in Cleanthes (ap. Epictetum *Ench.* 53) and Seneca's translation of him (*Ep. mor.* 107, 10), ducunt volentem fata, nolentem trahunt.

22. Diog. Laert. VII 87f. (*SVF* III 4). For some of the moral consequences which follow from the *logos* common to men and the universe, see I. G. Kidd, Chapter VII p. 158.

23. *SVF* I 537, especially lines 10–21.

24. Cf. Rieth, *Grundbegriffe* pp. 157f., who cites Chrysippus' approval of Homer *Od.* I 32ff. where Zeus denies the gods' responsibility for sufferings which men bring upon themselves (*SVF* II 925, 998). It appears that Cleanthes and Chrysippus gave different explanations of the connexion between divine planning and fate. According to Chalcidius *In Tim.* CXLIV (*SVF* II 933) Chrysippus asserted that 'events which are *ex providentia* are fated' is an analytic statement, but Cleanthes denied the conversion 'all fated events are *ex providentia*'. This suits Cleanthes' comments in his *Hymn to Zeus*, whereas Chrysippus would be claiming that even evil actions contribute directly to the οἰκονομία of the universe, cf. Plut. *Stoic. rep.* 1050Cff. (*SVF* II 937). I have discussed the Stoic concept of evil in *Philosophical Quarterly* xviii (1968) 329–43.

25. On a Stoic-Christian interpretation, God's knowing that something will take place does not entail that the *contrary* event is impossible, Origen (*SVF* II 964), cf. Plutarch *Stoic. rep.* 1055E.

26. This could imply, without further explanation, that other things also have some degree of autonomy, a point made against the Stoics by Alexander, *Fat.* XIV pp. 183f.

27. *Fat.* XIII p. 181, 13ff. (*SVF* II 979). Theiler, op. cit., pp. 65ff. tries to argue that the doctrine set out here and similarly in Nemesius (*Nat. hom.* 744ff.) derives not from Chrysippus but from Philopator, a Stoic of the early second century A.D. I see no reason to assume its *originating* from Philopator on the basis of Nem. loc. cit. 745B. Nor do I find the doctrine that man is in some sense the *Werkzeug* of 'divine fate' inconsistent with doctrines of Chrysippus subsequently discussed above. It is orthodox Stoicism that man should make himself consciously such a *Werkzeug*.

28. ὥστε αὐτὰ τὴν ἐξ ἑαυτῶν τε καὶ καθ' ὁρμὴν κίνησιν ἐξ ἀνάγκης οὕτω πως ἐνεργεῖν.

29. See 'The Stoic Concept of Evil' *Phil. Quart.* xviii (1968) 337–41.

30. A good example of the misunderstanding to which this concept gave rise is Nemesius' criticism, *Nat. hom.* 744f. Migne (*SVF* II 991). His further criticisms in that context concerning the necessity of acting in the same way given the same causes will be discussed subsequently, p. 188.

31. Especially 41–4. The passage has been much discussed. For background to the causal distinctions made there see Rieth, *Grundbegriffe*, pp. 134ff.; Pohlenz, *Grundfragen* pp. 106–12

32. A presentation to the mind is a necessary but not sufficient condition of action, cf. Cic. *De fato* 44. The agent's assent is a necessary and sufficient condition since assent entails there being something, though not necessarily one particular thing, to which its response is given.

33. So Chrysippus ap. Diogenianum (*SVF* II 998). Actions of this kind were called συγκαθειρμένα or *confatalia*. Evidence about the terms is scanty, but it would seem to follow that all 'free' human acts are *confatalia* for the Stoics since they are jointly dependent on external circumstances and volition. Chrysippus used this concept to answer the 'lazy' argument that destiny denies significance to human action, see Cic. *De fato* XIII 33.

34. *Fat.* XXVI p. 196, 24ff. I have given alternative renderings of ἐφ᾽ἡμιν since the phrase has this ambiguity. To translate it 'in the power of us', as is generally done without explanation, begs the very point under discussion.

35. *Fat.* XXVII–XXVIII especially p. 197, 17–30. Since Aristotle recognises a similar theory (*EN* III 1114b 1–12; X 1179b 20–3; *EE* θ 2) Alexander may be mis-applying this to the Stoics.

36. Clement *Strom.* VII p. 839 (*SVF* III 224).

37. Alexander recognises elsewhere (*Quaest.* III p. 121f. =*SVF* III 537) that in Stoic theory the acquisition of moral character is contemporaneous with the acquisition of maturity of reason. See also *SVF* III 214, 216.

38. Clement *Strom.* I p. 336 (*SVF* III 225).

39. Ibid.

40. Diog. Laert. VII 91.

41. See Plutarch *Comm. not.* 1061E–1062E who fails to grasp the point of the theory. Similarly, Aristotle regards certain changes, such as the recovery of health, as taking no time at all, *Ph.* VIII 3, 253b 21–30; I 3, 186a 13–16. See G. E. L. Owen, 'Tithenai ta phainomena' (*Aristote et les problèmes de la méthode*, Symposium Aristotelicum; Louvain 1961) pp. 99ff.

42. Clement *Strom.* VI p. 789 (*SVF* III 110). Furley, *Two Studies*, p. 191, notes that Aristotle does not seek a criterion of voluntary action in whether a man can act otherwise *now*.

43. Clement *Strom.* VIII p. 930 (*SVF* II 347) where a distinction is drawn between 'that on account of which' (δι᾽ὅ) and 'that which brings something about' (ποιη-τικόν). Both terms are expressed in a 'cause' (αἴτιον), but the fact that p occurs on account of q does not make q the αἴτιον of p. 'Medea would not have killed her children had she not been angry; she would not have been angry had she not been jealous . . .' A series of antecedent conditions can be traced back indefinitely, but only Medea is the sufficient and necessary condition to which liability (αἴτιον) applies.

44. *Noctes atticae* VII 2 (*SVF* II 1000).

45. The difficult phrase *proinde ut proprietas eorum est ipsa et quàlitas* is an attempt to render the concept of ἰδίως ποιόν, on which see J. M. Rist, Chapter III pp. 45f. The original of the whole Latin sentence may have been αἱ δὲ ἡμέτεραι διανοήσεις οὕτως εἰσὶν αὐταὶ καθ᾽ εἱμαρμένην ὡς ἐστὶν αὐτῶν τὸ ἰδίως ποιόν, cf. Plotinus *Enn.* III 1, 2.

46. *Per naturam* is less likely to be a strong personification than an adverbial construction such as *per iram, per ludum*. On *utiliter* see n. 48. Cleanthes postulated the inheritance of mental characteristics (*SVF* I 518), and for the Stoics' interests in embryology cf. Plut. *Stoic. rep.* 41. But in Epictetus' view (*Diss.* I 12, 27–34) heredity cannot count against moral responsibility. Aristotle (*EN* III 1114a 31–b 25) considers and rejects the view that moral character is genetically determined. For the influence of heredity and training on character in Epicurean theory see Furley, *Two Studies*, pp. 123f.

47. This account differs from Cicero *De fato* 41–4 and Alex. Aphr. *Fat.* XIII pp. 181f. (*SVF* II 979) in making no explicit reference to impulse and assent; both terms are in fact embraced under *voluntas*. Pohlenz, *Die Stoa* i p. 104, who asserts that for Zeno and Chrysippus the inner life is controlled by fate, fails to explain that fate here means the individual's character.

48. This is entirely consistent with Clement's evidence (n. 38). Chrysippus considers here two different types: (1) good nature and good upbringing (*utiliter ficta*); (2) bad nature and bad upbringing (*inscita . . . fulta*). To preserve this parallel *ficta* should be taken first with *per naturam salubriter* and then with *utiliter*,

cf. Ariston ap. Stob. *Ecl.* II p. 215 (*SVF* I 387) where becoming χρήσιμοι (*utiles*) is made to follow from good upbringing.

49. Clement (n. 38) lays greater stress on the effects of education. On the place of *praecepta* in Stoicism see I. G. Kidd, Chapter VII pp. 164ff.

50. Nemesius *Nat. hom.* 744f. Migne (*SVF* II 991); Alex. Aphr. *Fat.* x p. 176, 21f.; xv p. 185, 7–21.

51. The theory known as *apokatastasis*, Arius Didymus (fr. 37 Diels *Dox. graec.* p. 469 = *SVF* II 599); see also *SVF* II 597; 624.

52. Whether identity of substance entailed numerical identity was apparently debated in the school, Simplicius *In phys.* p. 886, 11 (*CAG* x = *SVF* II 627).

53. 'What each man lives is only the present, this moment of time', Marcus Aurel. *Med.* III 10, cf. ibid. VII 29, XI 1. See Goldschmidt, *Le système stoicien*, pp, 186–210 for the bearings of this theory on the autonomy of the moral agent.

54. See Sambursky, *Physics of the Stoics*, pp. 75–7.

55. Reesor shows convincingly, *Phoenix* XIX (1965) 289, that 'a possible event is one in which the predicate . . . follows from the principal cause'. That is, in the statement 'the gem is broken', 'is broken' follows from the internal nature ('break-able') of the gem.

56. Dio Chrysostom XIV 16 (*SVF* III 356). Some pertinent questions concerning the validity in Stoicism of real freedom are raised by Gerard Watson, Chapter X p. 223.

57. Ibid. Diog. Laert. VII 121 (*SVF* III 355).

58. Philo *Quod omnis probus* 45 (*SVF* III 360).

59. *Diss.* I 1, 7–14; I 12, 25–7; I 17, 21–8. In 'Aristotle's Legacy to Stoic Ethics' *BICS* xv (1968) 79–82 I have tried to show that the Stoic psychology of action is basically similar to that of Aristotle.

60. Cf. Marcus *Med.* III 16; IV 1; Epictet. *Diss.* II 14, 7–8 etc.

61. *Diss.* I 1, 24; I 17, 26.

62. E.g. ἀκώλυτον, ἀνανάγκαστον, ἀπαραπόδιστον *Diss.* I 6, 40; III 3, 10; IV 1, 100.

63. *Diss.* I 17, 27. The phrase, ἀπόσπασμα θεοῦ, as a description of the human soul, may belong to the Old Stoa, Diog. Laert. VII 143; cf. Bonhöffer, *Epictet und die Stoa*, p. 76.

64. Epictet. *Diss.* I 14, 6.

65. Ibid. IV 1, 69, contra Pohlenz, *Griechische Freiheit*, p. 101, 'Epictetus does not ask whether assent is determined'.

66. *Diss.* IV 1, 54–75.

67. ἐὰν θέλῃς ἐλεύθερος εἶ, *Diss.* I 17, 28.

68. See in particular *Diss.* I 7, and above p. 96.

69. Panaetius stressed the importance of acting appropriately to one's individual nature (Cic. *De off.* I 107ff.) and this is also emphasized by Epictet. *Diss.* I 2, and Marcus, *Med.* IV 32.

70. *Diss.* I 14; IV 7, 6–11.

71. See however *Diss.* I 12, 24–6.

72. *Diss.* I 8; I 18, 2–14. For the responsibility of the teacher see *Diss.* III 21, 12; 17.

73. *Diss.* II 1, 21ff., 'Only the educated (τοὺς παιδευθέντας) are free'; II 24, 21–3.

74. Cf. *Diss.* I 18, 4. For Posidonius' concern with the training of character see I. G. Kidd, Chapter IX pp. 205f.

75. *Die Stoa* i p. 124.

76. Epictet. *Ench.* 53 (*SVF* I 527).

77. Hippolytus (Diels *Dox. graec.* p. 571, 11 = *SVF* II 975).

78. See also the doctrine of *confatalia* p. 183. When Pohlenz, *Die Stoa* i p. 106, says 'Even the wise man will not alter the external course of events' he fails to see that certain external events are human actions.

79. See p. 187.

80. By 'necessary reactions' I mean both the gamut of attitudes embraced by *oikeiosis* (see p. 126) and certain impulses which are retained even when this faculty has been shaped by *logos*: among those cited by Epictetus are sexual attraction (*Diss.* i 6, 9; cf. ii 20, 19); blushing (iii 7, 29); desire to communicate in speech (ii 24, 16). Seneca notes (*Ep. mor.* 58, 4) that the unpleasant experiences he enjoyed in a cave at Naples would also affect the mind and colour of a Stoic sage: 'quaedam nulla effugere virtus potest . . . non est hoc timor, sed naturalis adfectio inexpugnabilis rationi'.

81. For the sources of διαστροφή (moral corruption) see *SVF* iii 228–36, especially Chalcidius (229) discussed in *Phil. Quart.* xviii (1968) 336f., and S. G. Pembroke, Chapter VI p. 146 n. 89.

82. A paraphrase of Marcus *Med.* iii 3.

83. On 'being a man' and what this entails see Epictet. *Diss.* ii 9, 1–12; iv 5, 20–1.

IX

Posidonius on Emotions

I. G. KIDD

My purpose in this chapter is strictly limited. I do not intend a general survey of Posidonius' ethics, nor of all the evidence relating to this division of his philosophy. I am concerned with one reporter, Galen, and with one work of Posidonius, the Περὶ Παθῶν (*On emotions*). On the other hand I do not propose here to examine the many problems of detail raised by each of the fragments reported by Galen. My aim is to ask whether a coherent account of Posidonius' views on emotions can be derived from a strict selection of that evidence in Galen's *De placitis Hippocratis et Platonis* which can with certainty be related to Posidonius; by that I mean those passages where Galen mentions Posidonius by name. Also, since Posidonius' discussion of 'emotions' (*pathē*) was clearly a key point in his system, I wish to ask how it was related to other subdivisions of his ethical philosophy. And indeed this must be an integral part of my enquiry, since here I merely follow the lines of Galen's own report. I should like first to raise briefly some problems concerned with the evaluation of the evidence; secondly to discuss what the evidence says; and lastly to review in the light of this some general characteristics of the system as judged by some of the ancient reporters and critics. So my paper is largely descriptive.

There are great advantages from the point of view of evidence in examining the doctrine of the emotions and Posidonian ethics, but also some difficulties arising from the same source. The advantages are obvious; a comparative wealth of evidence in Galen's *De placitis*, which not only uses Posidonius' Περὶ Παθῶν, but quotes verbally from the work, and, what is no less important, includes pages of sustained argumentation on the subject. But the disadvantages of such a situation are sometimes ignored. It can be dangerous to rely so much on one reporter, for not only can reported argument be manipulated by an interested party, but even direct quotation can be misleading outside the context. For example, it was to Galen's advantage to use Posidonius in support of Plato against Chrysippus, and one must allow for the possibility that in doing so he represented Posidonius as more of a Platonist than he was. There would seem to be two methods of therapy open for such a one-eyed view. First, some counter-checks, although slight compared with the bulk of Galen, do survive in men like Seneca, Diogenes, and Clement. Secondly, as for instance understanding of the Stoic evidence in Plutarch's *De Stoicorum repugnantiis* can be shown to depend a good deal on our knowledge of Plutarch, so much more work is required on Galen himself.[1] But there is another difficulty; not only are we concentrated largely on one work written by one reporter, but on the evidence of one work by Posidonius, the Περὶ Παθῶν; so that our evidence for his ethics is slanted from this point of view. Now I cannot help but be reminded of the confusion, to my way of thinking, that has sometimes been caused in the case of Panaetius, by regarding his Περὶ Καθηκόντων ('On Appropriate Acts') as his fundamental ethical work. It is true that Posidonius does say himself that the understanding of the 'emotions' (*pathe*) is fundamental for all his ethical dogmas, and the Περὶ Παθῶν and Galen deal with subjects like good and evil, virtue, the End. Yet this does not exclude the possibility that Posidonius also approached these topics from another direction. Another *aporia* may emphasise this point. It was characteristic of Stoics to illustrate the interdependence of the three divisions of philosophy by similes, often by that of a fruit garden.[2] Sextus Empiricus tells us that Posidonius deliberately changed the usual similes to that of a living being, precisely to emphasise the organic relationship between the parts.[3] Nevertheless Galen's evidence of the Περὶ Παθῶν indicates that on occasion at least, Posidonius was prepared to discuss ethics on its own. All these difficulties then may increase wariness in examining Galen's evidence, but cannot block the obvious route towards the bulk of what evidence we have. Galen is an obvious starting point.

At this point a question arises on which I must be ruthlessly

brief: does the Galenic evidence show signs of structural
arrangement? The main lines of argumentation and the
quotations in the *De placitis* are found in Books IV & V, the other
books containing only incidental references. In Book IV there
are three main long passages: one on the argument for the
cause of *pathe* (348, 5–351, 2),[4] one on weakness of soul and its
training (369, 7–376, 13), the third on emotional movements as
distinct from intellectual; training and education; and various
aporiai (391, 5–403, 12); all of course involving, indeed based
on, criticism of Chrysippus. At the beginning of Book V, an
important prologue looks back to Book IV, explaining that
Galen has selected from many statements of proof (*apodeixis*),
and will now in Book V proceed with inconsistencies of Chrysippus. These cover such topics as: disease of soul; 'cure' (*therapeia*); the case of children and the cause of evil; causes of 'false
assumptions' (*pseudeis hypolēpseis*); education; 'virtues' (*aretai*);
'goods' (*agatha*); 'end' (*telos*). Then at 451, 2–454, 7 he turns to
a positive account of what one gains by Posidonius' right understanding of the *pathe*, only to return at 454, 7 to other *aporiai* or
'causes of puzzles discussed', which look back to Book IV and
must be supplemented by it. The book then ends with an
epilogue for the polemic against Chrysippus. Even such a brief
outline reveals the overlap of the two books, and the danger of
speculation on the structure of Posidonius' Περὶ Παθῶν. It seems
safer to accept Galen's scattered largesse and to proceed as one
can and thinks best.

For the importance of *pathe* to Posidonius, one may begin
with the rather startling quotation, *De plac.* 448, 7–11, that the
enquiry into good and evil, ends and virtues depends on the
right enquiry into emotions; startling, because it is difficult to
imagine this statement coming from any other Stoic. Could a
Stoic promote *pathe* to be the key to the door of ethics? Chrysippus[5] made ethics depend as a whole and in its parts on explanations from physics. Yet we may not doubt that this statement
comes from Posidonius, for it is not a report but a verbal
quotation from Book I of the Περὶ Παθῶν, and it is borne out by
the whole account in *De placitis*, indeed traced in detail by
Galen in positive terms through the different sections of ethics
in 448, 11ff. But Posidonius, of course, was not elevating *pathe*

as such. What he reiterates is that ethics depends on understanding the *cause* of the emotions. Which brings one to Galen's
own rephrasing, earlier in Book ɪv, 397, 5ff., of the original
quotation: Galen says that the whole of ethics depends on the
knowledge of *psyche*. And this does not seem so startling for a
Stoic, and need not be incompatible with the Chrysippean
evidence, especially when we remember that Chrysippus is
quoted from his book on Φυσικαὶ Θέσεις, and Posidonius from
his work *On Emotions*. Posidonius also could talk in more
physical and cosmic terms,[6] and thought that physics should be
taught first.[7] So the fundamental difference between the two
men lay in psychology: Posidonius held that the crucial piece
of knowledge about the soul lay in recognising three distinct
faculties of it, and Chrysippus was wrong in admitting only
one, the rational.[8] On the contrary, the psychic capacity for
feeling anger, and the capacity for desire are irrational and as
such quite distinct from the capacity to think, *De plac.* 461, 4–6.
So *pathe* could never be regarded as a kind of reason or judgement, however perverted, as Chrysippus maintained; they were
movements of irrational capacities, and there must be admitted
for the human spirit irrational capacities as well as a form of
rational activity. Whether this, as is often claimed, was unorthodox or heretical psychology for a Stoic does not concern
me here, except that such terms do not appear to occur in the
discussion.[9] On the other hand Posidonius attacked Chrysippus
for contradicting facts and for inconsistency, and also for not
interpreting Zeno and Cleanthes rightly as he, Posidonius, did.

It is not altogether clear exactly what Posidonius meant by
three 'faculties (*dynameis*) of soul' and the Platonic analogies in
Galen may possibly confuse rather than help. One can only
cite what evidence is available. The most important piece is
that Posidonius rejected the term 'parts' (*merē*) of soul, and so
any theory of local separation. He also rejected the term *eidē* or
species, and insisted simply on distinct capacities (*dynameis*), *not*
localised in any specific way (*De plac.* 476, 2–6; 501). He also
maintained that the soul was a single unitary substance (*mia
ousia*, 501), and thus he was deliberately rejecting the Chrysippean argument that a single substance necessitated a single
capacity (501).

On what basis and by what method did Posidonius challenge Chrysippus on emotions and psychology? Galen says that frequently in Περὶ Παθῶν he pressed a proof (*apodeixis*), which is given in a most important passage, *De plac.* 348–50. The proof is based on asking the right question: namely, what is the cause of the *plenonazousa hormē*? ('Impulse in excess' was the accepted definition of *pathos* by the Stoa.)[10] The answer to this question cannot be reason (*logos*), since reason could not exceed (*pleonazein*) beyond its own activity and measure (πράγματά τε καὶ μέτρα). It is therefore clearly evident (πρόδηλον οὖν) that a distinct capacity or power must be responsible for the excess of the impulse going beyond the measure of reason, as the 'irrational' weight of a runner's body carries him *beyond* the finishing line or goal set by his rational choice. I want to point out that what is at stake is *not* the definition of *pathos*, for the proof depends on the *agreement* of Posidonius and Chrysippus on the School definition, but rather the crucial formulation: 'what is the cause of . . .', which is not only characteristic of Posidonius' thinking, but a deliberate methodology since he related all Chrysippus' mistakes to the failure to ask such questions. But more of this later. Apart from 'proof' (*apodeixis*), which Galen thought also characteristic of Posidonius, (and to which also I shall return), Posidonius appears from an obscure passing reference, *De plac.* 487, to have also held that *pathe* belong to a class of phenomena which carry within themselves an 'indication' (*endeixis*), of their character and cause furnished by an immediate experience of which we have only to be reminded. And one may add that he also used purely *ad hominem* arguments, (e.g. *De plac.* 348–50).

But it is time to turn to a survey of how Posidonian psychology in relation to the emotions affected his approach to other divisions of ethics. According to the Galenic evidence, the topics concerned are: good and evil; virtue(s); the end; the principle of perversion in regard to 'what is to be chosen' (*haireta*) and 'what is to be avoided' (*pheukta*); modes of education or training; the *aporiai* concerning the origin of 'impulses' (*hormai*) from emotions. It will be convenient to work back from the last item.

Each capacity involves an appetency (*orexis*), and each *orexis* is differently orientated; of the irrational capacities, called animal-like, one seeks pleasure, the other power, victory and success, and from these *pathe* arise. The divine rational capacity seeks wisdom and good, and from it arises 'knowledge' (*epistēmē*). Posidonius insists that all these 'objects of *orexis*' (*orekta*) are native to the human psyche (*oikeia*), and therefore man has three 'natural affinities' (*oikeiōseis*), not one as Chrysippus held (*De plac.* 399; 438f.; 452, 3–10). Now what strikes me here especially is the difference of approach from the Chrysippean doctrine of *to prōton oikeion* as evidenced in *SVF* II 178ff. For one thing, the latter applied only to animals and young children before the age of fourteen, while Posidonius refers to adult humans. Also the *orekta* are quite different. The idea of self-preservation etc., in Chrysippus is not mentioned by Posidonius, while Posidonius' pleasure is expressly denied a place among *ta prota kata physin* by Chrysippus. Of course the principle of *oikeiosis* is the same; the difference lies in the interpretation of the factual situation, in Posidonius' insistence that in the adult human there is a native affinity to pleasure, a natural impulse towards *pathe*. And following from this, since *pathe* are caused by an irrational capacity, Posidonius broke the stark Stoic separation between adult man and other animals, by now explaining what seemed to him a fact, the occurrence of *pathe* in animals and children.[11] More interestingly, he could also explain the phenomenon that people do not actually feel afraid through being *logically* persuaded of an impending disaster, but only when they have a vivid mental picture akin to perception (as he put it); and one may feel terrified simply from a vivid description. This, he said, is because the irrational (*to alogon*) cannot be moved by reason (*logos*), but only by an irrational impulse or 'emotional movement' (*pathētikē kinēsis*) (*De plac.* 453, 13–454, 7; 443, 9–11).

This last point is fundamental for his discussion of 'modes of education or training'. The brief statement in *De plac.* 452, 10–453, 11 contains the whole point: the irrational (*to alogon*) and 'the emotional aspect (*to pathetikon*) of the *psyche*' can only be helped or harmed through what is irrational (*dia tou alogou*), that is through irrational movements (*dia kinēseōn alogōn*) such as music, rhythms, habitual practices. Only the rational (*to logikon*) can be helped or harmed by knowledge (*episteme*) or ignorance and stupidity (*amathia*). In other longish passages, e.g. *De plac*. 400–3, 369–76, Galen reports Posidonius' concern with *ethos* and *ethismos* in the training, healing (*iasis*), care (*therapeia*) of the character (and personality). And connected with this he also recognises the importance of external irrational forces moulding the character, like physical and climatic factors, and sought to understand them by the sciences of physiognomy (*De plac*. 442, 7ff.), and geography. And there is the interesting passage in Seneca, *Ep. mor*. 95, 65–7 which adds to the familiar methods of *praeceptio, suasio, consolatio, exhortatio*, the peculiar Posidonian topic of *descriptio*, i.e. *ethologia*; that is, I suppose, the examples of history. At any rate, emotional disturbance cannot be cured by the medicine of reason. It must be exhausted, soothed, calmed, cajoled, ordered, urged, persuaded, until it becomes quiet and able to listen to reason, *De plac*. 454, 15–456, 14. But only the rational can be taught.

Which brings me to perversion and the cause of evil, αἰτία (*aitia*) τῆς κακίας. This is a particularly famous and embarrassing problem for the Stoics, and one eagerly seized upon by their critics.[12] Their difficulties are revealed by the number of different answers given by the sources, answers which are not only different but inconsistent with each other. For how could the idealistic view of the perfection of man's rational being be squared with the recognition that the world is full of fools not sages? In two main passages (*De plac*. 438, 12–443, 4; *Scripta Minora* vol. II, pp. 77–8), Posidonius again accused Chrysippus of being unable to explain the cause (*aitia*) of evil. For how could we be corrupted, as Chrysippus said, from without, from, for example, the bewitching influence of other men, or, more vaguely, from the very nature of things (ἐξ αὐτῆς τῶν πραγμάτων τῆς φύσεως), if we have only one *oikeiosis*, a natural affinity to the rational, wise and good?[13] Posidonius added that it is a fact, and Chrysippus admits it, that however you isolate and quarantine human beings, some will turn out to be bad. And how did the first men fall into evil ways? And if Chrysippus goes on to mention the persuasive allure of *phantasiai* one must still ask why we are convinced by them, one must still ask for the *aitia* why pleasure or power and pain offer a persuasive *phantasia* of good and bad. This can only be explained, says Posidonius, if we have an innate attraction to pleasure, a natural liability to emotional disturbance. The root of evil is within us (ἰδία ῥίζα); the power of evil is derived from the seed within; its cause is not external. How does this actually work according to Posidonius? The evidence seems to lie in a short, corrupt and difficult passage in the argument (*De plac.* 442, 1–7), where Posidonius goes on to show the causes of all false assumptions. There appear[14] to be two kinds of mistakes: theoretical mistakes caused by ignorance, and practical mistakes caused by the 'emotional pull' (διὰ τῆς παθητικῆς ὁλκῆς).[15] Now the experience of pleasure as good, of victory and success as satisfying, in order to become an emotion in the full sense of the word, a motive for action, requires a sense of conviction, a 'yes' on the part of the individual. It is this conviction, this assent (*synkatathesis*) which leads to action, which is brought about by the 'emotional pull', and which constitutes a wrong assumption. It thus becomes clearer in detail how for Posidonius emotions were not mistaken judgements in the Chrysippean sense, nor the result of mistaken judgements, as Zeno may have suggested, but on the contrary, mistaken assumptions were the result of the emotional pull. Moreover, the evidence is explicit on wherein the mistake lay. To quote from *De plac.* 452, 3–10, it lies in mistaking for *haplōs oikeia* (that is to say, for what is native or akin to man in an absolute sense) what are merely akin (*oikeia*) to the irrational capacities (*alogoi dynameis*), namely pleasure (ἥδεσθαι), and power (κρατεῖν), the objects of *orexis* of the brutish aspect of soul; but the only things which are *haplos oikeia* are wisdom, good, beauty, the objects of *orexis* of the rational and divine. This, I think, crystallises Posidonius' position more clearly than anything; one can see the characteristic Stoic cast of thought, and yet the quite individual and original approach. For one thing, it is clear that the concept *oikeion* for him is not necessarily related to the term good, however relative. Posidonius is not concerned here with 'the preferred' (*proēgmena*), with what has relative worth (*axia*) in a moral context, but with native drives which upset the moral balance. He is in the peculiar position for a Stoic of condemning the hedonist mistake not because the hedonist regards pleasure as akin to man, for it is, but because he fails to understand what aspect of man it is akin to. And here I may turn briefly to the notorious statements in Diog. Laert. VII 103 and 127–8, that wealth and health were in the class of goods for Posidonius, hilariously enlarged by Epiphanius, *De fide.* 9, 46 to the position that wealth and health were the greatest good for Posidonius.[16] This view seems to me decisively exploded by Seneca *Ep. mor.* 87, 31–40, both in statement and argument. But so it is by Galen. The attainment of wealth could never be an object of *orexis* which was *haplos oikeion*. As Seneca puts it in a Posidonian way, wealth can *inflant animos*, incite men to evil. But no doubt the satisfaction of wealth was regarded by Posidonius as *oikeion* (to the *alogoi dynameis*, that is), which may have given rise to the misconception that it was a kind of good. The fact remains, and is really so clear from Galen, that Posidonius, despite his recognition of native irrational drives in man, was as adamant as any Stoic in excluding these from the final absolute good and end.

Much the same situation occurs with virtue(s) (*arete, aretai*). Posidonius attacked Chrysippus for inconsistency in holding to one capacity, one 'natural affinity' (*dynamis, oikeiosis*), and yet also to a plurality of virtues, other, that is, from knowledge or prudence (*De plac.* 662, 3–8; 584, 4–10; 462, 12–463, 8). Ariston was more consistent. Posidonius spoke of two kinds of virtues: irrational capacities whose native virtues (*oikeiai aretai*) were derived from habituation (*ethismos*), and the virtue of reason (*logos*) itself, the training of which lay in the science of the constitution of reality (ἐπιστήμη τῆς τῶν ὄντων φύσεως, *De plac.* 446, 7ff.). In other words, there is a clear distinction between virtue without qualification (*arete haplōs*) which can be taught (Diog. Laert. VII. 91), and the virtues of the irrational capacities of the *psyche*, which cannot. And one must beware of comparing the virtues (*aretai*) of the irrational capacities with *kathekonta*; for to Posidonius, 'appropriate acts' do not derive from the development or perfection of the faculty of enjoying pleasure or being courageous, but are constituted simply in obedience to reason, that is, intellectual virtue.

And so we come to the End (*telos*). The reports on this contain some of the more obscure and difficult passages in the Frag-

ments, but I shall use only what seems to me clear from the
evidence. One approach, *De plac.* 448, 11ff., is once more from
the *pathe* and is contained in a quotation: 'The cause of the
pathe, that is of lack of harmony (*anomologia*) and of the life of
misery (κακοδαίμων βίος), lies in not following in everything
the *daemōn* within, which is kin (συγγενής) to the one which
rules the whole world, but rather to live in subjection to the
worse and brutish (ζῳώδης).' There are thus two alternatives,
and the other is the *telos* for man; namely that the irrational
capacities should follow reason in every respect (*De plac.* 445,
15). The end involves seeing that the aim of one's irrational
desires is not worth attaining in itself. It is true that the desires
of the irrational capacities are not foreign to man and so cannot be eradicated or ignored, but since they are devoid of any
intrinsic value, or since they positively pervert, they should be
subdued completely. Galen says that Posidonius criticised his
predecessors' account of the *telos* on two counts. The first is
precisely that they ignored the *pathe*. The obstacle, as it were, to
the *telos* was as important as the goal, because it is involved in
it. It was only if we recognised the innate power of the *pathe*
and their cause that we could successfully avoid *anomologia*.
That is why the definition given in Clement (*Strom.* II, p. 129,
1–5) adds to the positive section: 'to live in contemplation of
the truth and order of all things . . . .' (τὸ ζῆν θεωροῦντα τὴν
τῶν ὅλων ἀλήθειαν καὶ τάξιν καὶ συγκατασκευάζοντα αὐτὴν
[L: αὐτὸν Sylburg] κατὰ τὸ δυνατόν), the characteristic
negative: 'in no way led by the irrational part of the soul'
κατὰ μηδὲν ἀγόμενον ὑπὸ τοῦ ἀλόγου μέρους τῆς ψυχῆς); except
that 'part' (*merous*) is inaccurate. The other criticism (*De plac.*
450, 2–451, 2) is so obscure in detail that I embark on it in such
a general paper as this with reluctance.[17] But it does seem to me
that in this passage Chrysippus' followers are reprimanded for
contracting the *telos* definition of ὁμολογουμένως ζῆν to 'to do
everything possible for the sake of the first natural things'. In
Posidonius' view this is simply to make the aim equivalent to
pleasure, and one can see from my earlier account why this
could well be so in Posidonius' view. This is no way, he thought,
to cut through the dilemmas presented by the critics of the
Stoa, that is by bringing the indifferents 'meanly' more into

prominence in the interpretation of the end as his predecessors
had done; the way was rather by his own approach to interpreting the phrase which he as all other Stoics accepted:
ὁμολογουμένως ζῆν.[18] Again, what is most noticeable here is the
uncomprisingly Stoic position adopted by Posidonius. And
there does emerge from the evidence a consistent account of the
relevance of *pathe* throughout the different parts of ethics; and
the system constituted by this account is undoubtedly a Stoic
system.

I would like finally to glance at some general characteristics
of this system, but still and always from the base of ancient
evidence. Such diverse figures as Galen, Strabo, Seneca, Cicero
and Pliny admired Posidonius as a philosopher of the first rank;
and some of them, apart from referring to the content of his
philosophy, also cited what appeared to them certain peculiar
or outstanding formal characteristics. It would be interesting
to ask how far these apply to Galen's account of Posidonian
ethics. Perhaps the most famous label is what Galen and Strabo
(and Seneca) refer to as a propensity to inquire into causes,
to aitiologikon. It is also the most obvious trait. Even from my
brief review, the importance for Posidonian argument of asking
the question, 'What is the cause of . . .' must be clear. And anyone who reads through Galen must be struck by the frequency,
almost the inevitability, of this approach. To each and every
aporia which Posidonius contests with Chrysippus, Posidonius
applies the question: 'What is the cause of this situation, this
phenomenon?'[19] πολὺ τὸ αἰτιολογικόν indeed. But there is a
difficulty, not often faced. Galen much admired this trait;
Strabo criticised it, and Strabo was a Stoic: 'In Posidonius', he
says, (II 3,8), 'there is much enquiry into causes . . . precisely
what our School sheers off from . . .'. Now, of course Posidonius
was not the first Stoic to concern himself with causes. On the
contrary, that everything has a cause was a fundamental dogma
of Stoicism. So why is Posidonius' aetiological activity considered unStoic? Fortunately Strabo gives the hints: Posidonius'
activity is Aristotlizing, and Stoics shun it on account of the
concealment of the causes. And indeed Chrysippus while holding that nothing in nature happens without a cause, also held
that one cannot know every cause, but some must remain

obscure (*adēla*) to the human mind (*SVF* II 973; 351). As our
evidence shows, Posidonius was not prepared to let an enquiry
off the hook for such an excuse (cf. especially *De plac*. 395, 11–
396). He is not merely content to accept that there is a cause
for everything, he wishes to know what each of them is. The
matter goes deeper still. Alexander in *De fato* xxv (*SVF* II 949)
accuses the Stoa of an infinite regress in causation, so that no
cause can be called first or last. And he complains that this
would destroy the very basis of science whose special concern is
with first causes. Again this fits very well with what we know
of Posidonius. We know from Geminus, the pupil of Posidonius,
quoted in Simplicius, *In Aristotelis Physica*, 11, 2, (193b 23) that
Posidonius, without doubt the most scientific of the Stoics, held
that the main duty of the philosopher-scientist (i.e. in the
physikos logos) as distinct from the ordinary scientist, mathe-
matician, astronomer, was precisely a search for such causes.

No doubt connected with the foregoing is another characteristic selected by both Strabo and Galen: *apodeiktikos*, given to
proofs;[20] connected, because in the Geminus fragment the
philosopher-physicist will demonstrate (*apodeixei*) the phenomena, from the causes, that is. But it is Galen who really presses
this characteristic, *De plac*. 362, 5ff.: Posidonius is used to
following proofs (*apodeixis*) more than any other Stoic. But
what, pray, about Zeno and Chrysippus and their contributions
to Stoic logic in the hypothetical syllogism, apart from the
many examples of argument surviving in the evidence? But,
says Galen, Posidonius' proofs derive from his training in geometry; this is why he is the most scientific (*epistēmonikōtatos*) of
the Stoics.[21] It may be that we should have regard for Galen's
spectacles here. A question to be asked is what kind of proofs
does Galen relate to geometry and mathematics. We know that
Galen had a lifelong interest in both of these topics, ever since
he received his first mathematical lessons from his architect
father. He was particularly interested in scientific proof, and
wrote a vast work, now lost περὶ ἀποδείξεων (*On Proofs*). But
in three chapters (16–18) of the *Institutio Logica*, he introduces
what he regards as a peculiarly mathematical logic, distinct
from the categorical and hypothetical syllogism. His treatment
seems confused, but the new species of mathematical syllogism

he appears to have in mind is based on the relational syllogism, and a feature of his treatment of this is that he holds that such syllogisms owe their validity always to an unexpressed self-evident axiom. In other words, the two mathematical features apparently are the relational or proportional form, and the dependence on an axiom. Moreover, Posidonius is mentioned by name, as saying that this species of syllogism is 'conclusive by force of axiom'. Relational syllogisms cannot be traced, I think, to Chrysippus, and it is not impossible that these chapters of Galen depend to some extent on Posidonius. However, there seems no trace of the relational syllogism as characteristic of Posidonius' argumentation on the emotions as reported by Galen. On the other hand, conclusion by force of axiom is relevant to Posidonius' aetiological methodology in the Περὶ Παθῶν as elsewhere, so that this is what would seem to be in Galen's mind in the reference to mathematical logic. Fortunately, one other aspect of proof which Galen, however obscurely, connects with the foregoing is clear to any reader of Posidonius, and that is his respect for facts. Galen, *De plac.* 362, 7ff. pursues his point thus: 'It is *because* of Posidonius' addiction to geometric proofs that he was ashamed to contradict the evidence of the data and to contradict himself.' It is certainly true that Posidonius will argue the rejection of a thesis of Chrysippus (e.g. on the weakness of soul, *De plac.* 369–76) because the deduced conclusions do not square with the facts (οὐχ ὁρᾶται γιγνόμενον), or do not cover all of them. As in the famous story of his classic observation of the tides in Spain, so in a historical-ethical field stories are rejected if there is no corroboration of phenomena. *Per se ipsum explorator factus* (Priscianus Lydus). But this care in assembling data, whether from the senses or from what he regarded as clearly perceptible to the mind, was not only the instrument of destruction of others, but the flesh of his own theories. He was certainly the most scientific of the Stoics in the sense that his theoretical explanations had to accommodate, were tied to, tested by, were indeed the explanation of the experience of phenomena. Still, in the end, the phenomena, according to Geminus, had to be deduced from the causes.

It is hardly surprising that Posidonius earned his third title of Aristotlizer (τὸ ᾿Αριστοτελίζον);²² Platonizer, too, as is clear from the approving Galen. Strabo, the Stoic, thinks he goes too far. But neither considers him to be an Aristotelian or a Platonist. Galen, himself, an adherent of the Academy and Peripatos, points out differences where they seem most close;²³ and Posidonius' system is most certainly a Stoic one, and was always so regarded. It is indeed true that Posidonius had a strong admiration for Plato and Aristotle, but so, of course, did other Stoics; Chrysippus, Antipater and Panaetius, for example; and, according to Posidonius, Zeno and Cleanthes. But Posidonius refers more often to 'the ancients' (οἱ παλαιοί), and he attacked Chrysippus for ignoring 'the old account' (τὸν παλαιὸν λόγον).²⁴ Yet he was neither an antiquarian nor an eclectic. It is rather the case that he believed in the historical development of philosophy. Certain leading figures in the past had made a contribution to be admired—Pythagoras, Plato, Aristotle, Zeno, Cleanthes;²⁵ but their achievements were not simply to be accepted, but to be added to or continued. This concept of the progress of philosophy Seneca (*Ep. mor.* 33, 5f.) thought characteristic of the Stoa and lacking in Epicureanism. It is perhaps most evident in Posidonius. In the progression of knowledge Posidonius saw himself dealing with certain aspects of philosophy, certain *aporiai*, which he felt had been inadequately treated before him. In ethics *one* such outstanding topic was the problem of emotional disturbance. And so in the Galenic evidence Posidonius seems less concerned with the idealistic plane occupied so noticeably by the early Stoa. As Panaetius showed himself at least equally concerned with *kathekonta* (appropriate acts) as with *katorthomata* (morally right acts), so Posidonius appears more preoccupied with *pathe*, evils, vice (*kakia*), their origins and cure, than with goods and virtue. Determined to recognise the factual evidence of the imperfections of the human soul and character, the things according to nature with which he is concerned in the περὶ Παθῶν are the perverting ones, rather than with self-preservation, 'the preferred' (*proegmena*), 'goods' (*agatha*). But this is only one aspect of the matter. When it came to the *telos* Posidonius showed himself more rigorously uncompromising than other Stoics with regard to giving some place to the 'indifferents' by 'contracting' the definition of the End. And he believed no less than the others in the possibility of the Sage. Galen, for once, criticises him and points out the apparent contradiction (*De plac.* 408–411). The Sage, said Posidonius, is entirely free from suffering. On the other hand, the danger is much greater than Chrysippus thought. The soul is not liable to disease and suffering from chance external influence or outward factors only; it is always susceptible to disease from its own innate irrational drives; the great majority of men are in a diseased or disease-like state.[26] The diseases of the soul, i.e. emotional disturbances, are of our own making; they come from natural causes. Man has to fight a chronic illness. But the opportunity for self-cure is also derived from human nature apparently, or rather from its relationship to the structure of the universe. The key for this in psychology occurs in Tertullian, *De anima* XIV 2, where there is a distinction made between the concept of *hegemonikon*, which implies a ruling element and sub-servient elements that are in our own *psyche* as well as in the universe (cf. Porphyry, *De an.* in Stob. *Ecl.* I p. 369, 5 = *SVF* II 831; and Seneca, *Ep. mor.* 92, 1), and the concept of *logikon*, which implies rational and irrational elements. However, it does rather seem that the old challenge to Chrysippus: 'Why is everyone *not* a Sage?', has now to change for Posidonius to 'But how can anyone become a Sage?'

NOTES

I acknowledge gratefully my huge debt to the late Ludwig Edelstein, on whose unpublished *Fragments of Posidonius* I have had the opportunity of working. But of course Edelstein must not be held responsible for any of my arguments or conclusions.

1. Professor Phillip De Lacy is at present engaged on the *De placitis*.
2. E.g. Diog. Laert. VII 40.
3. Sextus *Adv. math.* VII 16–19.
4. The references to the *De placitis* throughout this essay are to page and line of Iwan Mueller's edition.
5. Plutarch *Stoic. rep.* 9 = *SVF* III 68.
6. E.g. in *De plac.* 449.
7. Diog. Laert. VII 40–1.
8. I am not talking here of divisions of *psyche*, which Posidonius, according to Tertullian *De an.* XIV 2, numbered seventeen. There the classification derives from

the two distinct concepts of *hegemonikon* (i.e. controlling aspect in relation to serving parts) and *logikon* (rational as opposed to irrational).

9. See e.g. Edelstein, 'The Philosophical System of Posidonius', *AJPh* lvii (1936) 306, 316; Pohlenz, *Die Stoa* i, 224ff.; Zeller *Phil. d. Gr.* III 1, 600ff.

10. E.g. *SVF* I 205; III 377; 378; 384; 391; 412; 462; 479.

11. Cf. Pohlenz, *Hermes* lxxvi (1941) 1ff. [See S. G. Pembroke, Chapter VI, p. 121, Ed.]

12. For a recent examination see Long, 'The Stoic Concept of Evil', *Ph. Q.* xviii (1968) 329–43.

13. [S. G. Pembroke, Chapter VI pp. 122ff., raises questions about the relation of Chrysippean *oikeiosis* to moral action. Ed.]

14. Because this depends on emendation. Sense demands the following lacuna: καὶ γὰρ καὶ ταῦθ' ὁ Ποσειδώνιος μέμφεται καὶ δεικνύναι πειρᾶται πασῶν τῶν ψευδῶν ὑπολήψεων τὰς αἰτίας ἐν μὲν τῷ θεωρητικῷ < . . . > διὰ τῆς παθητικῆς ὁλκῆς. Now, ἐν μὲν τῷ θεωρητικῷ would suggest ἐν δὲ τῷ πρακτικῷ at the end of the lacuna. At *De plac.* 446, 7ff. it is stated that the παιδεία and ἀρετή of reason is ἐπιστήμη τῆς τῶν ὄντων φύσεως. The opposite of ἐπιστήμη in influence on τὸ λογικόν is ἀμαθία (*De plac.* 453, 11). Edelstein suggested for the lacuna: <σκέμματι γιγνομένων διὰ τῆς ἀμαθίας, ἐν δὲ τῷ πρακτικῷ>.

15. The expression, 'emotional pull', may have been coined by Posidonius.

16. Cf. also my argument in *CQ* N.S. v (1955) 188ff. (= Chapter VII pp. 162f.)

17. For a different recent interpretation see Long, 'Carneades and the Stoic Telos', *Phronesis* xii (1967) 84–6.

18. E.g. Diog. Laert. VII 87.

19. *De plac.* 454, 7ff. for a general statement by Galen.

20. Strabo II 3, 5.

21. *De plac.* 653, 14f.

22. Strabo II 3, 8.

23. E.g. *De plac.* 463, 3–6.

24. E.g. *De plac.* 396, 1–3; 584, 4–7; 405, 14f.; 401, 10f.

25. E.g. *De plac.* 401, 11–15.

26. *Pathos* in Greek could mean 'disease'. See Cic. *Fin.* III 35.

X

The Natural Law and Stoicism

GERARD WATSON

There are subtler points for investigation in the philosophy of the Stoics than their statements on natural law, but no doctrine attributed to them has been more influential. It is also a fact that no doctrine attributed to them is less satisfactory to write about. A passage from Sir Ernest Barker's *Traditions of Civility* may be cited to illustrate the difficulty. He has been talking about the origin of the idea of natural law, and he continues:

But it was among the Stoic thinkers of the Hellenistic age that the movement first attained a large and general expression; and that expression . . . became a tradition of human civility which runs continuously from the Stoic teachers of the Porch to the American Revolution of 1776 and the French Revolution of 1789. Allied to theology for many centuries—adopted by the Catholic Church, and forming part of the general teaching of Schoolmen and the Canonists —the theory of Natural Law had become in the sixteenth century, and continued to remain during the seventeenth and the eighteenth, an independent and rationalist system, professed and expounded by the philosophers of the secular school of natural law (p. 312).

We might suspect a certain looseness in a term which has won such a variety of admiration. But the term survives. The events of the last thirty years in Europe have served to revive the notion. Since the Nürnberg trials at least it has again become fashionable to demand that 'crimes against humanity' be tried at the bar of natural justice. The Universal Declaration of Human Rights in 1948 has been read by some as the natural law for the twentieth century, and natural law has also been invoked rather dramatically in the Catholic Church quite recently. One of the events of 1968 was undoubtedly the appearance of the papal encyclical *Humanae Vitae*. The Pope there said that the Church's teaching on marriage was 'a

teaching founded on the natural law'. The debate on contraception which followed was also marked by a recurrence of the
question: 'Is it in accordance with the natural law?' And in this
debate within the Catholic Church when the natural law is
mentioned the Stoics are frequently invoked. Arntz, for instance,
in an attempt at a serious understanding, refers to the Stoics and
St Thomas as the 'two peaks of its [natural law's] historical
development'.[1]

The impression is sometimes given that the Natural Law is a
body of unchanging rules, somewhere at some time worked out
and available for consultation in difficulties, a sort of secular
version of the Ten Commandments. 'Natural Law' is such an
awe-inspiring phrase that it seems almost sacrilegious to examine
it critically. It may help, therefore, in the discussion of the
natural law in Stoicism if we begin by taking the term out of
English. For it is undoubtedly a complicating factor that even
when discussing natural law in the Stoic context one tends to
use the term in English, with all the associations that have been
built up for it there over the centuries. One does not do that
with other terms that are specially associated with Stoicism,
terms like *pneuma*, *oikeiōsis*, εἱμαρμένη, καθῆκον. They are either
left simply in Greek or at most transliterated. What would the
term or terms for natural law be in original Stoic contexts?

Given the tradition of civility that Barker talks of, one thinks
immediately of a Latin version—*ius naturale*, *lex naturalis*, *lex
naturae* are terms to be found in Grotius, St Thomas Aquinas,
the *Digest*, St Ambrose and Cicero. And νόμος τῆς φύσεως
would suggest itself in Greek. We could therefore begin with
the coupling of *nomos* and *physis* in Stoicism and see how the
associated ideas were taken over and translated by their successors. It seems necessary to adopt such an approach if we are
to give any definition to our subject. For in fact what is really
meant in most contexts today when natural law is used is
morality or the ideal standard of behaviour. To write about
natural law then in Stoicism would be to write about Stoic
morality. But Plato and Aristotle also had systems of morality
and yet their names are not linked in the way that the Stoics'
are with natural law. I shall try to show that for later ages the
Stoics were particularly associated with natural law mainly

because of one man, Cicero. And Cicero's presentation of natural law will be our chief concern.

The term natural law is in the first place highly ambiguous because the many meanings of 'natural' and of 'law' when each is taken separately are compounded when the words are put together. Here the Greeks had the advantage over us. For at the beginning at least they could not have accepted the term so uncritically as we normally do. We have become so accustomed to the term 'natural law' that we find it difficult at first to realise just how paradoxical such a close juxtaposition of *physis* and *nomos* must have sounded even at the time of the first Stoics. For, as Guthrie says, the antithesis of *physis* and *nomos* had become 'the favourite catchword of Athenian thought in the second half of the fifth century, and the chief bone of contention between the Sophists on the one hand and Socrates and Plato on the other'.[2] Consequently there is a certain air of conscious paradox in the first important presentation of the term νόμος τῆς φύσεως in Greek literature, in the *Gorgias* of Plato.[3] Callicles has been contrasting nature (*physis*), which demonstrates (he says) that it is right that the strong should prevail over the weak, and convention (*nomos*), which is the defence relied on by the weaklings who form the majority of mankind. Living in accordance with nature means despising received ideas and behaving like Xerxes and his father, for instance, who acted on the principle that the strong has the right to impose his will on the weak: indeed, he says, with the awareness that he is coining a paradoxical phrase, such action is 'in accordance with natural law' . . . καὶ ναὶ μὰ Δία κατὰ νόμον γε τὸν τῆς φύσεως (483e). This is also, of course, a first clear indication of the ambiguity inherent in natural law. All that Callicles' position has in common with the majority of later expositions of natural law is that the law of nature entitles (or obliges) us on occasion to ignore the narrow prescriptions of particular law-codes. Aristotle in the *Rhetoric* (1373b) shows how the law of nature can be invoked in the courts when the letter of a particular positive law seems unfavourable.

The two instances cited, from Plato and Aristotle, are deliberately exploiting the ambiguity in the notion of 'natural'. But it seems unlikely that, in the case of men less subtle, where confusion existed it was also willed. One of the easiest and oldest confusions is based on the argument: what the animals do is natural, for it is unhampered by convention. Therefore, if a man is to act naturally, he should do as the animals do.[4] Herodotus (II 64) reports that all races except the Egyptians and the Greeks allow sexual intercourse in sanctuaries, because the animals have sexual intercourse there and if the gods were opposed the animals would not do it. Aristophanes plays with the idea (*Birds* 755f.):

> All that here is reckoned shameful, all that here the laws condemn,
> With the birds is right and proper, you may do it all with them.
>
> (Rogers' trans.)

Pheidippides and Strepsiades argue the point in the *Clouds* (1427ff.). Here, as in an earlier scene where the advice χρῶ τῇ φύσει . . . νόμιζε μηδὲν αἰσχρόν (1078) is given, Aristophanes is parodying fashionable philosophical debates. Strepsiades, however, points out, with example, that there are a number of things the animals do which men will not do.

The vigorous rebuttal of Strepsiades was, we may be sure, frequently echoed later, but the appeal to 'what the animals do' persisted. It is particularly associated at a later stage with the Cynics. They too had grown up with the *nomos/physis* antithesis, and the good life was, of course, 'in accordance with nature' (*kata physin*). But as Dudley points out, they apparently never found it necessary to define exactly what *kata physin* implied: 'strip away all the accretions of convention, tradition and social existence, and what is left is *kata physin*'.[5] Human reasoning was too prone to err in the conduct of life, therefore keep reasoning processes out of it as much as possible. Animals had preserved the 'natural' state much better than man.

That Cynicism and early Stoicism were closely connected is well attested.[6] What advance did the Stoics make on the position of the Cynics, or what had they to add to the suggestions of Aristotle or Plato? Much, of course, is due to their historical position and the period during which Stoicism developed. The achievements of Alexander can hardly have failed to affect their thinking, even if one does not assent to the theory that he was the first believer in the brotherhood of man.[7]

Even more important for their later reputation is the fact that leading Stoics became so much a part of the intellectual life of the expanding Roman state, and its developing consciousness of its mission, *paci imponere morem*.

It would be absurd, however, to attribute the Stoic pre-dominance in the field of natural law simply to the fact that their school flourished at this particular period of world history. We have to turn to the system itself. Certain points made else-where in this book may be briefly recalled in support of a struc-ture which would commonly be accepted as Stoic. The Stoics held that from birth every living thing has self-awareness, a *synaisthesis* of itself.[8] And in man the inborn concentration on the self leads him to draw towards himself and assimilate what is ordered to him and beneficial for him and to reject the harm-ful and unpleasant. This process of *oikeiosis* is the working of the primary impulses towards self-preservation. From this instinctive activity there grows eventually in man the capability of calling one thing good and the other bad, of saying 'yes' to this and 'no' to that. And from this power of discrimination ultimately there will develop the laws of thought and the principles of ethics.[9]

Oikeiosis should not be interpreted in the narrow sense. The Stoic ideal, the sage, has come to understand and accept all reality. The whole context of their thought forced on them a broad conception of law: man's responsibilities were not bounded by the particular state or community in which he lived.

The *Politeia* of Zeno . . . is directed to this one main point, that our life should not be based on cities or peoples each with its view of right and wrong, but we should regard all men as our fellow-countrymen and fellow-citizens, and that there should be one life and one order, like that of a single flock on a common pasture feed-ing together under a common law. Zeno wrote this, shaping as it were a dream or picture of a philosophic, well-ordered society.[10]

The *Politeia* of Zeno is a much discussed work and no attempt has been made here to solve the problems which it offers.[11] But there seems little reason to doubt this particular statement by Plutarch about it. We have no reason to believe that Zeno regarded this view of life as anything but Utopian: and we need not waste time in deciding whether the inhabitants of Utopia are sages or not. But Heraclitus too had talked of a law which was valid for the whole universe and which men should follow if they wanted to live properly. What advance did Zeno make on Heraclitus? Did he discuss the relation between the common law and the active principle in the universe? Did he discuss the problems which are inherent in the combination of prescriptive and descriptive formulae? We have for instance a statement from Cicero (*De natura deorum* I, 36) where an Epicurean says: 'Zeno . . . naturalem legem divinam esse censet, eamque vim obtinere recta imperantem prohibentemque contraria.[12] Quam legem quo modo efficiat animantem intellegere non possumus; deum autem animantem certe volumus esse'. The point is not developed, unfortunately, and we have no further information about the relation of description to prescription in Zeno. And it would be asking too much to expect to find it discussed by Cleanthes when he mentions the 'common law of God' in his *Hymn to Zeus*.

Such a discussion in the early Stoa there may have been. But it seems unlikely, and particularly so when we find no traces of such a debate in a natural law context among the fragments of Chrysippus. Chrysippus discussed so many things so keenly that to us it does seem extraordinary that he should have omitted this point. Two reasons for the omission may be suggested, however. Firstly, the explicit distinction is a modern one. It was not made many centuries later by Thomas Aquinas in spite of the importance of natural law in his ethical theory.[13] Secondly, we must never forget the origins of natural law and its early rhetorical flavour. The rhetoric may be inspiring at times as in the case of Antigone and the 'unwritten laws'; but it remains rhetoric. And rhetoric is not designed to promote clear thinking.

We must, then, simply accept this blurring of distinctions between description and prescription. We must also accept the fact that within prescription itself no clear line is drawn between law and morality. Many would now find this regrettable from the point of view of morality. But in Rome the natural law was invoked most frequently in a legal context and it was not felt desirable to emphasize that legality sometimes differed from morality. The continuity of ethics and politics seemed self-evident to most Greeks.

Keeping these points in mind, we may now turn our attention to the following passage from Diogenes Laertius (VII 87-8):

Living virtuously is equivalent to living in accordance with experience of the actual course of nature, as Chrysippus says in the first book of his *About Ends*;[14] for our individual natures are parts of the nature of the whole universe. And this is why the end may be defined as life in accordance with nature, or, in other words, in accordance with our own human nature as well as that of the universe, a life in which we refrain from every action forbidden by the law common to all things, that is to say, the right reason which pervades all things and is identical with Zeus, lord and ruler of all that is (trans. Hicks, Loeb Library).

The meaning of this passage seems, at first glance, to be obvious. The two senses in which nature is used are clearly contrasted. There is, for instance, no question of taking *physis* in the narrow sense as the principle of organic being.[15] Universal nature in the broadest sense is distinguished from human nature. Our own human nature is the nature of man, the species, rather than the nature of one particular man. Human nature is characterized by logos. The universal nature is the nature to which Diogenes Laertius and Cicero refer, the πῦρ τεχνικόν, where God, the active principle, is responsible for all order in the universe.[16]

But the form of the contrast may be misleading. We are told that we will live as we ought by conforming ourselves to the divine reason, and the juxtaposition implies that the divine reason provides some directions which human nature can perceive and try to follow. But what looked like a form of instructions turns out on closer examination to be only another exhortation. For men are to behave not simply in accordance with the principles that govern the rest of nature, that is, in accordance with *hexis* or *physis* or *psyche*.[17] In the early stages of life human beings will indeed behave like the other animals, assimilating what is useful, rejecting what is harmful, persisting in being. But as the child grows older the distinctive human principle, *logos*, develops and it begins to shape the impulses. Here specific guidance on the use of one's reason would be more welcome than the exhortation to follow nature.

In fact when the principle of following nature does not say too much it says nothing, because it becomes a mere tautology. A tautology, because as Diogenes also says, to live according to nature means for man to live according to reason. And the exhortation evidently does not help very much in choosing among those things which are *kata physin*.[18] God is the perfection of reason. But because man is not God he cannot embrace all things: he must choose. The common law (ὁ νόμος ὁ κοινός) does not offer any obvious criteria to help him in his choosing.

Moreover choosing implies freedom. But real freedom presupposes some degree of self-determination. It is difficult to see how this can be guaranteed within the Stoic system. What is the imagined model of agreement here for instance? Is it to be like a branch on a tree? Or a boat in a stream? Or are we to think rather of one colour in a pattern, or a theme in a piece of music? It could, of course, be objected that there *need* not be any picture behind the accord, but common sense would suggest that there is, and Stoic images in slightly different contexts seem to indicate a picture of the sort above. We could beg the question slightly. We could introduce the picture of a rower in the boat, or a man carried by a team of animals. It is still difficult to see what having a will of one's own can mean, if a man is going to be whirled or dragged if he does not agree. Ubi igitur virtus, si nihil situm est in ipsis nobis?[19] Yet what else can 'accord' mean than accepting the regular order of events?

It may be urged that it is unfair to present the Stoic position in such impersonal terms, that even the enemies of Stoicism acknowledged as a leading feature in their system the Stoic emphasis on Providence.[20] Indeed the Stoics thought of themselves as constrained only by reason and consequently for their own good, just as a law in a city binds citizens because it protects them.[21] But this still does not seem to escape the difficulty.[22] Human reason may be in agreement with divine reason either because it accepts the suggestions of divine reason or because the two are simply manifestations, from different points of view, of the same principle. In the latter case the agreement could be expected to be perpetual. This perfect agreement would have been realized in the case of the Sage. But this then looks like saving the Sage's freedom by deifying him, and apart from the other difficulties in this procedure it does not solve the problem of freedom and therefore of morality for ordinary mortals.[23] And since the Stoics were materialists the problem remained, however far they went in using personal language about providence. God expresses himself in the regular order of events: the *Logos* under this aspect is Fate. The 'common law' will ultimately assert itself by the very fact that the process will be complete.

What difference does human action make? By what criteria does one say that one action is good and another bad? Can right reason not be more closely or concretely defined? What models for 'natural' action should man follow? Should it be to do as the animals do?[24] And would this in turn mean that the right of the stronger should prevail? In the fragments that remain to us one does not find these questions discussed in the context of 'the law that is common to all'. Nor do we find any mention of primary and secondary precepts, any attempt to systematise the natural law into a code of rules. The Stoics did give advice for action in various concrete situations, as we shall see, but the term 'natural law' itself was evidently not felt to be particularly helpful in the discussion.

Why was it then that a natural law tradition was able to develop? For reasons similar to those which later assisted its revival in Europe, above all the need for an international standard. The leaders of the Middle Stoa found themselves in Rome. Panaetius was accepted by the leading circles in that city as their philosopher.[25] The second half of the second century B.C. brought the culmination of the first great Greek intellectual invasion, with Greek ideas in literature, drama, history and philosophy setting the tone. The Greeks in turn were greatly impressed by the Roman vigour, and aware, more perhaps than the Romans themselves, of the future that was opening out before them. But the empire which Polybius could foresee brought its own responsibilities with it. These responsibilities became clearer as the expansion proceeded. Virgil summarised the experience of the preceding century when he wrote:

> Tu regere imperio populos Romane memento
> (hae tibi erunt artes) pacique imponere morem,
> parcere subiectis et debellare superbos.[26]

Rome's international role forced on her the administration of international justice. Foreigners subject or allied to her tended more and more to turn to her as their law court. The inevitable result was a broader conception of justice, a realisation of the need for a law that would apply to all men. There are various indications of this in the literature of the Republic. But the leading proponent of the importance of the development of a law for all men is Cicero. And the main source for the ideas of Cicero on this matter was Stoic philosophy.

It was an interest which might have been expected in Cicero in any case, Rome's leading lawyer and would-be statesman. 'Our statesmen should surely have taken pains to become familiar with politics and law, and should have examined their origins'.[27] The less Cicero was allowed to engage in the practice, the more he turned to the theory of statesmanship. The theme of the natural law recurs again and again in the writings of his last years. There is, however, little point in trying to trace a development from De republica to the De officiis. Cicero made no attempt to present himself as an original philosopher: his philosophical writings were an attempt to help his fellow-citizens and to further the good of the community. What was meant first as a distraction from political activity finally became a substitute for it.

Cicero said that he wanted to make Greek thought accessible to Roman readers. The first of the philosophical writings, the De republica, seems to have drawn from a number of sources. The theme is the ideal state and the Roman state as an example of it. The ideal state suggests the inspiration of Plato and his influence is at times obvious. But Cicero does seem to give us a very broad hint when Laelius, having proposed the theme, says: 'Memineram persaepe te cum Panaetio disserere solitum coram Polybio . . .'[28] Unfortunately much of the dialogue has been lost. Unfortunately, because it touches on the very points that we would have liked to see discussed by Chrysippus. This is particularly the case in Book III.

In Book I there have been references to a law for the universe, but they are of a general nature. They are not so much an analysis of natural law as a testimony to the fact that such ideas were in the air. But in Book III the very notion of justice itself is discussed. It is treated historically. We know from Lactantius that Philus referred to the theories of Plato and Aristotle and Carneades' refutation of them.[29] Where our text begins again Chrysippus is mentioned, but it is very much in passing, as the usual difficulties against a notion of universal justice are raised. 'Ius enim, de quo quaerimus, civile est aliquod, naturale nullum; for if it were natural, then, like heat and cold, or bitter and sweet, justice and injustice would be the same thing to all men.'[30] The usual examples of different customs in religion and morals are given. But 'virtue does not allow inconsistency, nor does nature permit variation . . . Nihil habet igitur naturale ius . . . . And, they say, it is the duty of a good and just man to give everyone that which is his due. Well then, what is it first of all that we are to grant to dumb animals as their due?'[31] What follows is, unfortunately, lost. But according to Lactantius the argument pointed out that laws were made simply for utility and there is no natural law. People act for their own advantage: if they do not, they are regarded as fools. Nations and individuals, like Alexander, have shown that might is right.[32]

This last argument (formulated in III 23: 'not nature or choice, but weakness is the mother of justice') had been a commonplace since the Sophists. Much of the reply given by Laelius is again lost. Some of it is preserved by Lactantius. He quotes, for instance, one of the most famous descriptions of natural law in the 'almost divine words' of Cicero himself.

Est quidem vera lex recta ratio naturae congruens, diffusa in omnes, constans, sempiterna, quae vocet ad officium iubendo, vetando a fraude deterreat. . . . And there will not be one law at Rome and another one at Athens, one law now and a different one in the future, but there will be one law, eternal and unchangeable, which will bind all peoples at all times. And there will be one common master and ruler of men, that is, God, who is the author, interpreter and proposer of this law. Whoever will not obey it is trying to escape from himself, and in denying the true nature of man he will thereby suffer the severest penalties, even if he escapes what is commonly considered punishment.[33]

It seems that Laelius paid particular attention to the objection that nations in fact have acted on the principle that might is right and that empire is simply legalised robbery. This is the sort of theme that must have been keenly discussed in the Scipionic circle.[34] Conditions for a just war are put forward: it must be for honour or defence, that is to redress an injury or in the interests of security: war will only be waged after reparation has been refused and war formally declared. Defence is understood to include the defence of allies, and from there the transition to the imperial theme is easy. Laelius seems to have argued that Rome acquired its empire because it felt bound to defend its allies. Augustine tells us that it was argued that rule over subject peoples is just because subjection is advantageous for certain types of men.[35] As Aristotle had maintained earlier, some men are apparently intended by nature to be slaves. There is however some incongruity in Cicero's retention of a similar argument together with his assertion of one law for all men. Lactantius was clearly not impressed by the defence offered in this part of the *De republica* against Carneades. Having summarised Carneades' general objections to a natural law, he mentions some particular difficulties put forward by him, based on the premise that in some situations justice is against self-interest, and concludes: 'These are clearly subtle, tricky points which Cicero could not refute'.[36]

We look for further light on these problems to Cicero's next work, *De legibus*, where, as he says, he wants to cover the whole range of universal justice and law. The subject, he tells us (1 16), is one which demands consideration of what capacities man has by nature, what his purpose is in the world, and what are the natural bonds that unite men.

Lex est ratio summa, insita in natura, quae iubet ea quae facienda sunt prohibetque contraria. eadem ratio cum est in hominis mente confirmata et confecta lex est. . . . a lege ducendum est iuris exordium; ea est enim naturae vis, ea mens ratioque prudentis, ea iuris atque iniuriae regula (1 18f.).

People tend to think that only that is law which is written down. But 'I shall seek the root of justice in nature' (1 20).

As is obvious from these quotations, no attempt is made to preserve a clear distinction between what we might call the ontological and epistemological order. Cicero does not hesitate to glide from one order to the other. His whole purpose is to demonstrate the essential identity of the reason which directs the universe and the reason of the good man. This become quite clear in the sections that follow: man has been given a distinguished status by God because he has been given reason. 'Prima homini cum deo rationis societas' (1 23). Men then share law, which is right reason, with the gods. 'Virtus eadem in homine ac deo est neque alio ullo in genere praeterea; est autem virtus nihil aliud nisi perfecta et ad summum perducta natura; est igitur homini cum deo similitudo' (1 25).

Cicero proceeds then to derive 'the supreme Law which had its origin ages before any written law existed or any state had been established' (1 19) from nature. In doing so he follows a pattern which is to be found in his other philosophical works. It is primarily Cicero's account of natural law which represented the Stoic position for Christians like Lactantius and Ambrose and so influenced the Middle Ages. This can be sketched as follows.

In the case of man, 'nature' means 'reason'. Man owes his natural superiority to his reasoning powers, and consequently his ability to live in a wider present than the animals. But this ability brings with it wider obligations, obligations that in fact extend to all mankind. Law is man's great aid in guiding and helping him to carry out these obligations. And the model for all particular laws is the law of nature.

Man's perfection is the perfection of nature: 'est autem virtus nihil aliud nisi perfecta et ad summum perducta natura' (*De legibus* 1 25). The thought of this part of the *De legibus* is summed up in 1 35: we share the gifts of the gods, especially reason, and all men are bound together by a certain natural feeling of kindness and goodwill and by a partnership in justice. And, Cicero asks, having admitted this, how can we separate Law and Justice from Nature?

Although the source of *De legibus* 1 is notoriously disputed,[37] the Stoic colouring of this particular section is obvious. The notion of *virtus quasi perfectio naturae* is to be found elsewhere in Cicero where he is clearly drawing on Stoic sources.[38] One such place is the second book of *De officiis*. Here man is presented as the crown of creation and the being who, through his gifts, helps the rest of the world to fulfil its proper function. Man's gifts and crafts have led to the building of cities, and so were established *leges moresque* (*De off.* ii 15). This ability to form and use a community is the distinguishing mark of man, and the factor which is of highest importance in this development is *virtus*. 'As this point therefore admits of no doubt, that man can do the greatest good and the greatest injury to man, I lay it down as the peculiar property of virtue, that it reconciles the affections of mankind, and puts them to use' (ibid. ii 17).

Virtus itself has three properties, and in laying out these the second book of *De officiis* follows familiar Stoic paths. The exposition also shows clearly what the Stoics took to constitute the 'excellence' of man, his *virtus*, and why therefore man is in a special position in regard to morality. The first property that is mentioned is the ability to discern the true and genuine in each particular case, and yet not be limited to the particular but be able to perceive and estimate the relations and interactions between things. (This is 'the Dogmatists' thesis' that Sextus refers to, that is, that man differs from the irrational animals by the possession of internal reason and the ability to combine presentations and draw inferences. Man has a conception of logical sequence and grasps the notion of sign because of the sequence.)[40] The second property of virtue is its ability to control the passions and make our appetites subject to reason, and the third is that by which we treat our fellow men decently so that we have full enjoyment of all we need and full protection from what we want to avoid.

Cicero says in the middle of this exposition 'longiores hoc loco sumus quam necesse est' (ibid. ii 16). This unusual concession is due to some extent to his awareness that the present section of *De officiis* ii is a close parallel to the early portion of Book i. Book i has in fact examined human development from the start and it provides the basic theory which Book ii applies immediately to community life. In Book i Cicero is concerned to emphasize what is specifically human, and the evolution of some human qualities from instincts common to man and beast. So he starts off with the instincts of assimilation and rejection. The individual animal or man is thus established: and the self is extended through procreation and the care for the procreated.

It is from this point that the specifically human begins to emerge, for man through his intelligence becomes conscious of various bonds and logical consequences of actions, and is consequently aware of duties and concerns he must take upon himself. The animal on the other hand is moved only by what it can sense, and therefore by the immediately present. But in spite of his awareness of community values the 'selfish' element is always strong in man. It is encouraged by his appetite for getting to know the truth of things. His knowledge and awareness give him a sense of independence and an unwillingness to be subject to any man. But man is also intelligent enough to see that he must strike a balance between these attitudes: this he does through moderation, the sense of proportion in all things, which enables him to balance one demand against another.

If this is the proper development of man's nature it is easy to see that man should concern himself not only for those of his own household but for his fellow-citizens and all men.[41] Cicero talks most readily of the realisation of this ideal in terms of law, because he regards this as the necessary first step. Conventions must be agreed on if the community is to come into being: instincts must be controlled by what amounts to a community sense of moderation. And the laws which result are themselves a further civilizing influence. As is pointed out (*De off.* II 40) any community needs justice if it is to survive, even if it is only a community of thieves . . . 'Quin etiam leges latronum esse dicuntur, quibus pareant, quas observent.' It was the desire for justice, the equable, which at one time explained the power of the king, the moderator, and when the people could not be sure of equity at the hands of one good and just man, 'leges sunt inventae, quae cum omnibus semper una atque eadem voce loquerentur' (ibid. II 42). The laws would seem to be the recognition and expression of enlightened selfishness: 'For commonwealths and states were established principally for this cause, that men should hold on to what was their own. For although men did come together by the guidance of nature, yet it was with the hope of preserving their own property that they sought the protection of cities' (ibid. II 73).

Cicero himself is of course well aware that actual laws and law-codes have their limitations, and that some things 'propter depravationem consuetudinis neque more turpe haberi neque aut lege sanciri aut iure civili' (ibid. III 69). But these deviations only point up the perfection of the *lex naturae*, and *it* must look to equity for all: 'For there is a social tie between man and man which is of the widest extent, which though I have often mentioned it, yet needs to be mentioned oftener'.

This then is the picture which Cicero presents in the works between the *De republica* and his death, and which, as said above, was of primary importance for the tradition of natural law. It cannot however be said that natural law after Cicero had worked out answers to the questions that could have been put to Zeno or Chrysippus. At the end certain basic difficulties remain. In the first place, the material model of the world seems to leave little room for spontaneity and freedom. 'Things which are to be do not suddenly spring into existence, but the evolution of time is like the unwinding of a cable: it creates nothing new and only unfolds each event in its order' (*De div.* I 127). What then about our ordinary ways of thought and language which presume personal responsibility for one's actions?[42]

Moreover, if everything in the universe is material, it is difficult to see why man is specially privileged. We may grant that man as a class has superior gifts. But it must also be admitted that there are great varieties within the class of man. And if a particular class or nation, a *Herrenvolk*, is so organised that it can dominate all others, what effective *moral* argument can be used against it? Has an individual any absolute value *qua* individual? Cicero himself gets indignant at the notion that the propertied classes should be deprived of their property (*De off.* II 73), and says we must think of the good of individuals as well as that of the state (ibid. II 72). But an uneasy suspicion remains, as we shall see, about the sacredness of the rights of every individual.

For there does seem to be a difference in approach between the Greeks and the Romans in this respect, even allowing for the danger of clichés about national character. For the Greeks the law of nature is the decree of reason, the individual's last defence even against law, something to be remembered by a man who may be confronted with a number of precepts. We do not find the Romans examining and rejecting such an idea. But at the same time we must remember that among the Romans any theorizing that was done on the subject was done by people who were not primarily philosophers, but rather public men, like Cicero, the staple of whose higher education was training in the law.[43] The lawyer's criteria differ from those of the moral philosopher: the training and standards of the Roman lawyers were bound to influence their writing on law. The making of good legislation was their primary concern, and legislation necessarily concerns itself with the public rather than the private good. Regard for the public good is ultimately also for the good of the individual but the difference in approach is considerable. The Roman version of the theory, then, is significant for the change in level: for, while man still has his rights it is now a type of recognition from above. The emphasis is on public order rather than guarantees for the individual. The phrasing now is: for the sake of *State* welfare, justice for all is necessary. Therefore the best possible laws to guide people should be made.

The Romans were proud of their law: all other codes of law, including the Greek, were unbelievably underdeveloped when compared with the Roman, as Cicero remarked,[44] and in their constant efforts to develop it further they fell gratefully on the concept of natural law. It was the standard to which they could appeal when altering rigid laws to meet modern needs. And because these men were, like Cicero, practising lawyers who had to have a stock of precedents to hand, and had a keen appreciation of the suasory force of examples and of the necessity of giving something more than abstract arguments on natural law, even more attention was given to casuistry.[45] The unpleasantly totalitarian ring of one of these applications is another indication of the ambiguity of the natural law, and how uncomfortable it may be to have an external authority to make *your* decisions. Cicero says there 'and therefore nature's law itself, which protects and conserves human interests, will surely determine that a man who is wise, good and brave, should in emergency have the necessaries of life transferred to him from a person who is idle and worthless; for the good man's death would be a heavy loss to the common weal' (*De off.* III 31).

It must be stated that all along Cicero's instinct is for *humanitas*: but can he show that it is any more than a rhetorical plea?

An attempt is made to make *humanitas* a more effective criterion by specifying its obligations. This is in *De officiis* III, which deals with the clash of duty and expediency, a subject not treated satisfactorily by Panaetius, according to Cicero. One case of a clash of rights is suggested to Cicero by a very recent incident, the murder of Julius Caesar. He says: 'it often happens that what is accustomed under ordinary circumstances to be considered morally wrong is found not to be morally wrong' (III 19), and instances the killing of a tyrant. Some formula must be established to help us decide in these matters: 'erit autem haec formula Stoicorum rationi disciplinaeque maxime consentanea' (III 20). He begins then to establish a scale, first negatively, deciding what is *contra naturam*. The generic crime is 'to take away wrongfully from another, and for one man to advance his own interest by the disadvantage of another man' (III 21). Such an act destroys the very basis of human community life and society. This negative, therefore, follows from a positive because human society itself is that which is 'maxime secundum naturam'. Human society is like a body: one limb must not be allowed to weaken another. The human and divine law, which is obeyed by all who wish to live according to nature, forbids us to seek what belongs to another. We may, however, take a tyrant's life 'for we have no community with tyrants . . . it is a virtue to kill such a man, and all this class should be expelled from the community of mankind' (III 32). Such members of society are removed, just as bloodless and lifeless limbs that are harmful to the rest of the body are amputated.

With this solution Cicero appears to be content. It is a solution that has often been accepted through the centuries, and the analogy of the diseased limb appeals to common sense. But we should be very careful not to be too quick in establishing a general principle based on such an analogy. It is too easy to show that a person or group is a diseased limb in any particular society, is not filled with the spirit that animates the whole. But sometimes such an uncomfortable person or group might be the only healthy element left in society. Panaetius had, in his teaching, emphasised the importance of individual initiative.

Q   L.P.S.

But does the general system, or the body-limb analogy, really permit such initiative? Will it tolerate an uncomfortable reformer? Was Socrates 'natural'?

This brings us again to a point mentioned earlier, the contrast of law and morality. That this is still a live issue and not by any means an easy one to settle is clear from the Devlin-Hart controversy. Confusion of law and morality does harm to both. On the other hand, law cannot dissociate itself entirely from morality and the confusion which we might be inclined to blame Cicero for promoting was due not so much to looseness of thought as to the desire to make law as perfect as possible. Cicero recognised the limitations of positive law and wished to set a standard for it: 'sed aliter leges, aliter philosophi tollunt astutias; leges, quatenus manu tenere possunt, philosophi, quatenus ratione et intellegentia' (*De off.* III 68). But it would have been better if he had popularised some other term for this ideal than *lex naturae.*

Lex, then, is not *lex* in any restricted law sense in the *lex naturae* contexts of Cicero. The whole phrase is often better translated rationality or morality. It directs man's response to his total environment, it is the guide of his reason. And since everything is subordinated to the good of the totality, the law of nature does not mean that man may not interfere with the 'ordinary' functioning of a particular organ, for example. There is nothing sacred about the teleology of the *parts* of man himself in Stoicism. Chrysippus would have been surprised to be told that the use of the sexual organs is for procreation alone, and that any other use is contrary to the natural law. Teleological arguments that are associated with expositions of the Stoic providence go back much farther than Stoicism.[46] It was natural to add them to an exposition such as that of *De natura deorum*, but there is nothing specifically Stoic about them.

It may seem that this chapter has approached natural law in a rather negative spirit, picking out points only for criticism. The critical approach is due to the fact that, as mentioned at the beginning, natural law is very often used today with the meaning simply of morality, and the legal model has done damage to morality. Is there, then, nothing to be said *for* natural law, or why was it that Barker, to mention only one, was so enthusiastic about natural law as a 'tradition of civility'?

In the first place, the emphasis on the good of the totality, the insistence on the necessity of controlling purely selfish drives, is an essential element in the development of any society. The Greek Stoics had taught that it was not just convention that man should respect the rights of others, but rather that the awareness of and consideration for others was built into him, was in fact his nature. Therefore the more aware of his nature, the more natural, in a sense, man became, the more he took account of all men. The social conventions which the Cynics had despised were expressions of the real needs of man's true nature. The theory of natural law, especially in the Roman context, dramatised this awareness of the common good. The Romans applied practically what they learned from Greek theory and tried to make the Stoic insistence on the identity of nature and approved convention into a tradition.

The most obvious and effective channel for the preservation of this tradition was the Roman law itself. But it would take us too far afield to study the relations between philosophical and legal thought in this context or to say anything about the question of the origin of the triple distinction in the *Digest*. It will, however, be granted that the concept of natural law was bound to influence those people who were not given to philosophical enquiry, especially after its presentation by Cicero. Natural law became another *topos*. I have concentrated in this paper on the exposition by Cicero of natural law because for the thinkers of the succeeding centuries his influence is preponderant—Lactantius, Ambrose and Augustine are good examples of it. As Sidgwick said, 'there is probably no ancient treatise which has done more than his *De officiis* to communicate a knowledge of ancient morality to medieval and modern Europe'.[47]

But the Church Fathers also developed the habit of using 'natural law' simply as a term of approval for whatever idea they wanted to recommend at any particular time. When Ambrose, for instance, in his *De officiis ministrorum*, uses the language of 'imitating nature' (i 84) and the law of nature, the phrases evidently mean something other than what they meant for Cicero. Ambrose and Augustine became two of the four

Greater Doctors of the West. Together they took natural law from Cicero, baptised it, and handed it on for preservation in the Church. Augustine continued the shift of emphasis of Lactantius and Ambrose when he said: 'The eternal law is the Divine reason or the will of God which commands that the natural order be preserved and forbids it to be disturbed' (*Contra Faustum* 22, 7). The *Decretum Gratiani* (*c.* 1140), the oldest collection of Church law, is not saying anything new when it maintains: 'Mankind is ruled by two laws: Natural Law and Custom. Natural Law is that which is contained in the Scriptures and the Gospel'. This was simply taking over the teaching attributed to Isidore of Seville (d. 636): '*Ius naturale* is that which is contained in the law and the Gospel, by which each is commanded to do to the other what he would have done to himself and is forbidden to do to another what he would not have done to himself'.[48] After that the natural law began to look like a doctrine of the Church. But after the canonists and theologians there came all the secular thinkers and systems to which Barker alludes. The term 'natural law' had something to offer to all. What the specifically Stoic teaching had to contribute was an entirely different matter. The name has remained constant; but the content has to be examined afresh on each occasion.

NOTES

1. 'Natural Law and its History', *Concilium* (May 1965) 23. For an excellent account of the uses and abuses in Church history of the 'natural law argument' in regard to one particular problem, see John T. Noonan, *Contraception* (Cambridge, Mass. 1965). He shows how easy it was for Clement of Alexandria to accept the writings of Musonius Rufus as *the* Stoic teaching on marriage, and how early the tradition became established that severe Christian views were simply a continuation of the best pagan thought.

2. *A History of Greek Philosophy* ii (Cambridge 1965) p. 344. φύσις in Greek seems to have offered even more opportunity for misunderstanding than 'nature' in English. Aristotle's exposition of meanings in *Met. Δ* 4 does not exhaust the possibilities. See Ross's notes *ad loc.*, with references to earlier work by Burnet and Lovejoy. On φύσις in Heraclitus and other Presocratics see G. S. Kirk, *Heraclitus, The Cosmic Fragments* (Cambridge 1954) pp. 227–31. D. Holwerda summarises the senses in which the word is used up to Aristotle in *ΦΥΣΙΣ* (Groningen 1955). Holwerda (p. 6) disagrees with the statement of F. Heinimann that 'das Substantiv φύσις hat seine ursprüngliche verbale Kraft als "Werden", "Wachsen" immer

beibehalten', *Nomos und Physis* (Basel 1945) p. 89. Otherwise, however, he thinks, quite rightly, that this work of Heinimann is a 'liber optimus'. Heinimann also reviews the uses of νόμος. See too Kirk, op. cit., pp. 48–55.

3. I do not wish to imply that Plato was the first to suggest, even in this ironical fashion, the desirability of φύσις becoming νόμος. Even apart from Antiphon's words in the *Aletheia* fragment (DK B44) on the opposition between the laws of the city and the laws of nature, the very contrast of νόμος and φύσις had from the beginning suggested an ideal state of affairs where the two would coincide.

4. This confusion is also one of the longest lasting. Noonan, op. cit., p. 294, quotes from St Thomas's commentary on the *Sentences* where the use of certain forms of contraception was condemned as 'against nature, for even the beasts look for offspring' (*On the Sentences* 4, 31).

5. *A History of Cynicism* p. 31.

6. Diog. Laert. VI 104f.; VII 2f.

7. See the discussion in H. C. Baldry, *The Unity of Mankind*, esp. pp. 122f.

8. [See S. G. Pembroke, Chapter VI pp. 116ff. Ed.]

9. [On the formation of moral concepts see F. H. Sandbach, Chapter II pp. 28ff., and Pembroke, Chapter VI pp. 122ff. Ed.]

10. Plutarch, *De Alex. Magni Fortuna aut Virtute*, 329 a–b.

11. See again Baldry, op. cit., pp. 153ff.

12. Cf. *SVF* III 314f. and p. 228 below.

13. See D. J. O'Connor, *Aquinas and Natural Law* (London 1967) pp. 59–60.

14. See the discussion of this passage by Long, 'Carneades and the Stoic Telos', *Phronesis* xii (1967) 63–4.

15. See *SVF* II 708–13.

16. Diogenes Laertius VII 156 and 148; Cicero, *De natura deorum* II 57.

17. See Sextus Empiricus, *Adv. math.* IX 81ff.; Cicero, *ND* II 33f.

18. For discussions of τὰ κατὰ φύσιν, see I. G. Kidd, Chapter VII p. 155 and Long, op. cit. 62ff.

19. Cicero, *Acad.* II 38. [The Stoics themselves did not claim that 'nihil situm est in nobis', see Chapter VIII pp. 182ff. Ed.]

20. Cicero, *ND* I 18ff. Cf. Diog. Laert., VII 138. See also M. Reesor, *The Political Theory of the Old and Middle Stoa*, p. 19.

21. See Cicero *De fin.* III 64 and *De leg.* I 22. Bréhier, *Chrysippe*, p. 210.

22. There are difficulties for *Pronoia* itself in the Stoic teaching. There seems to be some necessity limiting its action: see Plutarch, *Stoic. rep.* 37, Seneca, *Prov.* v 9, Galen, *Us. part.* XI 14. The gods are said to care for individuals, Cicero, *ND* II 164; yet it is also said that *magna di curant, parva neglegunt*, ibid. II 167.

23. See Seneca *Ep. mor.* 73, 13 and 53, 11. Bréhier, *Chrysippe*, pp. 214ff. [For further remarks on the dual perspective mentioned above see Chapter VIII, pp. 176ff. Ed.]

24. See Plutarch, *Stoic. rep.* 22, 1045A. [For Stoic arguments from animal behaviour see S. G. Pembroke, Chapter VI pp. 122f. Ed.]

25. Cf. Cicero, *De rep.* I 15.

26. *Aeneid* VI 851ff.

27. *De rep.* V 5.

28. *Ibid.* I 34.

29. *Inst. div.* V 14, 3–5.

30. *De rep.* III 13.

31. *Ibid.* III 19.

32. *Inst. div.* V 16. [For a probable attack by Carneades on *oikeiosis* in relation to justice see S. G. Pembroke, Chapter VI pp. 128f. Ed.]

33. Cicero, *De rep.* III 33.

34. Cf. *De off.* I 34ff.

35. For the reconstruction of *De rep.* III 34–8, see the text and apparatus of K. Ziegler (Teubner, Leipzig 1915).

36. *Inst. div.* v 16.

37. For a summary of views cf. Reesor, op cit., p. 41.

38. See *De fin.* III 33 and IV 35, and *Acad.* I 20 with Reid's note *ad loc.*, which gives references to Seneca, Galen and Sextus. Cf. Schmekel, *Die mittlere Stoa,* p. 270.

39. *Adv. math.* VIII 275ff.

40. [See further, Chapter V p. 87. Ed.].

41. See *De fin.* II 45 and v 65.

42. For another approach by Cicero to the Stoic Fate, see *De fato.* For a modern treatment, see M. Reesor, 'Fate and Possibility in Early Stoic Philosophy', *Phoenix* xix (1965) [and Chapter VIII above. Ed.].

43. See Cicero, *De leg.* III 14 on the difference between himself and the early Stoa.

44. *De oratore* I 197.

45. In *De officiis* Cicero makes it quite clear that there was a tradition of casuistry in Stoicism itself. The Stoics became concerned with casuistry largely owing to the difficulties raised by Carneades. There is reference to a particular branch of ethics, the παραινετικὸς καὶ ὑποθετικὸς τόπος (rejected by Ariston of Chios), which dealt with particular problems, such as those of marriage, treatment of slaves etc. Cf. Seneca *Ep. mor.* 94 and 95, and I. G. Kidd, Chapter VII p. 164.

46. Teleological thought was evidently very popular in Athens at the end of the fifth century. See Willy Theiler, *Zur Geschichte der teleologischen Naturbetrachtung bis auf Aristoteles.*

47. *History of Ethics* (Papermac edition 1967) p. 95.

48. *Decretum Gratiani*, I pars, dist. I, proem. See E. Hölecher *vom Römischen zum Christlichen Naturrecht* (Augsburg 1931) p. 62.

SELECT BIBLIOGRAPHY

The following list contains full details of books or articles on Stoicism to which frequent or occasional reference is made in the notes. In addition, a few works cited there on different or more general subjects are included. But the list is not exhaustive in this respect, nor does it contain titles of any works on Stoicism which are not mentioned elsewhere in the book.

Collections of texts and fragments are cited first. The Greek commentators on Aristotle are referred to by page and line in the appropriate volume of *Commentaria in Aristotelem Graeca (CAG)*.

DE VOGEL, C. J., *Greek Philosophy*: *a collection of texts with notes and explanations*, 3 vols. (Leiden, 1950–59).

DIELS, H., *Doxographi Graeci* (Berlin, 1879).

DIELS, H. and KRANZ, W., *Die Fragmente der Vorsokratiker (DK)*, 6th. ed., 3 vols. (Berlin, 1951–52).

ARNIM, J. VON, *Stoicorum Veterum Fragmenta (SVF)*, 4 vols. (Leipzig 1903–24, reprinted Stuttgart, 1964).

PEARSON, A. C., *Fragments of Zeno and Cleanthes* (London, 1891).

USENER, H., *Epicurea* (Leipzig, 1887).

ACKRILL, J. L., *Aristotle's Categories and De Interpretatione* (Oxford, 1963).

ADORNO, F., 'Sul significato del termine ὑπάρχον in Zenone Stoico', *La Parola del Passato* xii (1967) 156–61.

ARNIM, J. VON, *Arius Didymus' Abriss der peripatetischen Ethik*, Akad. der Wiss. in Wien, Phil.-hist. Kl., Sitz. 204, 3 (1926).

—, *Hierokles, Ethische Elementarlehre* (Papyrus 9780), Berliner Klassikertexte, Heft iv (1906).

BALDRY, H. C., *The Unity of Mankind in Greek Thought* (Cambridge, 1965).

—, 'Zeno's Ideal State', *Journal of Hellenic Studies* lxxix (1959) 3–15.

BARTH, P., *Die Stoa*, 2nd ed. (Stuttgart, 1908).

BARWICK, K., *Probleme der stoischen Sprachlehre und Rhetorik*, Abhand. zu Leipzig, Phil.-hist. Kl. 49, 3 (Berlin, 1957).

—, *Remius Palaemon und die römische ars grammatica*, *Philologus* suppl. xv, 2, (Leipzig, 1922).

BEVAN, E., *Stoics and Sceptics* (Oxford, 1913).

BONHÖFFER, A., *Epictet und die Stoa* (Stuttgart, 1890).

BRÉHIER, E., *La théorie des incorporels*, 2nd ed. (Paris, 1920).

—, *Chrysippe et l'ancien stoicisme*, 2nd ed. (Paris, 1950).

BRINK, C. O., 'οἰκείωσις and οἰκειότης: Theophrastus and Zeno on Nature in moral theory', *Phronesis* i, 2 (1956) 123–45.

COLE, THOMAS A., *Democritus and the Sources of Greek Anthropology*, American Philol. Assoc. Monograph No. xxv (Western Reserve University, 1967).

CHRISTENSEN, J., *An Essay on the Unity of Stoic Philosophy* (Köbenhavn, 1962).

DAHLMANN, H., *Varro und die hellenistische Sprachtheorie*, Problemata 5 (Berlin–Zürich, 1932).

DE LACY, P., 'The Stoic Categories as Methodological Principles', *Transactions and Proceedings of the American Philological Association* lxxvi (1945) 246–63.

DE LACY, P. and E. A., *Philodemus: on methods of Inference*, American Philological Assoc. Monograph No. x (Philadelphia, 1941).

DIRLMEIER, F., *Die Oikeiosis-Lehre Theophrasts*, Philologus suppl. xxx, 1, (Leipzig, 1937).

DUDLEY, D. R., *A History of Cynicism* (London, 1937).

DYROFF, A., *Ethik der alten Stoa*, Berliner Studien N.F. 2 (1897).

EDELSTEIN, L., *The Meaning of Stoicism*, Martin Classical Lectures xxi (Cambridge Mass., 1966).

—, 'The Philosophical System of Posidonius', *American Journal of Philology* lvii (1936) 286–325.

FURLEY, D. J., *Two Studies in the Greek Atomists* (Princeton, 1967).

GERCKE, A., *Chrysippea, Jahrb. für Klass. Phil.* suppl. xiv (Leipzig, 1885).

GOLDSCHMIDT, V., *Le système stoicien et l'idèe de temps* (Paris, 1953).

GOULD, J. B., 'Chrysippus: on the criteria for the truth of a conditional proposition', *Phronesis* xii (1967) 156–61.

GRUMACH, E., *Physis und Agathon in der alten Stoa*, Problemata 6 (Berlin, 1932).

HALLER, R., 'Untersuchungen zum Bedeutungsproblem in der antiken und mittelalterlichen Philosophie', *Archiv für Begriffsgeschichte* vii (1962) 57–119.

HEINIMANN, F., *Nomos und Physis* (Basel, 1945).

HICKS, R. D., *Stoic and Epicurean* (London, 1910).

HIRZEL, R., *Untersuchungen zu Ciceros philosophischen Schriften*, 3 vols. (Leipzig, 1877–83).

KNEALE, W. and M., *The Development of Logic* (Oxford, 1962).

LERSCH, L., *Sprachphilosophie der Alten* (Bonn, 1840).

LONG, A. A., 'Aristotle's Legacy to Stoic Ethics', *Bulletin of the Institute of Classical Studies* xv (1968) 72–85.

—, 'Carneades and the Stoic Telos', *Phronesis* xii (1967) 59–90.

—, 'The Stoic Concept of Evil', *Philosophical Quarterly* xviii (1968) 329–43.

MATES, BENSON, *Stoic Logic* (Berkeley California, 1953).

PHILIPPSON, R., 'Das "Erste Naturgemässe" ', *Philologus* lxxxvii (1932) 445–66.

POHLENZ, M., *Die Stoa*, 2nd. ed. (Göttingen, 1959).

—, *Grundfragen der stoischen Philosophie*, Abhandl. der Gesellschaft der Wiss. zu Göttingen, Phil.-hist. Kl. 3, 26 (1940).

—, 'Die Begründung der abendländischen Sprachlehre durch die Stoa', *Nachricht. von der Gesell. der Wiss. zu Göttingen*, Phil.-hist. Kl. N.F. i 3 (1939) 151–98.

—, *Griechische Freiheit* (Heidelberg, 1955).

—, 'Plutarchs Schriften gegen die Stoiker', *Hermes* lxxiv (1940) 1–33.

—, 'Tierische und menschliche Intellegenz bei Poseidonios', *Hermes* lxxvi (1941) 1–13.

—, 'Zenon und Chrysipp', *Nachricht. von der Akad. der Wiss. zu Göttingen*, Phil.-hist. Kl. N.F. i 2 (1938) 173–210.

PRAECHTER, K., *Hierokles der Stoiker* (Leipzig, 1901).

REESOR, MARGARET, *The Political Theory of the Old and Middle Stoa* (New York, 1951).

—, 'Fate and Possibility in Early Stoic Philosophy', *Phoenix* xix (1965) 285–297.

—, 'The Stoic Categories', *American Journal of Philology* lxxviii (1957) 63–82.

—, 'The Stoic Concept of Quality', *American Journal of Philology* lxxv (1954) 40–58.

—, 'The "Indifferents" in the Old and Middle Stoa', *Transactions and Proceedings of the American Philological Association* lxxxii (1951) 102–10.

RIETH, O., *Grundbegriffe der stoischen Ethik*, Problemata 9 (Berlin, 1933).

—, 'Über das Telos der Stoiker', *Hermes* lxix (1934) 13–45.

RIST, J. M., *Stoic Philosophy* (Cambridge, 1969).

SAMBURSKY, S., *The Physics of the Stoics* (London, 1959).

SCHÄFER, M., *Ein frühmittelstoisches System der Ethik bei Cicero* (München, 1934).

SCHMEKEL, A., *Die Philosophie der mittleren Stoa in ihrem geschichtlichen Zusammenhange* (Berlin, 1892).

SCHMIDT, R., *Stoicorum grammatica* (Halle, 1839).

SCHUHL, P.-M., *Le Dominateur et les possibles* (Paris, 1960).

STEIN, L., *Erkenntnistheorie der Stoa* (Berlin, 1886).

STRAATEN, M. VAN, *Panaetius Rhodius Fragmenta*, 3rd. ed., Philos. antiqua 5 (Leiden, 1962).

STRAATEN, M. VAN, *Panétius, sa vie, ses écrits et sa doctrine* (Amsterdam Paris, 1946).

THEILER, WILLY, *Zur Geschichte der teleologischen Naturbetrachtung bis auf Aristoteles* (Zürich, 1925).

—, 'Tacitus und die antike Schicksalslehre', *Phyllobolia für Peter von der Muehll* (Basel, 1946) 35–90.

UEBERWEG-PRAECHTER, Ueberweg, F., *Grundriss der Geschichte der Philosophie*, ed. K. Praechter, 12th. ed. (Berlin, 1902–28).

VERBEKE, G., 'Stoicisme et Aristotélisme dans le *De Fato* d' Alexandre d'Aphrodise', *Archiv für Geschichte der Philosophie* l (1968) 78–100.

WASZINK, J. H., *Plato Latinus* iv (London and Leiden, 1962).

WATSON, GERARD, *The Stoic Theory of Knowledge* (Belfast, 1966).

ZELLER, E., *Die Philosophie der Griechen*, 4th. ed. III i (Leipzig, 1876).

INDEX OF PASSAGES QUOTED
OR REFERRED TO

Bold figures denote a main entry or an entry on which critical or explanatory comment is made in the notes. Though not fully comprehensive the index aims to include all passages from ancient authors which are cited as primary evidence for Stoicism, and all other passages which are fully germane to the argument of each chapter. Cross-references to von Arnim's collection of Stoic fragments (*SVF*) are normally included, where appropriate, in the notes to each chapter and they are cited by volume and fragment number. Texts cited in the notes solely by reference to *SVF* are entered here under their ancient author.

R

INDEX OF GREEK AND LATIN WORDS

INDEX OF PROPER NAMES

Bold figures denote a main entry or an entry on which critical or explanatory comment is made in the notes.

57 Bee